Trauma in American Popular
Texts, 1980–2020

Sean Travers

Trauma in American Popular Culture and Cult Texts, 1980–2020

palgrave
macmillan

Sean Travers
Cork, Ireland

https://doi.org/10.1007/978-3-031-13287-2

This Palgrave Macmillan imprint is published by the registered company Springer Nature Switzerland AG.
The registered company address is: Gewerbestrasse 11, 6330 Cham, Switzerland

Note on Referencing and Citations

The referencing style of the Modern Language Association (MLA), based on the seventh edition of the MLA Handbook for Writers of Research Papers, is used in this book.

Acknowledgments

I would like to thank my parents, Anne and Steve, my aunt Marie, and my grandparents, Ettie and Sean, for their support.

I would also like to thank Dr Matthew Carter, Dr Graham Price, Stephen Black, Lara O'Toole, Shannon Spence, Max Nestorowich and Ryan Fay for their perceptive feedback.

Many thanks to Dr Maureen O'Connor, Dr Clíona Ó Gallchoir, Dr David Coughlan, Sharone O'Loughlin, Prof Graham Allen, Dr Tim Groenland, Dr Kerry Dodd, Dr Steve Gronert Ellerhoff, Dr Eoin O'Callaghan and Dr Michael Nott for their advice on this project.

My thanks to Dr Dara Downey, Dr Gabriele Biotti, Dr S. Jonathan O'Donnell, Dr Rebecca Stone Gordon, Dr Danel Olson, Dr CarrieLynn D. Reinhard, Dr Donna Alexander, Dr Dan O'Brien, Dr Orla Lynch, Victoria Koivisto-Kokko, Martin O'Connor, Dr Johnny Goodwin and Brian J. Showers for their encouragement during the production of this book.

Final thanks go to the staff at Palgrave Macmillan including Camille Davies and Raghupathy Kalynaraman and the anonymous readers for their valuable suggestions.

Declaration

This is to certify that the work I am submitting is my own and has not been submitted anywhere else. All external references and sources are clearly acknowledged and identified.

July 2022 Sean Travers

Contents

List of Figures

CHAPTER 1

Introduction

Trauma has become a central paradigm for reading contemporary American culture. Since the early 1980s, an extensive range of genres increasingly feature traumatised protagonists and centre on traumatic events. In particular, trauma has become an important facet of contemporary American popular culture. Indeed, trauma is a frequent trigger for a turn to super-heroics in Hollywood blockbusters; major US television series recurrently centre on catastrophic apocalyptic events and warfare, while American video games increasingly use trauma as a short-hand to fill in character backstories and motivations. Paradoxically, contemporary horror has been found to feature realistic depictions of Post-Traumatic Stress Disorder (PTSD), with supernatural themes including possession and hauntings being apt metaphors for traumatic symptoms, while the fluctuating visual style of American animation increasingly exploits its capacity to represent traumatised states of mind. As trauma scholars Lucy Bond and Stef Craps observe, 'today, trauma is a big business' (3).

That is not to say that trauma in popular culture has been overlooked. While trauma has been predominantly associated with high culture in the late twentieth century, research on trauma in popular culture has grown significantly in recent years. The following study aims to add to this scholarship, examining trauma in late twentieth- and twenty-first-century American popular culture and cult texts. The main aim of this book is to uncover new themes and formal techniques of trauma representation, the

S. Travers, *Trauma in American Popular Culture and Cult Texts, 1980–2020*, https://doi.org/10.1007/978-3-031-13287-2_1

central argument being that certain popular and cult texts produce innovative representations of trauma. Examining film, television, animation, games and cult texts, I develop a series of original paradigms through which to understand trauma in popular culture. Divided into five sections, I explore five modes of traumatic representation, which will structure the book. These are: popular trauma texts' engagement with postmodern perspectives; analytical frameworks termed 'competitive narration', 'polynarration' and 'sceptical scriptotherapy'; and perpetrator trauma in metafictional games. A further key topic is gender and cultural diversity in popular trauma representations. These chapters address a range of representational sites and subjects, including feminism, queerness, race and Internet culture, among others, and provide an accessible foundation for future scholarship. This book outlines and explores some of the major avenues of analysis regarding trauma in contemporary American popular culture in a way that will ideally hold interest for students and researchers. I aim to provide what one could call a collection of jumping-off points for advancing the scholarly conversation about the centrality of trauma in contemporary American popular culture. This topic offers fertile ground for academic analysis that invites a wide range of interpretive approaches. Therefore, my book aims to be a usefully suggestive rather than a comprehensive or exhaustive selection of such approaches.

I bring an interdisciplinary interpretive framework to my selection of texts. This methodological approach allows the study to bring the texts together with the argument that contemporary American popular culture is amongst the most pioneering areas of trauma representation. Trauma in popular forms is also a cross-media field and incorporates methods of representation from other media, in particular literature. Therefore, it would be reductive to ignore literary representations of trauma and literary theory that are relevant and useful. I use specific textual examples from 1980 to 2021 to support my claims. Some of the examples I have chosen are not overtly popular culture but can instead be defined as cult texts; I argue for their inclusion through their shared characteristics with popular works and the similar type of fan engagement they generate. Although the selection of primary texts considered cannot be exhaustive, each has made a distinct and innovative contribution to trauma representation. Each text both informs and most effectively illustrates my trauma paradigms, which are critical tools that can be applied to myriad popular and contemporary works. Again, it is subsequently hoped that this analysis of trauma in contemporary American popular culture might be more broadly applicable to a wider understanding of the textual processes of trauma, contributing to larger conversations in cultural trauma studies as a whole.

To outline the structure of the book, Chap. 2 examines trauma and postmodern perspectives in two horror cult texts: Mark Z. Danielewski's *House of Leaves* and Stanley Kubrick's *The Shining* (1980). Popular culture produces innovative trauma representations via its engagement with postmodern themes and perspectives rather than solely its aesthetic. In certain popular and cult texts, trauma is attributed to postmodern conditions, specifically, Jean-François Lyotard's characterisation of postmodernism as incredulity towards metanarratives. This refers to scepticism towards the overarching grand narratives that purport to explain how the world works, including history and religion. This perspective is depicted as traumatic because it produces feelings of nothingness in individuals and reveals life to be meaningless. *House of Leaves* represents this trauma through a house haunted by literal emptiness and its inhabitants searching for spectres to combat this emptiness. By contrast, *The Shining* represents Lyotard's concept of micronarratives, the individual, localised narratives that replace metanarratives in postmodernity. The resulting fragmentation and pluralism produce a traumatic sense of incoherence and meaninglessness. *The Shining* represents this phenomenon and the failure to construct overarching discourses in postmodernity that give life meaning, particularly cultural production. The film does this through an overdetermined haunted site, with the haunted hotel containing too many sources of terror to form a coherent horror film; through its struggling author-protagonist and his arbitrary, meaningless manuscript; and through a strategy that I term 'narrative crash', a labyrinthine narrative structure that avoids closure and employs techniques that resemble technical difficulties in order to represent the break-down of the film.

Chapter 3 explores an analytical framework that I term competitive narration in Tim Burton's *Batman Returns* (1992) and David Lynch and Mark Frost's franchise *Twin Peaks* (1990–2017). Feminist trauma scholars critique dominant cultural trauma theory because it is phallocentric, excluding the types of trauma frequently experienced by women, ethnic minorities and LGBTQIA+ individuals. Likewise, canonical trauma fiction usually features white male protagonists. While popular culture is also phallocentric, it is nevertheless more likely to engage with the trauma of a more diverse range of characters. This chapter argues that certain popular and cult texts critique canonical fiction's neglect and mythologisation of women's trauma through a technique that I term competitive narration.

This technique takes two forms. The first form, which is evident in *Batman Returns*, features one plot overtaking another. The narrative centred on the traumatised, putative protagonist Batman is overtaken by a female secondary character, Catwoman, whose narrative centres on women's oppression. The second form of competitive narration critiques the cultural tradition of displacing ostensibly taboo traumas commonly experienced by women to the supernatural, such as family violence. This technique, which is apparent in *Twin Peaks*, features two narratives vying for the viewer's attention, except neither one overtakes the other and emerges as the main plot, producing a narrative that consists of contradictory plotlines. *Twin Peaks* offers competing realistic and supernatural explanations for the series' traumatic events, it renders dominant trauma concepts in supernatural terms and the female murder victim returns to disrupt the male-centred detective narrative.

Chapter 4 investigates a framework termed polynarration in texts by writers diverse in terms of gender, race and sexuality: The Wachowskis' *Sense8* (2015–2018), Rebecca Sugar's *Steven Universe* (2013–2019) and Nia DaCosta's *Candyman* (2021). Whereas *Batman Returns* and *Twin Peaks* feature female characters overtaking male-centred narratives, *Sense8*, *Steven Universe* and *Candyman* feature diverse groups of characters acquiring interconnectivity abilities that enable them to supernaturally share traumatic experiences and help one another recover. This produces unique narratives where a singular traumatic event is told from a range of diverse perspectives as characters' consciousnesses and/or bodies amalgamate. In contrast to canonical trauma fiction, the supernatural is employed to further explore rather than conceal the trauma of diverse individuals. *Sense8*, *Steven Universe* and *Candyman* formulate fantastical metaphors to depict these experiences specifically. The groups' interconnectivity abilities can be read as metaphorical for online communal healing, a mode of recovery significant for diverse and underrepresented individuals, because the Internet is more accessible than the phallocentric domain of trauma culture.

Chapter 5 discusses a framework that I term sceptical scriptotherapy in Brit Marling and Zal Batmanglij's *The OA* (2016–2019) and Sam Esmail's *Mr Robot* (2015–2019). Sceptical scriptotherapy features characters narrating traumatic events by reworking them into alternate, therapeutic narratives. *Mr Robot* and *The OA*'s protagonists take on new identities and displace their traumatic experiences to more palatable narratives. In canonical fiction, characters' imaginings of alternate scenarios are conventionally represented as futile responses to trauma and a way of denying agency for perpetrator-protagonists. Likewise, a dominant critical trauma conception is that sharing and narrating traumatic events exactly as they happened are essential for recovery. Conversely, in works that employ sceptical scriptotherapy such as *Mr Robot* and *The OA*, escapist fantasies are depicted as the only way that victim-protagonists can take agency over their recovery. This is significant regarding the types of trauma experienced by diverse groups, which are frequently structural traumas beyond individuals' control, comprising everyday insidious experiences of inequality and oppression.

Lastly, Chap. 6 investigates the transmission of perpetrator trauma in two metafictional games: Dan Salvato's *Doki Doki Literature Club* (2017) and Toby Fox's *Undertale* (2015). Dominant trauma theory valorises the practice of transmission to represent trauma victims, meaning to simulate in readers the protagonists' traumatic symptoms through experimental formal techniques. How symptoms specific to trauma perpetrators, including feelings of responsibility, guilt and moral contradiction, are conveyed in this way is a more unique topic. Conversely, games employ their increased level of interactivity to transmit to players perpetrator trauma symptoms, granting players agency to virtually perpetrate immoral acts. However, the concept of transmission is increasingly subject to criticism, while games' interrogation of players' moral frameworks does not translate to a real-world context. Responding to these issues, this chapter examines games that employ metafiction as a means of exploring player immorality in relation to the game medium specifically. *Doki Doki Literature Club* and *Undertale* interrogate players' culpability in the medium's sensationalism of violence and expected play patterns of replayability.

This book is carefully structured, and my research thoughtfully designed to ensure thematic unification of contemporary American popular culture. I chose this particular order of chapters because I aim for the earlier chapters to inform the later ones in terms of theoretical paradigms, topics, themes, form, media and socio-cultural and historical contexts, and to draw significant comparisons in terms of trauma representation. The trauma paradigms examined in the earlier chapters draw upon, subvert and/or incorporate more familiar concepts of trauma than the later chapters. Chapters 2 and 3 discuss more well-known concepts such as flashbacks, dissociation, the gaze in cinema and circling as a form of evasive narration, whereas Chaps. 4, 5 and 6 talk about lesser known concepts such as online communal healing, scriptotherapy and perpetrator trauma.

Analysing the male-centred texts in *House of Leaves* and *The Shining* in Chap. 2 before the texts with diverse casts of characters in Chaps. 3, 4 and 5 evidences a striking contrast between how trauma is perceived and defined depending on whom is represented. Examining Chap. 3 before Chaps. 4 and 5 demonstrates the differences in approach to trauma and feminism between earlier straight white male writers in the 1990s and contemporary twenty-first-century writers diverse in terms of gender and race. I also aimed to order chapters according to media, examining more traditional media in the field of trauma studies including literature and film in the earlier chapters (Chap. 2 to the beginning of Chap. 4), and more unique media in the field such as animation and games in the later chapters (the later section of Chaps. 4–6).

Existing Criticism

This book joins a complex and multiform multidisciplinary field. The field of trauma is constantly moving and paradigms need updating in terms of both new objects of study and new theoretical titles. Psychological discourse has foregrounded resilience much more than the first couple of decades, for instance. This book makes a significant contribution to knowledge in three respects: through its pioneering interdisciplinary methodology, in considering a wide range of media and by bringing diversity to the texts examined in terms of gender and race. Breaking away from understanding trauma defined solely according to dominant criticism, which stems principally from psychoanalytic theory, this study combines trauma criticism with theories from fields more appropriate to analysing the specific themes, techniques and media of popular trauma representations. Therefore, this book follows and extends interdisciplinary trauma studies on popular culture. While there is scant space in this Introduction for an analysis of the wide-ranging critical literature on this research area, I wish to take a moment here to survey existing interdisciplinary studies on trauma in popular culture. The most significant of which include Linnie Blake's *The Wounds of Nations: Horror Cinema, Historical Trauma and National Identity*, Adam Lowenstein's *Shocking Representation: Historical Trauma, National Cinema, and the Modern Horror Film*, Roger Luckhurst's *The Trauma Question* and Alan Gibbs' *Contemporary American Trauma Narratives.* Luckhurst's landmark study analyses trauma across a range of high- and low-brow cultural forms, such as Stephen King's trauma Gothic, 'misery memoirs', and trauma auteurs of film including David Lynch and Atom Egoyan, as well as utilises a range of theories such as film studies. Luckhurst does this in order to produce a state-of-the-art assessment of the widespread impact of trauma studies on cultural production. Luckhurst said he aimed to 'extend the range of cultural reference from the relatively narrow body of texts that typically feature in cultural trauma theory' during the time of his book's production (*Trauma* 15), that he 'wanted to move beyond Modernist aesthetics of fragmentation and aporia and into popular culture' to demonstrate 'the reiteration of traumatic subjectivity in different kinds of register' (*Trauma* 15). Luckhurst asserts the importance of popular culture to the representation of trauma, stating that 'Hollywood representations are as important as those of the avant-garde in the co-constitution and diffusion of the trauma paradigm' (*Trauma* 179). He also acknowledges that trauma in cinema incorporates both high and low forms and it is therefore difficult to label trauma cinema as either high or low culture: 'a significant mark of trauma in cinema is its constant movement between high and low forms … [it is] progressively difficult … to situate their cinema of trauma as either marginal or mainstream' (*Trauma* 179). Luckhurst suggests that what he considers the now derivative trauma aesthetic can be avoided in two ways. First, consider narrative experimentation as a 'possibility' rather than a necessity for trauma representation, which would 'open up the different kinds of cultural work that trauma narratives undertake' (*Trauma* 89). Second, regard trauma fiction 'not as a narrow canon' of high-cultural avant-garde works, but as 'a mass of narratives that have exploded across high, middle and low-brow fiction since the late 1980s, texts with wildly different ambitions but that frequently share the same narrative devices' (*Trauma* 89–90).

Blake's and Lowenstein's later studies examine historical trauma in international avant-garde and popular horror cinema, and incorporate diverse theories from cinematic genre studies, historical materialism and postmodernism. Blake explores how horror film criticism can 'enable us to shift the emphasis of trauma critique away from high-modernist cultural artefacts and onto popular cultural forms', and highlights how forms such as horror have been excluded from dominant trauma theory (4). Combining trauma and horror studies, Blake focuses on 'the social, cultural and political function of horror cinema', exploring how horror films employ the conventions of the genre to represent traumatic historical events including the Holocaust, Vietnam and the atomic bombing of Hiroshima and Nagasaki (5). Blake explores a range of international horror films, including the body horror of the American 1970s, avant-garde German Reunification horror, and more recent supernatural Japanese horror. Lowenstein's study takes a similar approach, exploring what he terms the 'allegorical moment' in horror cinema, meaning that which conforms neither to realist representation nor to experimental modernist techniques when representing historical traumas. Lowenstein draws upon Lyotard's theory of the differend as a means of 'finding new idioms' for the 'unrepresentable' experience of trauma (5). Lowenstein's study demonstrates how horror cinema can be seen as evading the concept of trauma as unspeakable and unrepresentable, which he says silences victims (5). Lowenstein argues that 'when traumatic experience becomes equated solely with the "unrepresentable", then this respect for victims/survivors transforms, paradoxically, into a silencing of both experience and representation' (5). Lowenstein surveys a range of critically neglected international horror films which disrupt the boundaries between high and low cinema, between experimental avant-garde and mainstream film, and argues that these texts more adequately represent national traumas including the Holocaust, Hiroshima and Vietnam. Similar to Blake, Lowenstein also argues that these horror films challenge 'comforting historical narratives and notions of national identity intended to soothe public anxieties in the aftermath of national traumas' (n.p.).

Gibbs does not focus on popular culture but shifts the focus from psychoanalytic approaches to trauma to theories from alternative fields, primarily narratology. Gibbs also incorporates cult texts such as *House of Leaves*, and war films such as Sam Mendes' *Jarhead* (2005). While this project also takes an interdisciplinary approach, I combine trauma theory with a unique methodology, including postmodernism, narratology, feminist film theory, animation and game studies and queer theory. In positing original paradigms for reading trauma in popular culture, I explore new topics of trauma representation. Of these topics, the relationship between trauma and postmodernism has been considered by Gibbs, who examines ontological trauma, and Lowenstein, who employs Jean-François Lyotard's concept of the differend. My analysis focuses on postmodern scepticism as a theme in popular trauma texts, a new topic which aims to add to Gibbs' and Lowenstein's criticism. In terms of media, my project contributes to the developing critical tendency to broaden the boundaries of what is defined as trauma culture. I widen the scope of critical enquiry to consider games and animation, which are amongst the most active and pioneering areas of trauma representation. Among the most significant scholarship on trauma in games include Tobi Smethurst and Stef Craps' article 'Playing with Trauma: Interreactivity, Empathy, and Complicity in *The Walking Dead* Video Game', and Smethurst's articles 'Playing Dead in Videogames: Trauma in *Limbo*' and 'We Put Our Hands on the Trigger with Him: Guilt and Perpetration in *Spec OPS: The Line*'. Regarding diversity in popular trauma representations, Tim Rayborn's and Abigail Keyes' *Jessica Jones, Scarred Superhero: Essays on Gender, Trauma and Addiction in the Netflix Series*, and April Kalogeropoulos Householder's and Adrienne Trier-Bieniek's *Feminist Perspectives on Orange is the New Black: Thirteen Critical Essays* acknowledge women's engagement with trauma in popular culture. Cassandra Chaney and Ray V. Robertson examine post-traumatic slave syndrome in popular culture (2016), and Nikola N. Stepić analyses queer cultural memory in the work of Ryan Murphy (2017).

Definitions, Cultural Trauma Theory and Cultural Contexts

It is also necessary to outline this book's definition of terms, and the socio-cultural and historical contexts for American trauma representation. Definitions are required to denote the differences between canonical texts, popular culture and cult texts. By popular culture, I refer to non-canonical cultural forms including television series, horror films, comic book adaptations, animation and video games. I also include in this definition of popular culture 'cult' texts that blur the boundaries between high and low culture. A number of popular texts can be defined as cult works, which can be seen as experimental or avant-garde to a degree. *House of Leaves*, *The Shining* and *Twin Peaks* analysed in this study are very much cult works. Cult texts share a number of formal and thematic similarities with the high-cultural avant-garde works valorised by dominant cultural trauma theory, including experimental formal techniques, 'ambiguous generic identity' and 'resistance to closure' (Pheasant-Kelly, 'Strange' 95). What distinguishes these texts from high-cultural works is that 'the term cult is usually understood through audience involvement' (Pheasant-Kelly, 'Strange' 95). For example, Mark Jancovich and Nathan Hunt claim that 'cult features are not intrinsic to the texts themselves, but emerge through fan responses' (Pheasant-Kelly, 'Strange' 95). Furthermore, Janet Staiger argues that 'cult engagement involves more intense displays of interest than seen in normal viewing activities'

(Pheasant-Kelly, 'Strange' 95). According to Staiger, this includes 'expressing opinions, speculation, gossip and predictions' and 'a tendency to repeat memorised lines of dialogue' (Pheasant-Kelly, 'Strange' 95). For instance, predictions for episodes of *Twin Peaks: The Return* (2017) were discussed in online forums such as *Reddit*, whereas we would generally not see this kind of engagement with more canonical trauma texts by Joseph Heller and J.D. Salinger. Frances Pheasant-Kelly observes that difficult topics, such as murder, incest and deformity, also promote 'cult spectatorship', in addition to a 'fascination with space' (95). Pheasant-Kelly identifies the unusual space of the Black Lodge in *Twin Peaks* as an example of such ('Strange' 95).

To define trauma, trauma essentially is an emotional and/or physical response to a distressing, disturbing event, resulting in clusters of symptoms. Trauma frequently involves being confronted with an experience involving 'actual or threatened death or serious injury, or a physical threat to the physical integrity of the self' (American Psychiatric Association 467–468), such as wars, rape, sexual abuse and natural and man-made disasters. However, trauma can also describe other significantly stressful events. Trauma may result from a sudden, overwhelming event outside the range of normal human experience, or it may result from a gradual series of everyday events. For instance, Stef Craps and Gurt Buelens describe trauma as resulting from everyday experiences of inequality and oppression such as sexism. Laura S. Brown describes insidious trauma as 'the traumatogenic effects of oppression that are not necessarily overtly violent or threatening to bodily well-being at the given moment but that do violence to the soul and spirit' (107). As Craps and Bond note, trauma's definition is unstable because of its transition from professional to popular discourse (4). Despite ongoing debate, and the symptoms of trauma being diverse, critics generally agree that their common denominator is an extreme stressor (event and or/series of events). Symptoms can include flashbacks and nightmares, a 'persistent avoidance of stimuli associated with the trauma in the form of avoiding thoughts or feelings associated with the trauma', a 'numbing of general responsiveness' or the 'inability to recall' the traumatic event, and an increased arousal including hypervigilance and exaggerated startle response (American Psychiatric Association 467–480). Trauma is not always involuntarily unavailable and unconsciously erased through amnesia; therefore a further symptom can be a conscious and deliberate repression of the event (Gibbs 11). Trauma sufferers may also have memories of partial memories of the event, or memories may be influenced by fantasies and desires, with the trauma being reworked in memory and affected by the sufferers fantasies (Gibbs 13). Symptoms can appear belatedly, days, weeks, months or even years after the event, or can come on acutely, persisting chronically (Luckhurst, *Trauma* 1).

Cultural trauma theory is the study of trauma within the humanities that largely focuses on how trauma is represented in cultural forms, such as literature and film. Cultural trauma theory is an interdisciplinary area of study, as trauma has been increasingly studied through a variety of approaches, including 'production, contexts, reception studies, political implications and social meanings' (Hodgin and Thakkar 2). For example, Blake defines cultural trauma theory as follows:

> Trauma Studies can thus be seen as a body of theoretical scholarship that addresses itself to cultural memory, to the modes in which traumatic events are representationally transmitted in time and space, to the politics of memorialising such events and experiences and to the cultural significance of vicarious modes of witnessing trauma. (1)

Cultural trauma theory is in contrast to clinical trauma theory. Clinical trauma theory refers to the study of real-life individuals who have experienced trauma. For example, Craps and Bond describe clinical trauma theory as 'psychiatric approaches to trauma' (*Trauma* 5). Dominant cultural trauma theory then refers to cultural trauma theories that have been significantly influential upon subsequent cultural trauma theory and trauma representations.

Rehearsing a full genealogy of trauma and PTSD is beyond the scope of this study and already covered in existing criticism. In summary, from the 1980s onwards, PTSD and trauma have reached 'far into culture' (Gibbs 1), effecting 'the rise of what is becoming almost a new theoretical orthodoxy' (Radstone, 'Theory' 10). PTSD was first designed through its inclusion in the 1980 third edition of the American Psychiatric Association's (APA) *Diagnostic and Statistical Manual of Mental Disorders* (*DSM-III*). The dominant trauma theorist Cathy Caruth has also been very influential. Essentially, Caruth's trauma theory draws upon Holocaust studies, post-structuralism, Sigmund Freud and the roots of PTSD as a concept in the experience of Vietnam veterans (specifically, the APA's definition of

PTSD as an event 'outside the range of usual human experience' (467–468)). Indeed, while PTSD was defined in 1980, the condition was discussed much earlier, such as, for example, in Freudian reports of shellshock during 1920 after World War I. Allan Young, for instance, notes that traumatic memory 'originates in the scientific and clinical discourses of the nineteenth century; before that time there is unhappiness, despair, and disturbing recollections' (141). Ben Shephard also asserts that Vietnam 'helped to create a new "consciousness of trauma" in Western society' (355).

First, Caruth claims that trauma is belated, meaning that a traumatic event is so overwhelming it cannot be assimilated into memory at the time of the event and is instead repressed and returns in the form of flashbacks and nightmares:

> there is a response, sometimes delayed, to an overwhelming event or events, which takes the form of repeated, intrusive hallucinations, dreams, thoughts or behaviours stemming from the event ... the event is not assimilated or experienced fully at the time, but only belatedly, in its repeated possession of the one who experiences it. (*Trauma* 4)

Caruth's characterisation of trauma as belated stems from Freud's notion of *Nachträglichkeit* ('belatedness' or 'afterwardness'), that traumatic memory is repressed from consciousness but returns in flashbacks and nightmares. Gibbs, for example, refers to the belatedness model of trauma as the 'Freudian-Caruthian model' (33).

Second, Caruth defines trauma as unspeakable or unrepresentable, which means that trauma should be represented in experimental and indirect forms. Caruth says that trauma 'must, indeed, also be spoken in a language that is always somehow literary: a language that defies, even as it claims, our understanding' (*Unclaimed* 5). For Caruth, trauma should be represented in experimental forms in order to convey rather than represent to the reader the suffering of the work's protagonist. Defined as transmissibility, this type of aesthetic draws upon techniques found in avant-garde modernist and postmodernist texts. These include the collapses of temporality and chronology or narrative and chronological fragmentation, dislocation, repetition, indirection, belated revelations of traumatic incidents, open endings/non-closure, non-linear chronologies, shifts in narrating voice and decentred subjectivity. For example, a writer may employ fragmented chronologies to represent a character's flashbacks of a traumatic incident in order to make the reader feel similarly disorientated. Fragmented narratives may be characterised by analepses, digressions, diversions, abrupt ellipses, prevarications in narrative trajectory and 'dispersal or fragmenting of narrative personae' (Gibbs 17). The literal character of traumatic memory is a further reason for Caruth that trauma cannot be adequately represented in straightforward or realistic language. For Caruth, traumatic memory is 'absolutely true to the event' (*Trauma* 5), so the event literally returns to the sufferer, but traumatic dreams and flashbacks are also 'nonsymbolic' in nature (*Trauma* 5). Caruth's concepts of trauma as unspeakable and the transmission of affect have roots in Holocaust studies in particular, stemming from the idea that Holocaust representations must cause emotional effect in the reader, a 'suffering approximating that of the victims' (Rothe 161). Conforming to Caruth's assertion that trauma is unrepresentable then, the trauma genre aesthetic is, as Luckhurst says, 'uncompromisingly avant-garde' (*Trauma* 8). As writers are encouraged to seek structures that are 'experimental, fragmented, refusing the consolations of beautiful form', they are 'suspicious of familiar representational and narrative conventions' (Luckhurst, *Trauma* 8). Craps and Bond similarly observe that adherence to 'the modernist aesthetic of fragmentation and discontinuity … has long been seen as a requirement for entry into the canon of valued trauma literature' (*Trauma* 9).

What is referred to as canonical narratives, then, are works considered by cultural trauma theory and literary and cultural criticism to be representative of the trauma genre because they largely conform to the aesthetic models and themes outlined in dominant cultural trauma theory. Despite ongoing debate about trauma representation and its definition in fiction, among the trauma writers critics generally identified as canonical include J. D. Salinger, Joseph Heller, Kurt Vonnegut, Toni Morrison, Robin Moore, William Lederer and Eugene Burdick, Philip Caputo and Tim O'Brien (although O'Brien has been found to both conform to and satirise elements of canonical trauma narratives). These texts are frequently presented from a white American androcentric perspective, and focus on combat trauma, featuring traumatised soldier-protagonists (of course, there are exceptions, such as Morrison's work). The primary focus lies on the traumatic experience of the veterans and invading US forces, as opposed to that of the civilians' as a result of military action. The received, elite, canonical conceptions of trauma generally conform to the Freudian-Caruthian model in regards to belatedness, amnesia and the unrepresentability of trauma. These representations entail characters experiencing belated symptoms such as involuntary flashbacks, nightmares, dissociation and 'cycles of repetitive, often self-destructive behaviour, without having access to the originating cause' (Gibbs 25). Such texts employ the experimental formal techniques outlined above to represent such symptoms, in order to 'transmit affect onto the reader' and create ostensibly convincing depictions of trauma (Gibbs 28). Two examples of canonical trauma fiction are Heller's *Catch-22* and Vonnegut's *Slaughterhouse-Five*. These are texts that attempt to employ experimental techniques that are familiar in the depiction of trauma such as fragmented, non-chronological narration. Both texts have long been interpreted as a formally rich evocations of trauma (Gibbs 56). *Catch-22* is set during World War II and follows the life of Yossarian, a US Army Air Force B-25 bombardier who witnesses the death of Snowden, a member of Yossarian's flight during a mission. The text employs circling as a form of evasive narration, a technique which involves a structure of repetition and circling towards the protagonist's traumatic experience (Yossarian's death), with selective and fragmented additions to initially synecdochical memories that gradually reveal this traumatising event to the reader. This technique mirrors belated and recurring flashbacks. Yossarian's traumatic experience in totality is deferred until the penultimate chapter of the novel. *Slaughterhouse-Five* is a semi-autobiographic anti-war novel that follows Billy Pilgrim, and chronicles his time as a soldier during World War II, as well as his early and post-war years. Billy is in a permanently dissociated traumatised state whereby he believes he retreats to an alien planet. He also claims to experience time travel, which is in actuality flashbacks, and the text's non-linear narrative reflects this. In terms of film, cinema has become among the key means for representing trauma according to the Freudian-Caruthian model. Luckhurst notes that the medium is suitable for the 'narrative temporalisation of experience in the twentieth-century', and its specific stylistic devices, such as *mise-en-scène* and montage, conventions for marking point of view and temporal shifts, have made it a 'cultural form closely attuned to representing the discordances of trauma' (*Trauma* 177). An example of such is the fractured imagery in Paul Haggis' *In the Valley of Elah* (2007). *In the Valley of Elah* depicts a military father's search for his son, and explores themes of the Iraq War and PTSD. In the film, the visual devices that structure the narrative are employed in a way to mirror soldiers' traumatic memory, specifically fractured imagery which mimic flashbacks, as images of violence and death intermittently inject narratively. Pheasant-Kelly says the 'narrative structure whereby scenes of gruesome death are abruptly inter-spliced with unspectacular ordinary scenes' ('Signifying' 7) renders these scenes 'more intrusive' and 'replicat[es] both the nature of traumatising events and the invasive effect of the flashback on normal life' ('Signifying' 8).

However, as noted, critics are increasingly seeking to extend the range of cultural reference from the then relatively narrow body of texts that used to typically feature in cultural trauma theory and move beyond Modernist aesthetics, which this book also aims to do. As Craps and Bond note, a new direction of cultural trauma research is a tendency to study 'popular, realist or indigenous literature' and increasing 'attention is being paid to the representation of traumatic experiences in media other than literature' such as film and video games (9). At the same time, Caruth's concepts of unspeakability and transmission have retained a hold on studies of trauma in popular culture, which this study aims to move beyond via its interdisciplinary approach and by formulating new paradigms more suited to the study of trauma in popular works that take into account the specific themes, forms and media of popular culture. While a number of the texts examined in this study are formally experimental, they employ more unique techniques beyond the conventional forms of trauma representation described above, and/or they rework these techniques to formulate new ones. Additionally, as noted, the experimental forms in my selected primary texts are frequently used to further explore rather than, as Lowenstein suggests, repress traumatic experiences.

CHAPTER 2

Trauma and Postmodernism: Mark Z. Danielewski's *House of Leaves* and Stanley Kubrick's *The Shining*

This chapter examines the relationship between trauma and postmodernism in two cult horror texts: Mark Z. Danielewski's *House of Leaves* and Stanley Kubrick's *The Shining*. There are a number of issues to be unpacked here: What is the connection between postmodernism and trauma? What is postmodernism? When does postmodernism begin and end, and has it ended? What particular aspect of postmodernism is represented in popular trauma texts? To begin with postmodernism's connection with trauma, the experimental forms of postmodernism have 'frequently become approved formulaic markers of trauma genre literature' (Gibbs 86). As noted in the Introduction, this stems from Caruth's theories of transmission and unspeakability, which are rooted in Holocaust studies and post-structuralism. In terms of theme, then, one of the most significant ways that popular culture is innovative in terms of trauma representation is its engagement with postmodern themes and perspectives in addition to an experimental postmodern aesthetic. When discussing *House of Leaves*, Gibbs says that one key characteristic that marks the novel off from earlier, paradigmatic trauma texts is that it 'not only employs postmodernist literary techniques as a means to illustrate the effect of trauma, but also explores concrete thematic links between postmodernism and trauma' (98). I argue that trauma attributed to the conditions of postmodernity is a theme more commonly found in certain contemporary popular and cult texts, specifically trauma deriving from the scepticism and nihilistic perspectives of postmodernity.

S. Travers, *Trauma in American Popular Culture and Cult Texts, 1980–2020*, https://doi.org/10.1007/978-3-031-13287-2_2

Postmodernism

It is essential to note that scepticism and nihilism are merely one aspect of postmodernity and that there are multiple interpretations of postmodernism. Postmodernism is a historical term and a concept that means a bewildering array of different things to different individuals. Essentially, postmodernism can be described as experimental or 'avant-garde', a 'continuation of the values and techniques of modernism' or a break with these techniques (Nicol 1). The term was originally defined in the 1940s to identify a reaction against the Modern movement in architecture, but the term began to be more widely used in the 1960s by cultural critics to describe a set of aesthetic styles and ideas developed from philosophy and theory which characterise literary and cultural production, and which are influenced by the context of postmodernity (Nicol 2). The characteristics of postmodern works include metafiction, pastiche to original production, a mixing of styles and genres and the juxtaposition of 'low' and 'high' culture. There is also disagreement regarding when postmodernism ends. Bran Nicol frames postmodernity as ending in the 1990s but notes that many critics argue that we are still in the postmodern period. I argue that contemporary American popular culture still incorporates many of the postmodern themes and conventions outlined above, ranging from comedy-drama television series including Dan Harmon's *Community* (2009–2015) and Rachel Bloom and Aline Brosh McKenna's *Crazy-Ex Girlfriend* (2015-2019), to films including Joss Whedon's *Cabin in the Woods* (2012) and Tim Miller's *Deadpool* (2016), to games such as *Doki Doki Literature Club* and *Undertale.*

There are a number of key postmodern theorists relevant to contemporary American popular culture and cult texts. As noted in the Introduction, the most significant of whom to this chapter is Jean-François Lyotard, who defined postmodernism as 'incredulity towards metanarratives' (xxxiv). This refers to scepticism towards the overarching grand narratives which purport to explain how the world works, such as history or religion. In other words, in postmodernity, our dominant discourses are viewed as artificial constructs rather than 'natural', made by us rather than 'given'. For instance, religious explanations of the world have, to an extent, lost their cogency, having been replaced with secular ones, with God and every other transcendent source of value beyond human beings considered to be a myth (Woodward, 'Postmodern' 56). Dominant discourses such as history are viewed as partial, selective and interpretive rather than exact and objective recordings of past events (Hutcheon 70). Language and identity are similarly viewed as human-made, in particular by poststructuralist theorists. Ferdinand de Saussure in *Course in General Linguistics* (1916) claims the relationship between the signified and the signifier to be arbitrary, while Roland Barthes asserts in 'The Death of the Author' that language speaks us and precedes us, that we cannot write anything original but arrange pre-existing linguistic structures into particular narratives (4). Lacanian theory similarly proposes that an individual's 'identity is a product of language' (Belville 48), and that language does not allow us to express anything individual because it has been constructed by other people (Lacan 209). Identity itself is also considered by postmodernism as something that is constructed by external forces rather than fixed from birth. Emphasising the role of dominant ideologies in the shaping of individual identity, postmodernist theory attends to the relationship between discourse and power in the construction of values, conventions and norms. Judith Butler demonstrates in her writing how identity and behaviour are constructed according to dominant conventions of gender (519), while Michael Foucault argues in 'The Subject and Power' that discourse shapes individuality, asserting that there are 'different modes by which, in our culture, human beings are made subjects' (777). Further, critics such as Jean-Paul Sartre and Arnold Weinstein assert in their writings that it is in fact 'nothingness' that lies beneath all forms of identity. For Sartre, 'existence precedes essence' (3), while Weinstein claims that 'nothingness is primal. ... Nobody lurks within all selves, ... our forms of being are culturally produced' (5). Jean Baudrillard, likewise, theorises the end of subjectivity, truth and history in the 1980s. Baudrillard was in line with structuralists and poststructuralists in his belief that subjectivity was produced by language, social institutions and cultural forms. For Baudrillard, capitalism homogenises, controls and dominates social life, and removes from individuals their freedom, creativity, time, individuality, self-determination and human potentialities. Baudrillard argues that commodities and technologies dominate people, taking away their human qualities and capacities, reifying individuals. The postmodern era, then, is underscored by a radical and increasing decline of our overarching concepts of reality, truth and self.

Trauma

It is scepticism, then, this particular perspective of postmodernity (to recall, there are multiple), which links postmodernism as a mode of thought with nihilism because of postmodernity's 'negation of existing ideologies' (Woodward, 'Postmodern' 51). Specifically, postmodern thought chimes with existential nihilism, which is defined as, essentially, 'the belief that life is meaningless … that existence itself … is ultimately senseless and empty' (Alan Pratt). Fredrich Nietzsche defines nihilism as 'the radical repudiation of value, meaning and desirability' (7). For Nietzsche, there is no objective order or structure in the world except what individuals give it (Alan Pratt). Alan Pratt goes on to say that this realisation, that metanarratives are merely constructs employed to give life meaning and that there is no objective order in the world except that which humans invent, produces in individuals a profound sense of 'nothingness' and lack of meaning,

> [When we] expose all cherished beliefs and sacrosanct truths as symptoms of a defective Western mythos … [w]hen we abandon [these] illusions, life is revealed as nothing; and … nothingness is the source of not only absolute freedom but also existential horror and emotional anguish.

Akin to an existential crisis, I propose that this experience can be read as a type of trauma, and that this trauma is a theme of certain popular and cult horror texts. While nihilism was certainly fashionable in the postmodern 1980s and 1990s, I argue that nihilism is a theme evident in American popular culture from approximately the 1980s to the present. The fashionable, more radical nihilists of the 1980s and 1990s such as Jean Baudrillard and Arthur and Marilousie Kroker were criticised at the time of production, and their philosophy of a wilful refusal of meaning arguably came to an end in the 1990s. However, Thomas S. Hibbs, in *Shows About Nothing: Nihilism in Popular Culture*, points out, 'nihilistic premises pervade our popular culture, infiltrating … horror films and violent movies of the week', in addition to 'the most successful mainstream sitcom of the last thirty years, *Seinfeld*, a show about the comical consequences of life in a world void of any ultimate significance or fundamental meaning' (6). We can add to this multiple works of contemporary cinema and television series, including Peter Weir's *The Truman Show* (1998), James Wan's *Saw* (2004), Raphael Bob-Waksberg's *Bojack Horseman* (2014–2020) and

Dan Harmon and Justin Rolland's *Rick and Morty* (2013–present). Highlighting the nihilistic scepticism of postmodernity specifically, Hibbs argues that:

> From *The Matrix* to *Inception*, many highly successful contemporary films begin from the assumption that what we have taken to be real is in fact a construct. ... Reality dissolves into a self-referential trap. Nihilism generates banality, an egalitarian sense of emptiness. (3)

This experience of realising 'what we have taken to be real is in fact a construct' as a source of trauma is yet to be explored, a topic the following will examine in *House of Leaves* and *The Shining*.

It is important to note that the postmodern condition, its scepticism and nihilistic tendencies are traumatic solely in fiction. This is not the case in reality. As noted in the Introduction, there is a significant difference between clinical trauma theory (the study of real-life individuals who have experienced trauma or psychiatric approaches to trauma) and cultural trauma theory (fictional representations of trauma). Both *House of Leaves* and *The Shining* feature characters experiencing traumatic symptoms in line with those in paradigmatic trauma fiction outlined in the Introduction, and both texts feature innovative reworkings of the themes and techniques found in mainstream fictional trauma representations. However, while *House of Leaves* and *The Shining* generate multiple interpretations, I argue that the symptoms, themes and techniques depicted in these texts evoke the postmodern condition.

There are a number of reasons for this reading. First, both *House of Leaves* and *The Shining* are very parodic of existing discourses, in particular discourses surrounding trauma. *House of Leaves*, in particular, has been found by critics to parody trauma theory (Gibbs; Bemong). *The Shining* similarly parodies horror and trauma texts that feature family violence. Both texts' depiction of the postmodern condition as traumatic, then, can be interpreted as part of these texts' parodic approach. Both texts also demonstrate a scepticism towards metanarratives and discourses, which is significant in texts which depict trauma, because trauma too is a discourse. *House of Leaves* undermines many major dominant trauma concepts, such as, for example, scriptotherapy (the act of writing as a means of healing from trauma), and communicating trauma to others as a means of therapy. The protagonists of both texts partake in these activities and their conditions exacerbate. It is also important to note my order of readings here. I examine *House of Leaves* first because Danielewski's text has previously been examined by existing scholarship in terms of the trauma produced specifically by postmodern conditions. For example, Gibbs explores the text in terms of ontological trauma, which he defines as postmodernity's challenge to major foundations of knowledge and Enlightenment thought, the undermining of 'previously cherished certainties' (109). *The Shining*, on the other hand, has yet to be examined in terms of this theme. I therefore aim for my analysis of *House of Leaves* in terms of postmodern nihilism to inform that of *The Shining*. Furthermore, *House of Leaves* depicts postmodern nihilism via more conventional, recognisable themes and imagery, specifically absence, and concepts such as nothingness and the decline of metanarratives. By contrast, *The Shining* depicts nihilism more uniquely via imagery of abundance, and lesser known themes including the exhaustion of art and micronarratives.

Second, there is an important point to be made about trauma in terms of gender and privilege. According to Brown, trauma is frequently an ongoing experience for women, children, people of colour and the LGBTQIA+ community.[1] As noted in the Introduction, the type of trauma frequently experienced by straight white males is a sudden, overwhelming event outside the range of usual human experience; in other words, those who are lucky and privileged enough that trauma is unusual, rather than an ongoing part of everyday life. That the male-centred texts *House of Leaves* and *The Shining* depict the postmodern condition—something that more likely causes unease and cynicism—as traumatic, can be read through this concept of trauma and male privilege. As explored in Chaps. 3, 4 and 5, this is in contrast to texts which feature diverse characters experiencing trauma that results from extreme, prolonged situations such as systemic racism and childhood abuse. That both *House of Leaves* and *The Shining* feature male protagonists is further significant in terms of this perspective on the scepticism of postmodernity. While not traumatising in actuality, men have been found to consider this phenomenon threatening, evident in misogynistic backlashes to feminism and movements such as Men's Rights Activism. Such movements employ hyperbolic language which borders on trauma discourse, and a number of men claim to be traumatised. However, such rhetoric is a cover-up for misogyny. This is evident in sexist online trolls, 'keyboard warriors' and incels. Indeed, incels are members of an online community of young men who consider themselves

[1] Explored further in Chap. 3.

unable to attract women, and in turn have inflicted violence against women in real life. I argue that the male leads of both *House of Leaves* and *The Shining* being traumatised by the decline of metanarratives evoke this reaction.

The grand narratives called into question and undermined in postmodernity are those largely made by, and thus made to benefit, dominant groups (straight white men), and by turns tend to harm and constrict everyone else, including women, people of colour and the LGBTQIA+ community. Major discourses such as history and religion are phallocentric metanarratives. Likewise, traditional constructs such as gender and identity are designed largely to be advantageous to men and detrimental to women. Further, with the decline of metanarratives comes the increasing inclusion and valuing of marginalised voices and perspectives. According to Tristan Bridges, 'as societies redistribute privileges that have been largely reserved for straight white men, this group feels threatened by their loss of entitlement and privilege'. According to Barbara Creed, 'there is a common group shared by feminism and postmodernism', despite feminism coming 'from a different theoretical basis' (52). Creed points out that feminism critiques grand narratives 'in terms of the workings of patriarchal ideology and the oppression of women and other minority groups', while 'postmodernism looks to other possible causes', particularly the 'reliance on ideologies which posit universal truths', such as history and religion (52). Creed says that 'feminism would argue that the common ideological position of all these "truths" is that they are patriarchal' whereas 'postmodern theory ... would be reluctant to isolate a single major determining factor' (52). Despite this difference, however, Craig Owens observes that 'both feminism and postmodernism endorse Lyotard's argument' that the grand narratives 'have lost their credibility' (Creed 47). Furthermore, Owens adds that both feminism and postmodernism present 'a critique of representation' (59), 'that system of power that authorises certain representations while blocking, prohibiting or invalidating others' (59); and that both agree that the dominant 'representational systems ... admit only one vision—that of the constitutive male subject' (58). It therefore appears fitting for texts which explore the thematic connections between trauma and postmodernism to write within the horror genre, and feature men haunted by the very nothingness produced by the pervasive scepticism towards this group and their discourses. While *House of Leaves* and *The Shining* do not exhibit a complete alteration of horror or trauma fiction's gender conventions (male characters are still at the centre of both works), these texts feature male protagonists haunted by a sense of nothingness and searching for monsters. This is in contrast to the horror convention of 'women being chased along dark corridors' (Botting 11). Significantly, not only are metanarratives and constructs of reality eradicated in the empty labyrinth in *House of Leaves*, but certain male characters in the narrative literally disappear along with these grand narratives. Jack, too, appears wiped out at the end of *The Shining*, similarly enveloped by the labyrinthine surroundings of the snow-covered maze he freezes in.

House of Leaves and *The Shining* were produced two decades apart yet both texts can be read as responding to periods of increasing inclusion. 1980 and 2000 are periods during which the phallocentric grand narratives were called into question. The early 2000s was a time of third wave feminism. Postmodern feminism and intersectionality were on the rise; therefore multiple diverse voices emerged, which contributed to the breakdown of overarching metanarratives in favour of micronarratives.[2] Through his theory of the end of metanarratives, Lyotard characterises postmodernity as an age of multiplicity, fragmentation and pluralism. Micronarratives are 'individual, localised narratives or temporarily useful interpretive constructions' (Nicol 12). These narratives do not attempt to present an overarching 'truth' but offer what 'a qualified, limited truth, one relative to a particular situation' (12). The postmodern condition, then, 'is more generally marked by a plurality of voices vying for the right to reality—to be accepted as legitimate expression of the true' (Gergen 7). During the time *The Shining* was produced, Kubrick was aware of this idea of postmodernity as a time pervaded by the paranoia of a Western male-dominated society resisting changes that increasingly included the voices of the marginalised, such as the Native American activism of the 1970s. Fredric Jameson, for instance, argues that Kubrick's evocation of a hotel stuck hauntingly in the 1920s is representative of 'nostalgia for the wealth and confidence in rigid racial and class hierarchies of the pre-war era' (Luckhurst, *Shining* 45). Jameson says that *The Shining* appears to project 'a longing to believe and the nostalgia for an era when belief seemed possible', as well as a time 'in which an American ruling class … enjoyed its

[2] Kimberlé Crenshaw, who coined the term, describes intersectional feminism as 'a prism for seeing the way in which various forms of inequality often operate together and exacerbate each other', such as the distinct forms of oppression faced by women of colour and trans women.

privileges [openly and] ... without guilt', in contrast to 'today, where ... the most repressed ... have begun to speak in their own voice and to project the demands of properly revolutionary subjects' (131). As we shall see, Kubrick includes a wealth of Native American imagery in *The Shining*, the blood pouring out of the elevator that 'haunts' the hotel has been read as suggestive of the blood of the Native Americans, the hotel is built on an Indian burial site, and Jack laments the 'white man's burden'. Examining *House of Leaves* and *The Shining*, two horror texts twenty years apart, demonstrates the pervasive white male reaction of fear and purported 'trauma' in the face of loss of privilege.[3]

House of Leaves

Mark Z. Danielewski's *House of Leaves* centres on a traumatised individual named Johnny Truant, an apprentice tattoo artist living in Los Angeles, and his experience of assembling a manuscript he discovers entitled 'The Navidson Record'.[4] The manuscript was previously edited by a man named Zampanò and it purports to document a film about the life of a family—Will Navidson, Karen Green and their two children—and their move to a house that contains an infinite labyrinth with unstable internal dimensions and possibly a dangerous beast.[5] Published in 2000 by Pantheon Books, *House of Leaves* is Danielewski's debut novel. The novel was on the best-seller list, won the New York Public Library's Young Lions Fiction Award and multiple dissertations have been written on *House of Leaves*. While the novel has generated extensive academic coverage, *House of Leaves* has also generated a strong cult following, the characteristics of which, as noted, usually emerge through fan responses. Prior to publication, Danielewski posted his manuscript on his personal website, with a PDF of *House of*

[3] In addition, both criticism on *House of Leaves* and Danielewski have noted how *The Shining* was among the influences on *House of Leaves*.

[4] In criticism on *House of Leaves*, 'The Navidson Record' conventionally refers to Zampanò's manuscript whereas *The Navidson Record* refers to the fictional film.

[5] *The Navidson Record*, in the fictional plane of Johnny's world, is itself acknowledged to be a work of fiction, the creation of Zampanò. Johnny notes in his Introduction: 'Zampanò's entire project is about a film which doesn't even exist. ... you will never find *The Navidson Record* in theatres or video stores' (xix–xx).

Leaves circulating in an underground scene.[6] Readers were fascinated by the book's experimental labyrinthine design and bizarre story about a TARDIS-like house that is bigger on the inside than the outside.[7] Over twenty years since its publication, the novel continues to inspire fan devotion. The many mysteries, ambiguous content to be decoded and typographical oddities Danielewski incorporates into *House of Leaves* prompt readers to share theories, express opinions and speculate about the novel online. The MZD fan forum website, for instance, sustains and develops the novel's cult following. The *House of Leaves* book club on Facebook has over 7000 members, with its moderator Dreebs Thornhill noting that '*House of Leaves* is a living, breathing thing. … It's one of those things you can't relax with until you've discussed it with someone else' (Lloyd). Danielewski has commented on this type and level of fan engagement with his text, noting that *House of Leaves* deliberately encourages fan interpretation and cult spectatorship. In an interview with Larry McCaffery and Linda Gregory, Danielewski says that 'intellectual engagement' with *House of Leaves* 'has never been my primary goal', that 'rather I've always wanted to create scenes and scenarios that verge on the edge of specificity without crossing into identification, leaving enough room, so to speak, for the reader to participate and supply her own fears, his own anxieties, their own history and future' (119–120). Moreover, the novel is listed and examined in the popular website *TV Tropes*, has its own page on *Fandom* and has been discussed on popular culture websites including *The A.V. Club*, *Bloody Disgusting* and *Wired*. *House of Leaves* has sparked much fan art on sites including *DeviantArt*, and readers have created video reviews and essays about the novel. Repeated and memorised lines of dialogue, another key characteristic of cult texts, are especially evident in the *House of Leaves* fandom, with individuals quoting from the novel on social media and getting lines from the text tattooed. Danielewski compares the novel to 'smart horror' films which generate fan speculation, such as Daniel Myrick and Eduardo Sánchez's *The Blair Witch Project* (1999): 'kids want to talk about it, read about it on the Internet' (Cottrell). Indeed, further estab-

[6] Furthering *House of Leaves*' status as a multi- or trans-media experience, Danielewski's sister Poe released a companion musical album entitled *Haunted*, and Danielewski released a companion novella entitled *The Whalestoe Letters*. Danielewski also wrote a script for a television adaptation of *House of Leaves* on his Patreon page, including a script for a TV pilot and three teleplays which function as a sequel or side sequel to the text.

[7] TARDIS is the time machine and spacecraft that appears in the television series *Doctor Who* (Chibnall et al. 1963–present).

lishing *House of Leaves* as a cult text is its ambiguous generic identity. As McCaffery and Gregory observe, *House of Leaves* is 'genre-expanding', that it is 'many different kinds of books rolled into one—part horror novel ... part family saga, part metaphysical speculation', blending genres from high and low culture (99). In particular, *House of Leaves* is heavily influenced by horror cinema, appropriating the content of various cinematic materials from horror film directors including Kubrick and Alfred Hitchcock, an array of B-horror films, horror video games and German expressionists, in addition to mirroring the grammar and syntax of cinema via the novel's unusual typography.

The following will examine two ways that *House of Leaves* represents the trauma produced by postmodern scepticism towards discourses and resulting feelings of meaninglessness and nothingness. First, the type of trauma experienced by the characters in the text can be read as stemming from this phenomenon. Second, the text represents this trauma metaphorically through the motif of the 'haunted house', with Danielewski reworking the 'haunted house' to formulate a new, postmodern variation of the architectural trope. Houses in literature (especially those of the haunted variety) not only serve as plot devices but also as metaphors for particular narrative themes, psychological structures of characters and cultural anxieties (Chandler 3). The deteriorating house in Edgar Allan Poe's 'The Fall of the House of Usher', for instance, can be read as symbolic of the decline of the family residing there (Beebe 1). The house in Danielewski's text similarly represents the postmodern rejection of metanarratives and resulting feelings of 'nothingness' because instead of being haunted by ghosts or apparitions, the house is depicted as a labyrinthine, non-sensical space haunted by emptiness. That is, the house is literally devoid of our basic principles of reality and plagued by the far more disturbing reminder of life's meaninglessness. In this way, Danielewski's house also furthers 'Gothic-postmodernism'. The Gothic novel re-emerged at the dawn of postmodernity (Belville 23). It was influenced by the changing times in which it is written, employing and reinventing Gothic forms to encompass the anxieties of the postmodern age; in particular, the profound loss of faith in the Enlightenment narratives and 'overarching concepts of truth and reality' (Belville 23). The dissolution of reality and subjectivity is frequently emphasised in Gothic-postmodernist literature through pervasive themes of 'uncertainty' and 'disruption' (Pinedo, 'Postmodern' 24, 20), and presented through traditional Gothic tropes such as supernatural occurrences and possession (Belville 200). According to Isabel Cristina

Pinedo, typical features of Gothic-postmodernism also include 'incoherence' (19), the blurring of boundaries between reality and the supernatural (24), and, most significantly, the undermining of basic assumptions about reality (23). Bret Easton Ellis' *Lunar Park*, for instance, has been described as a Gothic novel that mediates on the postmodernist 'unreliability of everything, to a dizzying and or terrifying degree' (Belville 196). Similarly, postmodern horror films throw into question basic principles of reality such as 'temporal order and causal logic' (Pinedo, 'Postmodern' 23). In Wes Craven's *A Nightmare on Elm Street* (1984), we see discrepancies in time and an absence of any logical explanation for its violent narrative events, whereas language itself 'collapses' in horrors such as Sam Raimi's *The Evil Dead* (1981) and Tobe Hooper's *The Texas Chainsaw Massacre* (1974), where the dialogue in the final half hour is replaced with screams and ominous music (Pinedo 'Postmodern' 23). *House of Leaves*' empty house, then, takes this idea of undermining our basic principles of reality a step further.

When discussing haunted houses, Anthony Vidler notes that this motif draws upon the tradition of the uncanny, that a common characteristic of these dwellings is that they initially appear to be ordinary homes until its residents gradually begin to experience unsettling events (30). While this is certainly the case in Danielewski's house, the events that unsettle Navidson and his family are not the usual creaking sounds or glimpse of what Vidler refers to as 'alien spirits' (17) but the house's violation of the fundamental laws of physics and an absence of any stable sense of geography. The unsettling events in Navidson's house begin with a minor discrepancy regarding its measurements. He discovers that the house's internal dimensions exceed those of its exterior in that it measures one quarter of an inch larger on the inside than on the outside, undermining the basic 'assumption that the outside encompasses the inside' (Hayles 791). The house continues to obliterate our basic assumptions of everyday reality as additional rooms start to appear, which, as Zampanò notes, 'while not exactly sinister or even threatening, … still destroyed any sense of security or well-being' (28). Eventually, a dark, doorless hallway emerges in the living room leading to an endless labyrinth which constitutes a similar 'alteration of space beyond physical possibility' (Shastri 99). The labyrinth consists of an infinite number of '[h]allways, corridors [and] rooms' (359). As it grows, the internal geographies become increasingly larger than the physical space it can actually occupy. Anything dropped in the labyrinth 'only slips into darkness and vanishes without a sound' (46) and compasses do not work there so it is impossible to navigate; the text asserts that 'the needle never stays still. North it seems has no authority there' (90) and that 'direction no longer matters' (433). The labyrinth is also shapeshifting, meaning its internal architecture constantly changes, expanding and contracting at random, and turning very short distances into mile-long treks.

Zampanò suggests that the house's mutations 'reflect the psychology of those who enter it' (165). This is reflective of the postmodern realisation that the discourses and structures we impose on the world to create order and meaning in it are human-made rather than natural, because it suggests that those within the labyrinth must 'create' their own systems of measurement when attempting to navigate this space. Zampanò proposes that the labyrinth functions 'like an immense isolation tank' (330) in that the individual must construct their own sense of time, temperature and meaning: '[d]eprived of light, change in temperature and any sense of time, … the individual begins to create his own … [and] projects more and more … personality on those bare walls and vacant hallways' (330). Danielewski's house is unsettling, then, because it draws attention to the artificiality and arbitrary nature of discourses such as our systems of measurement and time. It suggests that an inch is a specific length and a minute consists of sixty seconds because humanity has decided so. Indeed, the quantity of an inch or the duration of a minute is defined by human-made systems such as the Imperial System and The International System of Quantities. The way in which the individual must project meaning or what Zampanò refers to as 'personality' onto the bare walls and empty space of the labyrinth is therefore further evocative of the idea that the dominant features of reality and our systems of meaning are invented by us, and that reality is a blank space upon which we must impose meaning.

Trauma Produced by Postmodern Conditions

It is this characteristic of absence that haunts the house throughout the text. The labyrinth is constantly described by Zampanò as a 'blank' space consisting of bare walls and emptiness. In the climax of 'The Navidson Record', Navidson, repeating the clichéd error of many Gothic and horror protagonists, decides to explore the location of terror by himself. However, instead of encountering a ghost or terrifying apparition that would conventionally be lurking in the basement, he encounters a 'grotesque vision of absence' (464), and each of the structures and discourses we use to make sense of reality including time and geography literally start to disappear:

> the window has vanished along with the room … darkness below, above … [and] beyond. … Who knows how many hours or days pass … he no longer cares about the meaning of a minute or even a week. … he is slowly becoming more … disorientated. … Is he floating … right side up, upside down[?] … questions are sadly irrelevant. (464–465)

This anxiety is further evoked by the 'beast' that apparently haunts the labyrinth because it is strongly suggested that the creature is a fabrication concocted by individuals within this blank space in a desperate attempt to impose meaning on it. This relates to writings on nihilism and the postmodern condition outlined in the Introduction such as those of Nietzsche, in addition to Vonnegut, who argue that we impose meaning on life to conceal its meaninglessness; that we create provisional truths—what Vonnegut calls 'comforting lies'—which 'give life meaning in a meaningless world' (Praxmarer 37). In contrast to traditional Gothic novels and haunted house tales, which typically feature characters plagued by monsters, Danielewski's characters search for such creatures for this reason.

For instance, Zampanò notes, '[t]his desire for exteriority is no doubt further amplified by the utter blankness found within' (119), while there are implications that the beast is imaginary. The growls heard in the labyrinth are equally likely to be the sound of its walls shifting, which, as Zampanò says, 'stretch', 'bend' (346), 'recede and vanish' (432). Johnny's sighting of the beast at the beginning of his narration can be attributed to a traumatic flashback of the childhood abuse inflicted upon him by his mother Pelafina, as what he sees recalls both his memories of Pelafina and the content he has read in 'The Navidson Record', such as the beast's '[e]xtremely long fingers' (71) slashing 'the back of [his] neck' (72). This evokes Pelafina's attempts to strangle Johnny as a child. Holloway Roberts' suspicion that the beast is stalking him in the labyrinth can additionally be attributed to the idea of imposing meaning on life to conceal its meaninglessness. When the labyrinth emerges in his living room, Navidson appoints a team of professional spelunkers to explore it and document these explorations.[8] In 'Exploration #4', spelunkers Holloway, Wax Hook and Jed Leeder explore the labyrinth. Holloway grows increasingly paranoid, murders Jed and commits suicide.[9] The 'beast' is described as 'the creature Holloway hunts' (334), and in the tape Holloway makes of his final moments, 'he slumps in the corner to wait' for the beast, and calls out for it, 'scream[ing] obscenities [in]to the void', such as 'Bullshit! Bullshit! Just try and get me you motherfucker' (337). When no monster surfaces, the text notes that Holloway's 'energy dips' and his 'words [come] out like a sigh—sad and lost' (337). When he turns the camera on himself moments before shooting himself, he again appears to want to encounter the beast, and it seems to be the absence of the creature, and everything else, which drives him to suicide:

> There's something here. I'm sure of it now. … It's following me. … But it won't strike. It's just out there waiting. I don't know what for. But it's near now, waiting for me, waiting for something. I don't know why it doesn't. … Oh God … Holloway Roberts. Menomonie, Wisconsin. [chambering a round in his rifle] Oh God. (335)

We are told '[i]n that place, the absence of an end finally became his own end' (337). Here, Holloway repeatedly states his name, birthplace, university name and profession in order to combat the absolute emptiness of the labyrinth:

> Repeat[ing] his identity seems the only mantra [that] offers any consolation. … It is almost as if he believes preserving his identity on video tape can somehow hold what he is powerless to prevent: those endless contours of darkness stealing the Holloway from himself. (334)

Holloway's attempts to preserve his identity from 'the endless contours of darkness' and prevent himself from disappearing with everything else in the labyrinth are further representative of the anxiety produced by post-modern scepticism. As noted, postmodern theory asserts that human identity, like our dominant discourses and metanarratives, is a construct that is culturally produced, that what we say is merely an arrangement of ready-formed linguistic structures and our thoughts, personality and

[8] A spelunker is an explorer of caves.

[9] The explorations carried out by Navidson and his team of spelunkers are titled in *The Navidson Record* as Exploration #1, Exploration #2 and so on.

behaviour are shaped by ideologies and conventions. Such realisations result in a loss of self and identity for the postmodern subject. According to Maria Belville, the postmodern crisis of identity is often represented in Gothic-postmodernist works through themes of possession or 'fluid identity' (11). Holloway's death in *House of Leaves* furthers this idea in that his body literally disappears once he dies. Similar to the way in which all sense of time and geography vanishes before Navidson, we are told that '[f]ingers of blackness slash across the lighted wall and consume Holloway. ... the last thing heard [was] the sound [of] Holloway ripped out of existence' (338).

The house has a similar effect on Navidson. Navidson becomes increasingly obsessed with exploring the labyrinth's dark hallways to the extent that he is willing to risk his life in order to attain knowledge of it: '[t]he obsession just grew and grew until it was Navidson who was finally possessed by some self-destructive notion to go back there' (386). However, the labyrinth, as Zampanò says, 'remains meaningless' (60) and even by the end of the narrative 'still continues to elude [him]' (111). This produces traumatic effects. The text notes 'the level of damage inflicted ... upon Navidson' (397) and states:

> [Navidson] finds no relief. He grows quieter ... often wakes up seized by terror, and ... starts eating less. ... The house continues to fix his attention. (397)

A number of cultural trauma critics (outside of the text) have attributed Navidson's trauma to his guilt over his failure to rescue a starving Sudanese girl whom he photographed being stalked by a vulture, which won him the Pulitzer Prize (Bemong; Little). However, while Navidson experiences guilt over Delial, his trauma appears to have stemmed less from the death of this child and more so from the postmodern desire for presence 'in the face of absence' (Slocombe, 'Postmodern Nihilism' 87–88), as Holloway experienced. It appears no coincidence that Navidson begins to dwell on Delial upon moving to the labyrinthine house. Delial appears, in part, to be a mechanism that enables Navidson to deal with the meaninglessness of the labyrinth. The text notes 'the sudden importance of Delial' to Navidson 'after twenty years of silence' (17) and that he began to experience nightmares of the child only since moving to the house, 'Just like that. Out of the blue' (17). Also, the fictional psychological theories offered within the text that attribute Navidson's trauma to Delial (suggesting that only after 'finding' Delial and 'reaching an understanding about his own life' (399) will Navidson be able to properly escape the house), in actuality, 'skewer particular aspects of trauma criticism' (Gibbs 93). Gibbs suggests that these theories form part of Danielewski's parody of the trauma discourse (93). A number of these 'critics' are also noted by Johnny to be fictional: 'most of what's been said by famous people has been made up' (xx).

Moreover, when inside the labyrinth, Navidson, similar to Holloway and his search for the 'beast', appears desperate to find 'something' to combat the meaninglessness and emptiness of the labyrinth, initially focusing on Delial: 'and now I can't get Delial out of my head. Delial, Delial, Delial' (391), then shifting his thoughts to his deceased brother Tom: 'Tom, maybe he's the one I'm looking for' (393). The text also notes that: Navidson produc[ed] projections powerful and painful enough to 'occlude, deny and cover ... the blankness of that place' (387). Navidson's desire to find 'meaning where there is none' (Slocombe, 'Postmodern Nihilism' 87–88) can also explain why Navidson creates a space so complex he gets lost inside. Eventually, like Holloway, when faced with the absolute emptiness of the labyrinth, Navidson begins to fear the eradication of his own existence along with everything else in the labyrinth, again evoking the postmodern loss of self and identity in an age of pervasive scepticism. For Navidson, the labyrinth was 'a place that would threaten no one else's existence but his own' (422).

We can also attribute Johnny's trauma to the postmodern incredulity towards metanarratives. Johnny experiences traumatic symptoms having encountered the disturbing content of 'The Navidson Record', experiencing nightmares which parallel its content and fearing the dimensions in his room will shift. Similar to Navidson and Holloway, then, what appears to traumatise Johnny is the house's eradication of the dominant entities of reality. Johnny warns the reader that once we read it, 'you'll watch yourself dismantle every assurance you ever lived by' (xxii–xxiii). As with Hibbs' interpretation of *The Matrix* (The Wachowskis, 1999), we can relate Johnny's fear to the postmodern view of everything as artificial. His previously cherished certainties undermined, Johnny starts to suspect that everything, including himself, is a product of the manuscript's invention, including his memories and past experiences:

> I am nothing more than the matter of some other voice, ... inventing me, defining me ... every association I can claim as my own ... is relegated to nothing; forcing me to face the most terrible suspicion of all, that all of this has just been made up. (326)

These fears evoke poststructuralist views of language as speaking and preceding us, and postmodern arguments that identity is a socially produced construct rather than a natural fact. This is further underscored in Johnny's remark that his memory is 'built upon story after story, so many, how many? stories high, building what? and why?' (297–298). The motif of building here can be seen as evoking the postmodern realisation that identity is 'constructed'. As with Holloway and Navidson, Danielewski reworks the tradition of having houses reflect both the social structures of characters and their psychological structures. Like our dominant discourses, both the house and its inhabitants are empty constructs.

The motif of building also evokes the creation of meaning in order to combat meaninglessness. Johnny's footnotes offer multiple anecdotes from his life such as his escapades with his friend Lude. It has been observed by Gibbs that Johnny's 'self-confessed procrastination, making up entertaining false stories' to conceal his past traumas is again drawing upon a practice familiar from a number of earlier trauma texts (90). Indeed, Johnny says that these stories 'help [him] look away' (20). However, in contrast to more conventional trauma literature, Johnny never broaches 'the story [he's] been meaning to tell all along' (265) but merely concocts an increasing number of random, outlandish tales, including the killing of a dog by a woman he met at a nightclub, his murder of a woman named Kyrie and an unrelated story of a mother grieving over the loss of her baby. Johnny also admits to fabricating a number of his traumatic memories, such as his mother's attempt to strangle him, and admits that he has 'lost sense of what's real and what's not. What I've made up' (497). Like Holloway and Navidson then, Johnny's 'stories' seem a similar attempt to overcome nothingness.

The Shining

Released in 1980, Stanley Kubrick's *The Shining* is an adaptation of Stephen King's 1977 novel of the same name. Reactions to *The Shining* upon its release were mixed, with King criticising the film's deviation from his novel. The film is now widely considered among the greatest horror films ever made and a staple of American popular culture. However, many initial reviews commented on how bizarrely un-terrifying, and seemingly meaningless, this horror film is. Janet Maslin of *The New York Times* noted 'the supernatural story knows frustratingly little rhyme or reason. … Even the film's most startling horrific images seem overbearing and perhaps irrelevant.' Kevin Thomas of the *Los Angeles Times* wrote 'the film is too grandiose to be the jolter that horror pictures are expected to be. Both those expecting significance from Kubrick and those merely looking for a good scare may be equally disappointed.' Roger Ebert said in the *Chicago Sun-Times* that 'one's immediate reaction is that maybe [Kubrick] was after something other than thrills in the film. If so, it's hard to figure out what.' Due to *The Shining*'s many ambiguities and symbolism, there has been much speculation about its meaning, plot and source of terror, and the film has generated myriad interpretations, to which this chapter will add one more.

Narrative Crash

This section will read *The Shining* in a similar manner to *House of Leaves*. The sense of nothingness produced by the postmodern decline of metanarratives can be read as the source of terror in *The Shining*. However, whereas *House of Leaves* evokes the feelings of nothingness that pervade in postmodernity through the metaphor of the disturbingly empty labyrinth, *The Shining* represents a different aspect of the trauma produced by postmodern scepticism: a strategy of constructing discourses purely as a means of combating this sense of nothingness, and the failure of this endeavour in postmodernity. The following examines how this phenomenon is represented in *The Shining* through a technique that I term narrative crash. Narrative crash involves a text employing a labyrinthine narrative structure which avoids closure. Texts that employ this strategy contain multiple narrative threads and subtexts, but to the extent that the text cannot form a cohesive narrative and ends by 'cutting-off' rather than providing a definitive conclusion, ending by opening another conjectural possibility to the text's already overloaded plot. We can read this as the text, in its attempt to fill the narrative void, collapsing or 'crashing' under the weight of its labyrinthine plot. This suggests the failure of creative endeavours to fill up or conceal the sense of emptiness produced by the depletion of fictional forms, and how in postmodernity we can no longer use literary discourse and cultural production to create meaning.[10] The structure of narrative crash can be described as what Katherine N. Hayles calls a series of 'inscriptions so densely overwritten that they have obliterated themselves' (793),

[10] Paul Auster's *Oracle Night* is also an example of a text with this kind of relentless storytelling structure.

or the occurrence of a computer crashing when too many programs are running at once. Indeed, further analogous to computers, the 'crash' of the narrative in such texts also simulates the breakdown of the device presenting the narrative. Texts which employ narrative crash represent the collapse of the narrative not only via inconclusive plots and narratives that terminate abruptly, but also through imagery and formal techniques which suggest production failure or technical difficulty.

This technique shares similarities to Vonnegut's and Thomas Pynchon's writings on metanarratives. As noted, Vonnegut says individuals impose meaning on life, as with religion, as a means of concealing its meaninglessness. This process aligns with Pynchon's imagery of labyrinths and deserts in *Gravity's Rainbow*. According to Will Slocombe:

> Pynchon's analysis of this human response is telling. … The response to the desert is to construct meaning: in the face of absence, we desire presence. The act of drawing ever more complex patterns on a blank sheet is tantamount to placing meaning on that which has no meaning … to construct meaning where there is none. ('Postmodern Nihilism' 87–88)

Slocombe also says that such postmodern texts are 'concerned with the attempt, by both language and culture, to overcome nothingness. When the text narrates, it is not to communicate, but to try to fill the void of silence that would otherwise be there' ('Nihilism and the House' 100).

Also relevant to narrative crash is how the postmodern incredulity towards metanarratives applies to literary discourse, which is frequently challenged by postmodern literature through metafictional strategies that foreground the text's status as artifice. A pervasive idea in postmodernity is that all forms of fiction and narrative content have been exhausted, that it is no longer possible to 'say or do anything new in the novel form following the achievements of modernism' (Nicol 50). This concern is voiced most famously by John Barth in 'The Literature of Exhaustion'. Barth suggests that instead of developing new ways of writing fiction, writers might alternatively produce works of metafiction. That is, to make the exhaustion of literature the subject matter of their work, as well as the process of representation. Accordingly, typical works of metafiction by postmodernist writers not only employ strategies to focus the reader's attention on their formal properties, but also lay bare their own process of construction by producing stories that are evidently in the process of being constructed (Nicol 76). For instance, works of metafiction often feature narrative digressions of commentary about devices and conventions of fiction, which parallel the 'main' story and narrate the author's attempt to produce it. Such texts may employ strategies such as intertextuality and genre-splicing, or as Nicol says, 'flit restlessly between different-tales-within-tales' and 'parallel versions of the same tale' (73). This gives what Nicol refers to as 'an overwhelming impression of relentless storytelling' (73), and appearing

> like a set of working drafts for a story ... a range of narrative possibilities considered by the author before he decides upon the final version. ... This explains the [story's] fragmented layout ... [and] other oddities ... such as why the characters and actions keep changing. (73)

Such strategies are evident in Barth's metafictional tale 'Lost in the Funhouse', which contains numerous reflections on how the story is evolving and on what will or could happen next (Van Der Ster 3). As the narrative progresses, the narrator continues to try out various endings all without success, to the point where the narrative ceases to progress. The protagonist Ambrose retreats to a dark corner of one of the corridors in the funhouse he explores, overcome by the complexity of the decisions he must make in navigating this space. Such an ending can be regarded as an analogy for the author's abandonment of this project when faced with the impossibility of producing original literature with the knowledge that fiction has been used up.

Lastly, narrative crash is in line with micronarratives (see page 27), and circling as a form of evasive narration (see page 17). Regarding micronarratives, the pluralistic perspective which is one of the characteristics of the postmodern condition has been noted to bring with it a frightening sense of meaninglessness and incoherence (Brent et al. 188). Nicol says of postmodern relativism: '[i]f there are no values, no norms, then nothing can have any real meaning' (200). It is this aspect of Lyotard's concept of micronarratives that narrative crash evokes in particular. Texts that I argue employ narrative crash open up multiple conjectural possibilities and potential interpretations, but to the extent that the text produces, as Brian McHale says of certain postmodern texts, 'too many' plotlines and interpretations, 'more than can possibly be integrated in a univocal reading' (142).

Labyrinthine Plot

It shall be argued that *The Shining* represents art's failure to produce meaning and combat feelings of emptiness in the nihilistic postmodern age. This aspect of the trauma of postmodernism is represented both formally through the film's labyrinthine structure, and thematically via the film's narrative of its protagonist Jack Torrance as a struggling author who seeks out the spectres of the Overlook Hotel as he procrastinates. To begin with the film's structure, *The Shining* contains multiple plots and in turn multiple interpretations. On the surface, *The Shining* appears to be a conventional haunted house tale. The narrative centres on Jack Torrance (Jack Nicholson), Wendy (Shelley Duvall) and their son Danny (Danny Lloyd) spending the winter in a haunted, off-season hotel. However, Kubrick's adaptation is filled with multiple potential, unfinished and seemingly unrelated plots, which can be taken as representative of an attempt to fill the void of the narrative in the wake of creative exhaustion. For instance, Elisa Pezzotta describes the film's structure as 'constituted by tableaux vivants and/or unrelated episodes, which are usually separated by ellipses and are full of unexplained enigmas' (116). Jarrell D. Wright observes that Kubrick throughout the film 'consistently miscues the audience', repeatedly 'priming viewers to expect' varying narratives, none of which he actually delivers (*True* 146).[11] Kubrick aimed to adapt King's novel in a 'more cinematic way', by reducing its details and refusing to provide clear-cut explanations for the narrative's supernatural events, and described the process as to 'lightly illustrate' the themes of King's novel (Hofsess). This approach stems from both the New Hollywood generation's incorporation of art cinema during the time of *The Shining*'s production, the writing of H.P. Lovecraft and Sigmund Freud's essay 'The Uncanny', which discourage analysing supernatural events too closely in horror (Hofsess). While this approach can be taken as an explanation for *The Shining*'s huge hermeneutic gaps, we can at the same time read the film's structure in terms of narrative crash.

[11] It is important to note here the level of intention behind the lack of closure and irreconcilability of *The Shining*'s various narratives. Rather than a failing of the film, my argument is that *The Shining* appears intentionally structured this way in order to underline the themes in the narrative which point to the perils, pitfalls and ultimate failure of artistic creation. Kubrick is characterised as an auteur and was renowned for organisational precision and controlling all aspects of filmmaking (Cocks et al. 'Deep Focus' 11).

The beginning of the film leads audiences to believe that the narrative will centre on Danny and his telepathy powers. Danny has an imaginary friend, Tony, who shows him glimpses of the future. This plot point implies a plot focused on demonic possession (Wright, *True* 146). The beginning of the film contains a number of lengthy scenes centring on Danny and Tony, including those in which Tony shows Danny a vision of the Grady Twins and the bloody elevator, the scene where Danny is visited by the doctor, and when Danny converses with Dick Hallorann (Scatman Crothers), the Overlook's chef. Hallorann informs Danny that his power is called 'shining' and that he, too, possesses this ability. These scenes imply that Tony is a sinister entity, as Danny implies that Tony tells him 'to do things' and that he is 'not supposed to' talk about Tony. Despite the incorporation of these scenes in the film, however, Danny's powers are misleading and what Jameson refers to as a 'false lead' (89). The film does not explain how or why Danny possesses his powers, nor does it explain the sources of the haunted house 'shinings' at the hotel. Danny's character arc and the way in which this narrative, as Jameson says, does not fully 'develop' (90) can be read as an unfinished subplot, as one of a number of narrative possibilities deliberately 'thrown up' and discarded in order to fill up *The Shining*'s screen time.

Myriad unrelated narrative threads unfold in the film in a similarly 'lightly illustrated' manner to Danny's telepathy subplot. For instance, *The Shining* has also been described by critics as an exploration of the family and domestic violence in America (Luckhurst, *Shining* 37). However, family violence is again a theme that is merely touched upon in the film: one that is, like Danny's subplot, neither wholly established nor resolved. We are informed that five months before the film's events, Jack drunkenly dislocated Danny's shoulder, but this act of violence is addressed in the film only in passing, briefly mentioned through Jack's contradictory account of events to the bartender Lloyd (Joe Turkel): 'I never laid a hand on him goddammit. ... I did hurt him once, okay? It was an accident!', and Wendy's rushed explanation to the doctor who visits Danny. The 'Fatherly Love Scene' where Danny encounters Jack in the Torrance apartment implies some act of violence takes place but only contains allusions to and non-diegetic indications of an impending attack. Luckhurst points out that Jack's expression of love for Danny here is 'undergirded with violent menace' (*Shining* 55), while the scene features melancholy music throughout but ends abruptly with a sudden jolt in the musical score. Rob Ager takes this sudden shift as indicative that Kubrick ended the scene just as Jack was about to harm Danny. Similar to the mutually exclusive narrative possibilities of 'Lost in the Funhouse', scenes such as the Fatherly Love Scene evoke the author's procrastination about where to take the story next when faced with a maze of depleted fictional conventions.[12]

The Shining not only generates large numbers of parallel texts, but also multiple subtexts. One way of interpreting these subtexts is that Kubrick is attempting to suggest multiple different concepts at once, to deliberately prevent the film from being reduced to a singular interpretation. One interpretation in Rodney Ascher's documentary *Room 237* (2012), which collects five distinct theories about the film's 'meaning', is that 'there [are] many layers to this film, that it's like three dimensional chess. [Kubrick is] trying to tell us several stories [at once].' There are a number of themes and narratives presented in a 'lightly illustrated' manner, which Wright suggests are both excessive and serve no obvious point in the apparent overarching narrative of the film (*True* 180). For instance, while Kubrick reduces the domestic violence narrative from King's novel, he incorporates the theme of European and American historical violence. According to John Lutz, alongside the ghost story of the film is a 'postcolonial narrative of American expansion at the expense of non-white victims', specifically, the genocide of the Native Americans (163). Kubrick did much research on Native American history while making *The Shining*, and the film is rife with allusions and references to this past atrocity, such as Native American imagery in the Overlook and how the hotel is built on an Indian burial ground. These references and iconography in *The Shining* lead Geoffrey Cocks in *Room 237* to read the elevator of blood sequence as representing the blood of the American Indians. However, *The Shining*'s layers of subtexts have generated a multitude of further, varying critical interpretations and conspiracy theories regarding the film's meaning and events. These include theories outlined in *Room 237*, such as the film as a coded confession from Kubrick regarding his contribution to the faking of the Apollo moon landing, a representation of the myth of the Minotaur, a metaphor for the Holocaust and an adaptation of Freud's 'The Uncanny'; as well as Jameson's argument that *The Shining* represents nostalgia for the pre-war era; the theme of corporate exploitation; and the myth of the American dream (Flo Leibowitz and Lynn Jeffress 46). Reading *The*

[12] This kind of structure also parallels with postmodern texts such as Pynchon's *The Crying of Lot 49*, which has been described as 'picking up' plots on an arbitrary basis and then promptly 'leaving them aside' (Nicol 98).

Shining in terms of narrative crash, I regard this crowded list of subtexts in an analogous manner to the film's multiple plots: as a series of deliberately unfinished concepts included in the film as a means of representing the attempt and failure to construct metanarratives that give life meaning and combat postmodern feelings of nothingness. Indeed, there are a number of obscure references in Kubrick's adaptation to dropped plot points from King's novel, and these scenes similarly give the impression that narratives and imagery are being 'randomly' inserted into the film to fill its running time. This is evident in the scene of the man in the bear costume kneeling before a tuxedoed man, as Kubrick omitted King's entire backstory associated with these characters. An analogously 'inexplicable' scenario is the Room 237 sequence, in which Jack encounters a young woman (Lia Beldam) who rises out of a bathtub and transforms into a rotting corpse (Billie Gibson). This scene is another allusion to an abandoned plotline from the novel, but in the film it has no reference to earlier events and the identity of the woman is kept ambiguous. Likewise, references to the hotel's bloody past appear to the casual viewer as meaningless images that crop up throughout the film because no narrative context is provided for them, such as that of the Grady Twins and the blood pouring out of the elevator in the vision Tony shows Danny. When the film was released, a number of reviewers complained that the elevator scene was 'suspended in the movie without meaning' (Cocks, *Wolf* 2), while critics observed how such images tended to 'confuse and frustrate rather than terrify' (Gamarra 97).

Exhausted Horror

Moreover, reading *The Shining* as an example of narrative crash is significant in terms of the film as a horror. Firstly, horror is an appropriate genre for the employment of narrative crash, in that by the time *The Shining* was released, this genre in particular was becoming somewhat exhausted and its themes had become clichés. For example, audiences had repeatedly seen films centred on telepathic children and possessions when *The Shining* was released (Gamarra 96). Secondly, in contrast to *House of Leaves* which represents the trauma of postmodern nothingness via a house haunted by absence, we can read *The Shining* as representing the attempt to combat and conceal this nothingness via representations of excess, that the film instead incorporates too many sources of terror. The film is packed with horror film tropes and appears to draw upon as many different types of horror as possible. According to Luckhurst, 'one of the central problems of the early reception of *The Shining*' was that '[i]t must have seemed to be a compendium of narratives, plots and images that had been endlessly rehearsed through the horror boom of the 1970s' (*Shining* 20). Jameson reads *The Shining* as a pastiche of multiple horror films and tropes (90). Bill Wyman suggests that one of the 'difficulties critics had with the film on its release may have been owing to disrupted viewer expectations', because, he says:

> Supernatural films are generally 'about' one supernatural issue. Here, Danny has 'the shining.' But the other supernatural manifestations are myriad and confused. [Jack] Nicholson … hallucinates as well, but the source of this—male rage, or insecurity, or isolation, or demons at loose in the hotel—remains unclear. … These are all discrete psychic conceptions, and they don't really jibe. … [Kubrick] took what he wanted from King's book, and added various layers of his own.

Not only is the Overlook built on an Indian burial ground (yet another common trope in horror narratives), but Ullman also informs Jack that Charles Grady murdered his family and committed suicide, which the police attributed to 'cabin fever' and 'a complete mental breakdown'. Additionally, Jack encounters a number of ghosts at the Overlook, including Lloyd the dead bartender in the Gold Room; the animated corpse in Room 237; and the butler Delbert Grady (Philip Stone) in the men's bathroom, who orders Jack to kill his family. The Overlook is thus haunted by multiple, somewhat unrelated sources of terror. Indeed, Jack eventually attempts to murder his family in the same manner as Charles Grady, but as Bob Haas et al. note, 'it could be the hotel itself or an evil presence in the hotel or a residue of the bad things that have happened there', that 'Kubrick elects never to tell us the cause' (109). While Haas et al. assert that the film's 'supernatural threat' and 'the guiding force behind Jack's metamorphosis' are 'ambiguous' (109), I propose that the film runs an entire range of narrative threads in relation to the source of evil in the plot, that Kubrick's film represents numerous supernatural threats and guiding forces behind Jack's villainous acts. Jack becomes influenced by a supernatural presence in the form of ghosts which appear to force successive generations to re-enact the original atrocities that took place in the hotel, such as Delbert Grady instructing Jack to 'correct' his family, as Charles Grady did. However, similar to Danny's telepathy arc, Jameson says that this plot point is, in itself, another kind of false lead, 'another kind of generic misreading, which seizes on some of the signals and conventions of the new genre of the "occult" film in order to project an anticipation of some properly diabolical possession to come' (89). Indeed, it is simultaneously implied in the film that Jack is the reincarnation of Delbert Grady, doomed to attack his family repeatedly, in the suggestion that Jack has 'always been the caretaker', while Jack is portrayed as sinister before he enters the Overlook, as he is aggressive to his family when he drives them to the hotel.[13]

The narrative is increasingly overladen with sources of evil and horror tropes as the film progresses. In the climax, when Jack breaks free of the store room and attempts to murder his family with an axe, there are numerous stereotypical horror signifiers. In addition to the axe-wielding psycho and telepathic child, Wendy encounters the following during her escape from Jack: the figure in the bear suit; a dead butler (Delbert Grady) with his head cleaved open; blood pouring from the elevator; and the body of Hallorann, who was killed by Jack. This overloaded sequence and its almost fragmentary structure as different types of 'movie monsters' appear can be read in a similar manner to Joss Whedon's *The Cabin in the Woods*, in which the source of terror is the exhaustion of the horror genre. Whedon's film concerns a group of scientists manipulating college students into a horror movie scenario as a means of entertaining a race of gods who threaten Armageddon if the ritual bores them. The scientists invent increasingly frightening means of torture via the varying monsters and horror clichés they keep in their facility. The facility scenes in *The Cabin in the Woods* are filled with recognisable 'movie monsters' that stem from a variety of horror genres, contained within its myriad cube prisons. In *The Shining*'s climax, multiple genres are similarly evoked. These include: the 'slasher' genre via Jack's pursuit of his family, with Wendy acting as the final girl (the trope of the last woman alive to confront the killer of the slasher film, usually the individual left to tell the story); the substandard quality of the bear suit recalls the costumes and aesthetics of B-horror monster movies; the image of the blood pouring out of the elevator evokes the amateur attempts found in horror 'home movies' to amp up the terror and shock value by adding unnecessary imagery of blood; and the murder

[13] Further adding to this idea is the film's ambiguity regarding the novel's supernatural content. As Wright says, Kubrick's film 'maintains a fine balance between rational and supernatural without forcing the audience into a choice between them' (*Reconsidering* 147).

of Hallorann can be read as an early evocation of the racist horror trope of the token Black character (how horror films often feature one Black character in the cast, who is usually the first of the characters to die).[14] In the novel, Hallorann survives Jack's attack. Like the cube prisons in *The Cabin in the Woods*' facility, a different horror trope or genre of monster lurks in the various rooms in the Overlook, as evident in the above sequence as well as Jack's encounters with ghosts in the Gold Room, Room 237 and the bathroom. The Overlook becomes something akin to a horror funhouse whereby the different areas of the hotel can be taken as representative of the possible directions the narrative could have taken. Like 'Lost in the Funhouse', the film is constructed to appear to be procrastinating with regard to which narrative direction to take next, and the amalgamation of horror tropes and monster characters resemble narrative possibilities.

Writer's Block

As noted, *The Shining* not only represents creative stagnation and the feelings of nothingness that accompany the decline of such discourses through its formal structure, but also within the thematics of the film via its narrative of Jack as a struggling author. Creative failure and the extreme scepticism characteristic of the postmodern have been noted as major themes of *The Shining* in previous scholarship. Cocks et al. note that Kubrick's 'use and interrogation of popular film genres, and his mordant view of the human prospect made him a powerful voice of postmodern scepticism about the whole enlightenment project' ('Deep Focus' 6). Jameson specifies that *The Shining* depicts a postmodern world in which 'stylistic innovation' is no longer possible (79), that *The Shining*'s conventional motifs of the horror genre distract the viewer from the 'obvious fact' that the film is ultimately 'the story of a failed writer' (93) and is 'about the impossibility of cultural or literary production' (93). John Hofsess in his interview with Kubrick also points out that while Kubrick pares back elements of King's narrative, Jack's 'frustrations as a writer' have been emphasised. Further, Tony Magistrale links the meaningless text that Jack produces in the film to the anxiety produced by postmodern conditions specifically:

[14] This trope became increasingly prominent in the 1980s.

> Jack fails to write. ... Jack suffers ... from the postmodern condition: the disintegration and blurring of all forms of coding-generic ... social ... linguistic ... and ultimately, of meaning. (104–105)

Indeed, in the novel, Jack is a writer of some achievement, whereas Kubrick's protagonist would like to be a writer (Jameson 93). Also, it is not so much the spirits of the Overlook that appear to haunt Jack but his inadequacy as a writer. As James Naremore observes, 'Jack becomes lively and sociable only when the ghosts appear' (194). For instance, Jack forgets his encounter with the woman in Room 237 when questioned by Wendy, whereas his bursts of temper stem from his difficulties with writing, evident in the scene where he screams at Wendy for disrupting his work.

For Jameson, Jack's 'book' is very explicitly a signifier of creative exhaustion: what he describes as 'a kind of ultimate and empty autoreferential statement about the impossibility of cultural or literary production' (93). Jack's manuscript is merely a repetition of the same sentence over hundreds of pages: 'All work and no play makes Jack a dull boy'. However, how this manuscript is revealed establishes creative exhaustion as the main source of terror in *The Shining*. Wendy's (and the audience's) discovery of it is more akin in its depiction to a traditional climax of a horror film, as opposed to the clichéd and overladen sequence presented at the end of *The Shining*, and the scene (which is not depicted in the novel) conforms closer to the generic expectations of the horror genre than any other ostensibly 'scary scene' in the film. Wendy cautiously approaches the typewriter. The subsequent low-angle shot from the perspective of the typewriter towards Wendy's face enables what Luckhurst calls 'an extraordinary reveal' (*Shining* 70), showing Wendy's horrified reaction to the pages that emerge from Jack's typewriter. The camera then zooms into Jack's manuscript beside the typewriter, the repetitive lines ominously filling up the frame. This shot is similar to the monstrous reveals in horror films, that is, the first full-fledged shot of the film's monstrous character or frightening element, such as the reveal of Norman Bates' dead mother in Alfred Hitchcock's *Psycho* (1960) or Samara Morgan's mangled face in Gore Verbinski's *The Ring* (2002).[15] Furthermore, there is a convention

[15] *The Shining* also appears to parody this convention in presenting an ordinary object such as a manuscript in this manner, calling attention to how monstrous reveals in horror films are usually disappointing to viewers as they do not meet the anticipation built by the preceding scenes in the film. This further gestures towards the failure of cultural production and exhaustion of the horror genre.

in horror texts whereby the monster or frightening element reflects the text's structure. For instance, the major 'adversary' in *House of Leaves* is the labyrinth which mirrors the labyrinthine structure of the novel via its experimental typography. Similarly, the manuscript in *The Shining* parallels the film's formal structure in its repetitive arbitrary nature and the way in which the pages are literally filled up with content without relating any kind of cohesive or meaningful narrative. The manuscript also contains modulations of the repeated line and typos such as 'All wori and no play makes Jack a dult boy'. Critics such as Ager regard this as an 'embedded message' by Kubrick, asserting that such spelling and grammar mistakes must be a conscious decision made by the meticulous auteur. These typographical disorders can be read as the manuscript reflecting the structure of the film in that it too eventually 'breaks down'.

Labyrinth Characters

Of course, among the major antagonists in *The Shining* is Jack. Because this chapter interprets creative exhaustion as the main source of horror in Kubrick's adaptation, we can regard Jack's varying transformations and villainous feats as part of the film's representation of 'writer's block'. Like the film, it is equally arguable that the characters within the narrative are represented as directionless and attempting to fill up the screen time with content. As Slocombe says, to 'cover up' the void of the narrative with 'a maze of words' ('Nihilism and the House' 102). Kubrick's characters have been described by Anthony F. Macklin as 'empty shells' who communicate in banal and mundane ways, and evidently devoid of motivation (93). Indeed, a number of scenes depict Jack performing repetitive actions such as throwing a ball, pacing the Colorado Lounge and typing variations of the same line. Reading Jack's characterisation in this light, we can regard his ennui and shifts in character in a similar manner to Danielewski's characters who actively search for monsters as a means of combating the unbearable emptiness of the labyrinth. For instance, similar to Holloway Roberts in *House of Leaves*, Jack appears to seek out monsters. Jack's transformation into the film's 'monster' proper only occurs having sought out 'monsters' in the various rooms of the hotel. What appear to be the conventional monsters in the film, such as the Overlook's ghosts, rarely, if ever, ambush Jack. Rather, Jack is generally the one to approach them. Jack approaches Lloyd at the bar, while he later enters Room 237 in search of the woman Wendy describes.

Kubrick's protagonist takes this notion of combating emptiness a step further by becoming the monster himself and inhabiting a whole host of varying roles as though 'trying out' different character personas, mirroring the narrative's generation of multiple plots. Numerous motivating forces behind Jack's metamorphosis are suggested in the film, from alcoholism to domestic violence to demonic possession, but I argue that this is similar to how metafictional stories like 'Lost in the Funhouse' appear like a set of working drafts for a story and feature characters and actions that keep changing. Kubrick's Jack becomes the film's villain because he is driven in that direction due to the 'horror' of creative failure. As the film progresses, Jack transforms from struggling author to abusive patriarch to murderous psychopath to beast (again similar to *The Cabin in the Woods*' collection of movie monsters, except Jack shifts between these roles).[16] When Jack attempts to kill his family, he not only undergoes a psychological transformation but a physical, animal-like metamorphosis as well, reverting to what Frank Manchel calls an 'apelike creature' (92). Luckhurst compares Jack in these scenes to the 'cripples and hunchbacks' of 1930s horror films (*Shining* 73). In addition to struggling artist, protagonist and antagonist (in the form of abusive father and ape-like 'movie monster'), Jack also inhabits the roles of: horror film victim, when the old woman chases him out of Room 237, complete with exaggerated and clichéd screams of terror; cartoon character, when he calls himself the 'Big Bad Wolf' and swings his axe whilst repeating lines from the 'Three Little Pigs'; a talk show host when he breaks down the apartment door and screams 'Heeeeeere's Johnny!'[17]; and an Overlook ghost in the way Jack mimics the Grady Twins' line 'forever and ever and ever' in the Fatherly Love Scene, and appears in the 1921 photograph in the hotel's lobby at the end of the film.[18] Naremore points out that Jack also inhabits the role of a confessional 'bar-fly' of the Western genre in the Gold Room scene, played by Nicholson in a 'broad, squirming style' (197).

[16] Danny also appears to change character roles in the film, similarly shifting from protagonist to antagonist, from child victim to the horror stereotype of 'evil child'.

[17] Jack's literary quotations further suggest literary exhaustion.

[18] Jack's characterisation, his multiple and shifting personae are also postmodernist in terms of theories of the unstable, decentred subject.

Narrative Break Down

I propose that Jack's intertextuality, that is, his abundance of character modes and cultural references, can also be read in terms of the 'crashing' of the narrative and characters breaking down. Before the narrative of *The Shining* is 'cut-off', there are a number of scenes which appear to simulate the crashing of the narrative under the weight of the labyrinthine plot it has generated. Characters appear like robots malfunctioning. For instance, language breaks down. This is evident via characters' inarticulate noises and screams, such as Jack's ape-like shrieks and Wendy's screams as she encounters masses of horror clichés. Also in the film are literal listings of names and objects in no apparent order, such as in the film's expository scenes where Hallorann describes the contents of the Overlook's kitchen.[19] Additionally, characters in the film communicate backwards, such as when Danny writes the word 'murder' in reverse on the Torrances' bathroom door. Characters also appear to physically break down, such as the close ups of Danny shaking and drooling at the mouth that are intercut in the Room 237 sequence, and shots of characters frozen, such as that in which Jack as he stares from the window in a trance-like state. By the end of the film, Jack literally crashes by freezing to death. The character not only, as Haas et al. say, 'slow[s] down' at *The Shining*'s end, but 'stops dead—literally' (120). The close-up of Jack in the snow-covered maze at the end of the film can be taken as representative of the breakdown of the text's protagonist and narrative. The narrative, having opened up too many plotlines, similarly gets lost in the maze and 'crashes', ending by opening yet another conjectural possibility rather than providing a definitive conclusion. As Sudha Shastri says of *House of Leaves*, *The Shining* ends with a 'token ending' that 'only leads to new beginnings without having adequately made sense of or resolved the stories it began to tell' (81). The image draws strong parallels with the conclusion of 'Lost in the Funhouse'. Ambrose is paralysed within the funhouse, a similarly labyrinthine structure which visualises literary exhaustion, with the funhouse's avenues representing a maze of depleted fictional conventions and the possible directions the narrative can take. Jack's breakdown can be taken as

[19] Also significant to note is Barthes' characterisation of language in the postmodern era as the destruction of syntax and its replacement 'by a parataxis, a regulated aesthetic of lists' (211).

similarly stemming from his efforts to fill the void of the narrative, having taken all of the various narrative directions.[20]

Moreover, not only do the characters within *The Shining* 'break down', but so too does the film itself, having generated too many plot lines. As noted, Kubrick employs techniques of art cinema. Art cinema deliberately exhibits an awareness of being works of art through experimental techniques such as jump cuts and flashforwards. According to Susan Hayward, in art cinema these techniques disrupt 'the notion of temporal and spatial continuity' (343) and are foregrounded over content (237). However, *The Shining*'s formal techniques can also be read as intentional representations of production errors and technical difficulties as the narrative breaks down. One of the ways in which *The Shining* simulates the crashing of the narrative is what Gibbs, in his analysis of *House of Leaves*, calls the 'indeterminate bleeding between initially separate discursive layers' (108). *The Shining* does this through what Pezzotta describes as the 'diegetic world' being 'evoked in the diegesis itself through the presence of scenes that either recall previous scenes, or foretell subsequent events' (142). The scenes in *The Shining* that 'work like flashforwards' which 'announce events that are to follow' (Pezzotta 142) can also be taken as representative of the film leaving visible the rough working drafts or storyboard sketches of scenes in the completed narrative. Kubrick never used the usual director storyboards to chart out action beforehand. Rather, he reshaped the narrative as it was being filmed, and this process, in certain scenes, appears to bleed into the finished film. An example of such is the unusual editing in the Room 237 sequence. When Jack sees the reflection of the woman he embraces in the mirror and realises that she has transformed into a corpse, he starts to stagger backwards out of the room while the old woman walks towards him with her hands outstretched. This sequence cuts back and forth to a shot of the old woman lying in the bathtub rising upwards out of the water as though the sequence is still a work in progress, being mapped out and presented simultaneously to the viewer. As noted, the sequence is also intercut with close ups of Danny trembling.

According to Pezzotta, the extradiegesis in *The Shining* is also recalled through 'the evocation of the making of the film' (142). Such instances include the incorporation of miniature models of props and film sets into scenes, such as the model of the hedge maze in the Colorado Lounge, and

[20] Kubrick altered Jack's death in his adaptation, and the film's hedge maze is an image of Kubrick's own invention (Giampietro).

the miniature replica of Jack's axe on Ullman's desk; the use of screen-titles; as well as intrusive non-diegetic elements evident in the film's music and editing strategies. *The Shining* heavily exploits its cinematic techniques and non-narrative elements, such as how the film's music is foregrounded to the point of disrupting the plot, rather than occupying a more traditional background role in comparison to character dialogue and action, as well as the manner in which the film's editing strategies overtly call attention to themselves. In contrast to traditional Hollywood practices, in which 'most cuts are specifically contrived to pass unnoticed' for the purposes of 'complete transparency in films' (Dmytryk 11), *The Shining* foregrounds its cuts and works to 'distance' the viewer from the action. For example, the shot of the Grady Twins in the corridor is intercut with three jump cuts of the Twins' bloody corpses, while Danny's vision of the bloody elevator is intercut with two jump cuts of the Twins. The horror effect of these scenes is not only reduced because they lack context, but also because their fragmented formal presentation draws attention to the film's editing process. The fragmented imagery makes these scenes appear similar to storyboard sketches of a scene rather than a completed sequence. Such scenes can be read in a similar manner to the techniques of metafictional texts that aim to foreground the agonising process of constructing a narrative with the knowledge that fiction or the particular genre the text works within (in *The Shining*'s case, horror) has been exhausted.

Furthermore, whereas almost every film contains continuity errors, *The Shining* contains so many 'inconsistencies' that they appear deliberate, especially considering Kubrick's status as a meticulous auteur. As Dru Jeffries observes, certain interpretations of *The Shining* offered in Ascher's *Room 237* rest upon the interpretation that Kubrick's 'mistakes' and 'continuity errors' are deliberate (17). For instance, a chair in the background of the Colorado Lounge disappears from one shot to the next in the scene where Wendy approaches Jack writing at his desk; a cartoon sticker of the Disney character Dopey vanishes from Danny's bedroom door; and as Luckhurst observes, 'in a single cut' the carpet pattern under Danny's feet in the hallway suddenly shifts 180 degrees (*Shining* 58). Further set design 'anomalies' (which strongly parallel *House of Leaves*) include doors which apparently lead nowhere, rooms that appear to move around the Overlook and the impossible window found in Ullmann's office (the hallways that surround Ullmann's office make it impossible for this room to have a window facing outdoors). In addition, The Torrances' television does not have a cord; the volume of the Torrance's luggage is too vast to fit in their

Beetle car; and there is a bizarre cut in the scene of the Torrances' Overlook tour where they are about to cross the street from the maze and get hit by a car.

As noted, the film ends by 'cutting-off', having generated too many disjointed plot lines to form a coherent narrative. The novel properly concludes with Wendy, Danny and Hallorann retreating to the Western Maine Mountains. Conversely, Kubrick's adaptation ends by opening yet another conjectural possibility in the implication that Jack is an immortal being.[21] The closing image shows Jack in the photograph of the Overlook's Fourth of July Ball in 1921.[22] The film 'ends' not with a definitive conclusion, then, but appears to 'crash' mid-narrative. As Slocombe says of *House of Leaves*, *The Shining* continues to pretend through relentless storytelling that 'the nihilistic void of the text is not there'.

Conclusion

House of Leaves and *The Shining* are therefore innovative representations of trauma. Both texts engage with postmodern themes and perspectives in addition to an experimental postmodern aesthetic, depicting the postmodern condition itself as a source of trauma. *House of Leaves* evokes Lyotard's theory of postmodernism as characterised by incredulity towards metanarratives and the accompanying feelings of nothingness via a house haunted by literal absence. Conversely, *The Shining* depicts this phenomenon via representations of excess and cultural exhaustion, evoking Lyotard's theory of micronarratives and the similar traumatic sense of nothingness. While my analysis focused solely on Danielewski's and Kubrick's texts, this topic is relevant to both trauma fiction and popular culture more generally. *House of Leaves* and *The Shining* introduce new approaches to horror and the haunted house genre, with *House of Leaves* appearing to establish the concept of the postmodern haunted house as defined by literal emptiness and *The Shining* providing important groundwork for subsequent meta-horrors such as *The Cabin in the Woods*. Both

[21] The contrast between the endings of the book and film further underscores the reading of Kubrick's film in terms of postmodernism. The book is realist, hence the closure of its ending, whereas the film's open ending is more in line with the non-closure of postmodern texts. Again, *The Crying of Lot 49* is an example of such. Pynchon's text contains numerous plots and opens up multiple interpretations, but 'the novel is cut short', stopping 'one paragraph short of full revelation' (95).

[22] In King's novel, this photograph is a painting, but it is never described.

texts provide insight into contemporary American culture's ongoing engagement with nihilism. Trauma stemming from the scepticism and nihilism of the postmodern age is a theme that appears in a number of contemporary American popular and cult works, ranging from the horror genre to superhero narratives to police procedurals. Derek Simonds' *The Sinner* Season 3 (2020) and Jac Schaeffer's *WandaVision* (2021) feature protagonists questioning the meaning and veracity of their reality, and experiencing traumatic symptoms as a result. Michael Haneke's *Funny Games* (1997 and 2007), Mary Harron's *American Psycho* (2000), Christopher Nolan's *The Dark Knight* (2008) and Bryan Fuller's television series *Hannibal* (2013–2015) feature antagonists characterised by the nihilistic aspect of postmodernity explored in *House of Leaves* and *The Shining*. These villains appear driven specifically by the feelings of meaninglessness and existential horror characteristic of the postmodern age, performing acts of violence and criminality out of ennui. Similar to narrative crash and *The Shining*'s generation of multiple seemingly unrelated plots, these antagonists' actions appear random and pointless because curiosity and experimentation are the motives. For instance, the home invaders in *Funny Games* take a family hostage for no apparent reason other than entertainment, and they subject the family to a series of increasingly torturous acts. Similarly, there is neither reason nor purpose for the chaos committed by Heath Ledger's Joker in *The Dark Knight*. The Joker sets fire to money, believes that life is pointless and declares that he has no plans, that he just does things. In Fuller's *Hannibal*, the titular protagonist commits heinous acts simply to see what happens, such as concealing his patient's encephalitis as he is curious about the outcome. In terms of structure, narrative crash is also a lens through which to read more formally experimental contemporary horror texts. David Lynch's *Inland Empire* (2006), Darren Aronofsky's *Mother!* (2017) and Charlie Kaufman's *I'm Thinking of Ending Things* (2020) feature a proliferation of seemingly unrelated narratives and characters faced with multiple sources of terror they can neither comprehend nor form into a coherent narrative. The concept of texts breaking down and engaging with the concept of running out of narrative content is also evident in *Community* and Glenn Gordon Caron's *Moonlighting* (1985–1989), and is of particular relevance to contemporary video games produced both in the US and internationally. Takayuki Sugawara's *Danganronpa 2: Goodbye Despair* (2010) and Arnt Jensen's *Inside* (2016) feature characters realising the game worlds they inhabit are fictional, as do *Undertale*, and *Doki Doki Literature Club*, the protagonists of which are depicted as attempting to fill the void of the narrative in order to prevent the player from switching off the game and remain in existence. Finally, as noted, the representation of characters traumatised by the postmodern condition can be read in terms of male reactions to periods of increased social change and male privilege. This crisis is also evident in later popular works, including Donald Glover's *Atlanta* (2016–present), which features white male protagonists experiencing 'trauma' (in actuality loss of privilege) as a direct response to Black liberation, as well as international texts such as Tatsuya Ishihara's Japanese animé series *The Melancholy of Haruhi Suzumiya* (2006–2009). The latter features male characters traumatised by empowered female characters specifically. Ultimately, this chapter aimed to extend existing explorations of the intersection between trauma and postmodernism and provide a striking contrast to the texts explored in the following chapters, which feature diverse characters traumatised by extreme, prolonged situations such as systemic racism and childhood abuse.

CHAPTER 3

Competitive Narration: Tim Burton's *Batman Returns* and David Lynch and Mark Frost's *Twin Peaks*

Chapters 4 and 5 examine trauma representations of diverse characters including women, people of colour and queer characters. This chapter examines the representation of women's trauma through a formal technique that I term competitive narration in works by three male writers from the 1990s: Tim Burton's *Batman Returns* and David Lynch and Mark Frost's *Twin Peaks*. Chapters Three and Four examine trauma representations of diverse characters in a selection of post-2010 texts by women, queer writers and writers of colour. I focus on these texts in order to investigate the potential differences between diverse trauma representations by earlier straight white male writers and more recent diverse writers in American popular culture.

Trauma and Phallocentricism

Canonical trauma representations are frequently phallocentric. This is in part due to Caruth's definition of trauma as a sudden, overwhelming event 'outside the range of usual human experience'. This model has come under criticism by feminist trauma scholars because it is applicable mainly to white, middle-class men and does not account for the types of trauma frequently experienced by women, people of colour and queer individuals. As noted in the previous chapter, the type of trauma experienced by these individuals tends to be the more insidious, 'everyday' traumas resulting from ongoing situations of distress such as domestic violence, child abuse,

S. Travers, *Trauma in American Popular Culture and Cult Texts, 1980–2020*, https://doi.org/10.1007/978-3-031-13287-2_3

poverty and 'repeated forms of traumatising violence such as sexism, racism and colonialism' (Rothberg, *Memory* 89). As Brown notes:

> the range of human experience becomes the range of what is normal and usual in lives of men of the dominant class; white, young, able-bodied, educated, middle-class, Christian men. Trauma is that which disrupts these particular lives, but no other. (104)

Post-colonial critics including Craps and Buelens also highlight the Western bias of Caruth's trauma model and its exclusion of insidious trauma deriving from colonialism and post-colonial experience, which have been shown to comprise everyday traumatic experiences of inequality, oppression and racism (*Studies in the Novel* 3–4). Craps and Buelens highlight 'the chronic psychic suffering produced by the structural violence of racial, gender, sexual, class, and other inequities' (*Studies in the Novel* 3–4) as potential causes of trauma. Likewise, Craps and Bond observe that there are 'blind-spots that have led canonical trauma theory to marginalise the experiences of non-Western and minority groups by prioritising "Western" atrocities such as the Holocaust and 9/11' rather than 'other traumatic experiences such as those associated with slavery … [and] colonialism' (*Trauma* 9).

As noted in the Introduction, canonical trauma representations in turn predominantly feature white male protagonists and present traumatic experiences from their perspectives. Of course, certain texts that deal with the trauma of diverse groups including women, people of colour and queer individuals have received considerable critical attention, such as the fiction of Morrison. Nevertheless, the texts considered by cultural trauma theory to be canonical trauma narratives, those regarded as the 'foundational trauma texts' and credited with constructing 'some of the key paradigms' of trauma representation (Gibbs 41), are predominantly presented from a white, American androcentric perspective. Renny Christopher, for instance, has criticised American Vietnam writers for ethnocentricity, critiquing celebrated Euro-American writers such as Robin Moore, William Lederer and Eugene Burdick, Philip Caputo and Tim O'Brien for stressing their own and their comrades' trauma and ignoring that of the Vietnamese. In such narratives, the traumatic symptoms of the soldiers, such as guilt stemming from atrocities they have committed and their nightmares and flashbacks of these events, are foregrounded. By contrast, the far greater suffering of the civilians such as the daily threat of rape and murder are either briefly referred to in asides or reduced almost to the level of statistics, described along the lines of 'x number of burned or decomposing bodies'.

Diversity and the Supernatural

Of course, numerous popular trauma texts also centre on white male characters, such as, for example, Doug Liman's *The Bourne Identity* (2002), Christopher Nolan's *Batman Begins* (2005) and Shane Black's *Iron Man 3* (2013). However, trauma representation in American popular culture since the early 2000s has nevertheless seen an increase in diversity, with texts increasingly focusing on the traumatic experiences of women, ethnic minorities and the LGBTQIA+ community. This is due to a number of factors, including: the increasing demand for diverse representation in contemporary popular culture and its production; the more immediate feedback on popular texts enabled by social media; and the increased creative freedom enabled by media-service providers in comparison to more traditional networks. As Reed Hastings says of platforms such as Netflix, the company can 'push the envelope with content and [allow] for innovation'. Also significant is popular culture's wider array of genres, particularly genres that incorporate the fantastic including fantasy, science fiction and horror. These genres can enable texts to generate more suitable representations for the traumatic experiences of characters diverse in terms of gender, race and sexuality. For example, superpowers in superhero narratives can be employed as metaphors for symptoms specific to the types of trauma largely experienced by women, such as mind-control as a metaphor for domestic abuse and date-rape in Melissa Rosenberg's *Jessica Jones* (2015-2019), and superpowers as a metaphor for gaslighting in Anna Boden and Ryan Fleck's *Captain Marvel* (2019). Likewise, Tananarive Due says in Xavier Burgin's documentary *Horror Noire: A History of Black Horror* (2019), 'black history is black horror'. An example of such is the representation of racial oppression in Jordan Peele's horror films *Get Out* (2017) and *Us* (2019).

It is also important to note the long-standing and problematic tradition in American culture to repress ostensibly 'taboo' topics by representing them in supernatural terms. While traumatic experiences such as sexual abuse are common, they are often relegated to the realm of the supernatural in culture as a means of repression. According to Judith Lewis Herman, sexual abuse in literature has been 'entirely enmeshed ... in myth and folklore' (*Father* 3), and '[t]he language of the supernatural ... still intrudes into the most sober attempts to describe' traumatic experiences such as 'chronic childhood trauma' (*Trauma* 98). Of course, the types of trauma commonly experienced by women and children such as rape and domestic violence are not always represented in a supernatural way. However, these experiences are often depicted in popular culture as it is more inclined to incorporate the supernatural (such as in the popular genres of horror and fantasy). This tradition can be regarded as evading family violence. According to Luckhurst, family violence in American culture is usually presented as 'an external evil' and either takes the form of a 'marginal figure' (*Trauma* 104) or is 'safely relegated to the supernatural' (*Trauma* 117).[1] Luckhurst notes that '[t]his device means that intra-familial violence is half-acknowledged but at once covered over by exteriorising it in an abjected, monstrous figure defined as the very opposite of the family' (*Trauma* 104). A marginal figure might include a serial killer or criminal outsider of the underclass (Richardson 100). Luckhurst adds that this convention 'also matches the model of trauma as something done to individuals, an event that breaches the subject from outside, turning them from agents to victims' (*Trauma* 104), evident in perpetrator trauma representations (see pages 221–224). In addition, this device matches how dominant trauma theory envisions trauma as an extraordinary event in order to give what Gibbs calls 'the illusion that is it not part of normal [American] life' (22).

Displacing abuse to the supernatural is a tradition evident in American fiction in particular. According to Laurie Vickroy, American culture 'redefines traumatic experience to suit mythical views of itself', shifting the focus 'away from its political implications and the fact that particular groups', especially women and children, are 'targets for abuse' (6–7). Similarly, Kalí Tal in *Worlds of Hurt*, which compares American attitudes towards incest and the Vietnam War, notes that two ways America copes with trauma are mythologisation and denial, or what she refers to as 'disappearance' (6). Tal asserts that survivor testimony has been 'overwhelmed and revised by dominant culture' (11) and that in particular, 'appropriation of trauma is obvious' when one examines 'cultural representations of institutionalised sexualised violence against women and children' (19).

[1] See Nathaniel Hawthorne's *The Scarlet Letter*, or for more recent examples, the fiction of Stephen King, including *Gerald's Game*, *The Shining* and King's long story 'The Library Policeman' in *Four Past Midnight*.

Certainly, as with the national violence of American history, American domestic violence has continually been subject to, as Mark A. Heberle says, 'mythic and ideological interpretations' (18). Heberle says of American political myth-making, 'storytelling becomes a vehicle for excusing trauma, revealing and covering it up, revising what has happened or inventing what has not' (203). There is a similar attitude in American culture towards intra-familial violence, what Diane Stevenson calls the 'secret violence of American life' (72), in that it too is consistently concealed behind somewhat 'more comforting fictions' (Melley 119). Specifically, that abuse and violence do not arise within the family circle but are 'constructed from outside' (Stevenson 75).

However, as this study argues, certain popular works diverge from canonical trauma representations and dominant criticism, and present innovative representations of trauma. I propose that this makes certain types of popular culture more suitable to represent the traumatic experiences of diverse individuals. Specifically, instead of using the supernatural to repress traumatic experiences common to groups such as women, the texts examined in this chapter and the following two chapters use the supernatural and popular fantastical genre tropes to further explore these experiences, as well as critique conventional representations of them.

Competitive Narration

One way that popular culture achieves this is through a technique that I term competitive narration. The technique takes two forms and can be used to analyse texts that potentially highlight and critique culture's phallocentricism regarding trauma. Similar to historiographic metafiction and traumatic metafiction, competitive narration draws the reader or viewer's attention away from the traumatic events being narrated as a means of foregrounding the processes of constructing this narrative, and exposes the androcentric bias of the genre it is writing within: the trauma genre.[2] The first type of competitive narration features one plot or character overtaking another. A subplot concerned with a female character (or queer

[2] Historiographic metafiction is a type of writing that works to draw the reader's attention away from the history being narrated to the process of narrating the history, in order to expose the Western bias and androcentricism of historical narrative. Gibbs defines traumatic metafiction as a type of writing that similarly undermines the discourse of trauma theory and dramatises the difficulties of constructing a trauma narrative (89).

character or character of colour) is written to distract the audience's attention from the 'main' plot concerned with the trauma of a more typical white, middle-class male protagonist. This can take the form of the female character taking up more screen time than the apparent male protagonist, or a text representing the female character as attempting to disrupt and 'break down' the narrative concerned with the false male protagonist, whose narrative is akin to a misdirect. My analysis examines this technique in relation to *Batman Returns.*

The first type of competitive narration combines feminist trauma theory, such as that of Brown, in addition to post-colonial critics including Craps and Buelens, with feminist film theory of the male gaze by Laura Mulvey in her essay 'Visual Pleasure and Narrative Cinema'. First, Mulvey argues that male characters in film generally drive the narrative forward and are positioned as both the protagonists and the characters with whom the viewer identifies. By contrast, women are relegated to secondary status, generally as love interests for the male lead and an 'erotic object' (19) for the male spectator to look at. Analysing texts in terms of the first type of competitive narration exposes this dichotomy in films, because it is a framework used to read texts where female secondary characters are depicted as overtaking the plot of male leads and swapping roles with them in order to foreground their trauma narrative. Likewise, in *Batman Returns*, the more conventional, male-centred trauma narrative of Bruce Wayne/Batman (Michael Keaton) is represented as overtaken by the trauma narrative of a female character, Selina Kyle/Catwoman (Michelle Pfeiffer). Second, Mulvey says that film provides not only what Freud calls scopophilic pleasure (viewing another, characteristically a woman, as an erotic object), but also signifies the threat of castration. Therefore, woman as representation induces not only fetishistic but also voyeuristic mechanisms to circumvent her 'threat' (Mulvey 25). This involves the male spectator asserting his control over the 'guilty' woman by subjecting her to either forgiveness or punishment (both common in film noir) (Mulvey 21). According to Cynthia A. Freeland, in terms of punishment, horror films often reinforce this 'conception of the active (sadistic) male viewer and the passive suffering female object' (18). Linda Williams adds that women are often punished in horror films for their appropriation of the gaze and patriarchal order is restored as a result of the punishment (563). Moreover, recent works contextualise the limitations of Mulvey's arguments, which is also relevant to this chapter. Pheasant-Kelly observes that cinematic signifying practices have undergone change, 'consistent with the development of feminism, equal rights and more generalised trends towards androgyny' ('Reframing' 197–198). For Pheasant-Kelly, this has led to strong female characters that 'propel' their own narrative ('Reframing' 195). Pheasant-Kelly also notes that, conversely, certain male characters 'correspond with the feminised position of Mulvey's original schema' in terms of 'visual objectification', 'instances of corporeal vulnerability' and passivity ('Reframing' 204), in addition to subversion of 'notions of the male hero' ('Reframing' 205). In *Batman Returns*, Catwoman is represented as subverting the traditionally female roles of villain/femme fatale, love interest/erotic object and victim, fulfilling particular superhero criteria that Batman fails to meet, and is repeatedly killed off in the film and resurrected. The structure of texts I analyse in terms of the first type of competitive narration such as *Batman Returns* also chimes with Freud's rhetoric of the fetish that Mulvey incorporates. How the young boy averts his gaze from the female genitals (which for him represent the threat of castration) towards more acceptable content such as a shoe (which becomes the fetish), or how the male spectator circumvents his castration anxiety through focusing on a more reassuring image of a woman's beauty or punishment, mirrors how female secondary characters such as Catwoman distract our attention from the male protagonist in the narrative. Reading this kind of representation in terms of texts exposing trauma fiction's androcentric bias, Catwoman's narrative disruption reflects how conventional trauma fiction and cultural trauma theory more comfortingly figure traumatic experiences as extraordinary events outside the range of usual human experience, as opposed to an ongoing part of everyday reality.

The second type of competitive narration features parallel plots that alternatively vie for the reader's or viewer's attention, except that neither one successfully overtakes the other and emerges as the main plot, resulting in a narrative that consists of alternative and contradictory sequences and plotlines. The second type of competitive narration is explored in relation to *Twin Peaks*, and combines feminist trauma theory, such as that of Herman, with postmodernist formal techniques, specifically narrative self-erasure (or denarration) and mutually exclusive narrative possibilities. Narrative self-erasure is when events are, as McHale explains, 'narrated, then explicitly recalled or rescinded' and 'replaced' with different events (101). An example of such is the line 'Of course it happened. Of course it didn't happen' (667) in Pynchon's *Gravity's Rainbow*. As noted, mutually exclusive narrative possibilities are found in Barth's 'Lost in the Funhouse'.

McHale says that in this story, 'two or more mutually exclusive states of affairs are projected' (102), events 'both do and do not happen' and 'the same event happens in two irreconcilably different ways' (106).

Batman Returns

Eschewing the campness of the 1960s television series, Burton's live-action *Batman* (1989) franchise put forth a darker, ostensibly more serious version of the character in line with that in Frank Miller's noir comic *Batman: Year One*. Similar to Miller's prequel, Burton foregrounded Batman's traumatic origins. Trauma is a frequent trigger for a turn to super-heroics generally. This trope aligns with the Freudian-Caruthian belatedness model in the way such characters are either instigated by a sudden traumatic event to *use* their abilities to fight crime or shown to *obtain* their powers via a sudden traumatic incident (Halfyard 30). Burton's Bruce Wayne is, in a number of ways, a typical trauma protagonist: Wayne is an affluent, straight white male character who continues a tradition of 'upper-class heroes' (Heldenfels 98). He has been affected by a singular traumatic event, the murder of his parents by a street thug when he was a child, and he experiences clichéd symptoms accordingly. For instance, Wayne experiences a flashback of his parents' murder when he sees Jack Napier/The Joker (Jack Nicholson) with his make-up removed, because, in Burton's adaptation, Napier killed Wayne's parents. The character's dual identity as millionaire philanthropist and masked crime fighter is analogous to dissociation or splitting, a symptom of trauma whereby an individual splits off a part of their consciousness from a traumatic experience and remembers it as occurring to someone else, thereby creating an 'alter personality' (Herman, *Trauma* 103). Wayne's assumption of the Batman persona can also be described as the character attempting to, in the Freudian/Caruthian sense of the term, fully grasp the traumatic experience, specifically the way in which trauma is understood as a mental wound that 'is experienced too soon, too unexpectedly to be fully known and is therefore not available to consciousness until it imposes itself again, repeatedly, in the nightmares and *repetitive actions of the survivor*' (Caruth 4, emphasis mine). This is evident in how, as Kelly Duquette observes, Wayne's crime-fighting persona provides him with multiple 'opportunities to (re)grasp the traumatic event' of his parents' murders and re-enact this trauma repeatedly (16).

Regarding Catwoman's trauma, Janet K. Halfyard asserts that the principal characters of *Batman Returns* are linked in that they are all 'dual personality characters ... people who have suffered some great trauma' (30). Burton says that what he likes about *Batman*'s characters includes their 'duality' and 'the fact that they're *all* fucked-up characters, the villains and Batman' (Salisbury 103, emphasis mine). Whereas Burton's *Batman* is, in many ways, a conventional representation of trauma, its sequel *Batman Returns* takes a more innovative direction regarding Catwoman's trauma narrative. Burton's Catwoman experiences a number of ongoing traumatic events, resulting from both physical violence and everyday experiences of inequality and oppression. Primarily, Catwoman's narrative foregrounds the more insidious, ongoing trauma of patriarchal domination. As noted, Brown describes insidious trauma as 'the traumatogenic effects of oppression that are not necessarily overtly violent or threatening to bodily well-being at the given moment but that do violence to the soul and spirit' (107). Kyle is continuously subject to the sexism of her boss, Max Shreck (Christopher Walken), the owner of a multi-million department store and business empire. Despite Kyle's attempts to move up in the corporate world and become part of the patriarchy, Shreck has her perform menial tasks such as making coffee for his fellow male corporate executives, and responds mockingly to Kyle's suggestion at an all-male board meeting, firmly re-establishing traditional gender roles: 'I'm afraid we haven't properly housebroken Miss Kyle. In the plus column though, she makes a hell of a cup of coffee.' Kyle's return from work also shows her experiencing the 'chronic psychic suffering produced by the structural violence of ... gender ... inequities' (Craps and Buelens, *Studies in the Novel* 3–4). Societal pressures and challenges faced by women are overtly foregrounded, such as pressures to marry when Kyle greets her empty apartment with 'Honey, I'm home! Oh, I forgot. I'm not married.' Kyle's exhausted appearance together with her concerns about paying rent indicate the low pay received by women and the undervaluing of their contribution to the workplace: 'I seem pathetic, but I'm a working girl, gotta pay the rent'. Kyle's messages on her answering machine lists varying, ongoing struggles of women, in line with what Brown calls '"normal" traumatic events' (101), that is, how women's experiences are 'daily blighted by abusive situations that, while part of their everyday life, are nevertheless traumatic' (Gibbs 16). These messages include the expectation for women to care for elderly family members rather than pursue careers (Kyle's mother says 'I'm disappointed that you're not coming home for Christmas. We must discuss why you insist on languishing in Gotham City as some lowly secretary' and Kyle corrects her mother's description of her as secretary to 'executive assistant'); and gender inequities in relationships in the message from Kyle's boyfriend, who ends their relationship because she beat him at a game of racquetball. Highlighting male fears of female competence, Kyle says, 'I guess I should have let him win'. The third message is from Shreck's store, which emphasises women's role as erotic object: 'Gotham Lady Perfume. It makes women feel like women and the men have no complaints either.' Further underscoring the menial nature of her job, the final message is Kyle reminding herself to collect Shreck's files. Kyle is subsequently murdered by Shreck at the office when she discovers his illegal activities, after which numerous cats resurrect her.

While Shreck's attempted murder of Kyle presents the kind of sudden, punctual trauma in line with the Freudian-Caruthian model, the trauma that instigates the creation of Catwoman aligns more with the prolonged, insidious suffering produced by gender inequities, evident in the lengthy scenes that show Kyle as gradually traumatised by sexism and corporate patriarchy. Moreover, as with *Batman*'s Joker, this is a new origin story for Catwoman, with the misogynistic business mogul Shreck being a new addition to the *Batman* canon. Kyle is murdered because she attempts to become part of the patriarchy, as Kyle suggests that Shreck let her in on his activities before her 'murder'. Patriarchal conditions, then, give Kyle concrete motivation as Catwoman: her mission being to disrupt the patriarchy that oppressed her and take revenge on Shreck. In contrast to The Joker, who is usually depicted as a terrorist or insane bank robber, Catwoman's first mission is not an act of random terrorism but to blow up Shreck's department store. That Kyle's traumatisation and transformation into Catwoman stems from patriarchal oppression is additionally suggested when she vandalises her apartment and destroys all signifiers of femininity following her murder. She breaks the paintings and mirrors upon her walls with a frying pan and spray-paints black lines across her pink walls and pastel coloured clothes. The frying pan in particular can be read as symbolic of oppressed femininity.

Overtakes the Narrative

Catwoman's feminist trauma narrative is represented as overtaking the film in a number of ways. The film has Kyle/Catwoman interrupt Wayne/Batman's dialogue and 'steal the scene' from him when Batman first encounters Oswald Cobblepot/The Penguin (Danny DeVito), and when Wayne meets with Shreck to discuss the power plant. When Batman, in typical superhero fashion, attempts to chastise and intimidate The Penguin for wreaking havoc on the city, Catwoman interrupts him by emerging into the street, somersaulting triumphantly, and saying 'meow' before the department store explodes behind her. Similarly, when Wayne begins to tell Shreck of Cobblepot's/The Penguin's criminal nature and his plans to prove this ('Oswald controls through a triangle gang, I can't prove it yet but we both know that I-'), Wayne is cut short when Kyle enters the room, and begins sharing random anecdotes about her past. The 'Catwoman theme' (Danny Elfman) also swells throughout the scene. This theme dominates the score throughout the film and is present in scenes supposedly focused on other characters. For example, the 'Catwoman theme' plays when Batman spies on The Penguin in his office. Thus, Catwoman even dominates scenes she is apparently absent from.[3]

Kyle/Catwoman also gets more screen time (33 minutes) than Wayne/Batman (31 minutes). While the difference appears minimal, it was nevertheless suggested to Burton that 'it was a case of too many villains spoiling the Batman, with Keaton again forced to take a back seat' (Salisbury 103). Burton responded that he did 'probably spend too much time' on his supporting cast, as Cobblepot/The Penguin gets 29 minutes of screen time and Shreck gets 19 minutes. However, Wayne/Batman also appears inconsequential in terms of the film's narrative. Phil Hardy suggests:

> [In] *Batman Returns*, after taking second place to Jack Nicholson's Joker on *Batman*, ... [Keaton] is actually a supporting player. His familiar trauma [is] ... not rehashed here, [and] ... is given far less weight than the appalling circumstances which create ... Pfeiffer's schizophrenic Catwoman. (45)

The murder of Wayne's parents and its resulting trauma are briefly mentioned in Burton's sequel, which is in stark contrast to the film's lengthy depiction of Kyle's/Catwoman's ongoing suffering. Likewise,

[3] This tactic brought to the extreme in *Twin Peaks*, evident in how 'Laura's Theme', dominates the score.

Wayne's/Batman's plot points that were central to the previous film, such as his alienated dual personality and his love interest Vicki Vale (Kim Basinger), are dispensed with in a few dialogue references.

Refusing Roles

Not only is Kyle/Catwoman the protagonist of the narrative by virtue of the character's increased screen time, but also by the way Burton depicts her as rejecting traditional Hollywood feminine roles and fulfilling particular superhero criteria that Batman fails to meet. Burton has Kyle/Catwoman reject traditional feminine roles of villain/femme fatale, love interest/erotic object and victim. For instance, when vandalising Shreck's department store, the reason Catwoman attacks the two guards is that they attempt to categorise her into these narrative stereotypes. One quips to the other: 'I don't know whether to open fire or fall in love' to which she responds, 'You poor guys. Always confusing your pistols with your privates.' Kyle's/Catwoman's relationship with Wayne/Batman also establishes the interpretation of the character as breaking out of the film's subplot and the traditional roles of villain, love interest and victim assigned to female characters to keep them there. Regarding Catwoman as an antagonist, Burton insisted that '[s]he was never bad' (Salisbury 103), and he depicts Catwoman rejecting the role of villain in a number of scenes. These include: Kyle's reaction when she and Wayne realise each other's secret identity (she anxiously asks: 'Does this mean we have to start fighting?'); when Wayne comments to Kyle that she has 'got kind of a dark side' and Kyle responds with 'No darker than yours, Bruce'; and Catwoman's alliance with The Penguin. Catwoman disapproves of The Penguin's grotesque schemes to garner power and status, and breaks their alliance when she learns he killed Gotham's beauty pageant contestant: 'You said you were going to scare the ice princess'. Catwoman's initial alliance with The Penguin appears related to overtaking Batman's role as the film's hero. Catwoman suggests they 'destroy' Batman by framing him for the kidnap of the pageant contestant, which would turn Batman into a villain: 'To destroy Batman, we must turn him into what he hates the most. Namely us.'

Catwoman is likewise depicted as rejecting the role of love interest. For instance, among the reasons Catwoman aligns with The Penguin to 'destroy' Batman is to avenge Batman's attempt to rescue her when she fell from a rooftop during their initial confrontation. Batman's act of heroism angers Catwoman because it positions her as a 'damsel in distress' and therefore the film's love interest rather than its protagonist. The damsel-in-distress trope is common to the superhero genre and its love interests: the hero's girlfriend is put in some type of danger (such as confrontations with antagonists, fires and great heights), and he must come to her rescue. In *Batman*, Wayne rescues Vale from dangers such as high buildings and The Joker. Catwoman in *Batman Returns* refuses to be rescued by Batman in this manner. When Catwoman loses the fight with Batman on the rooftop and falls from the building, Batman saves her. This gesture angers Catwoman and she stabs Batman in the stomach with her claws. Batman then pushes Catwoman from the building and she lands in a truck full of cat litter. Catwoman laughs that she is 'saved by kitty litter' rather than Batman. She reacts with anger when rescued and positioned in a traditionally feminine role of helpless victim, and reacts with glee when treated as an equal opponent. In so doing, Catwoman is depicted as resisting what Pheasant-Kelly calls 'a feminised position' in cinema ('Reframing' 206) and 'garners agency through refusing to perform victimhood' (Pheasant-Kelly, 'Reframing' 206).

Hero

Because *Batman Returns* is a superhero film, Burton has Kyle/Catwoman take on stereotypical 'heroic' characteristics, and mimic (or *copycat*) the actions and behaviour exhibited by Batman in both this narrative and the previous film. Not only is Batman overshadowed by the film's supporting cast (which is suggested in Alfred's (Michael Gough) observation to Wayne regarding The Penguin: 'Perhaps you think you should be the only lonely man-beast in the city'), but the character is given few action scenes and relatively little to do in the narrative. A number of scenes depict Wayne doing literally nothing. When the character is introduced, the city flashes the Bat-Signal into the sky and the film cuts to a shot of Wayne in the Batcave sitting in an armchair, as though waiting to be Batman. This is in contrast to the opening of the previous film, which shows Batman in crime-fighting action. The few scenes that depict the character's crime-fighting escapades often show him to fail in his endeavours. When driving the iconic Batmobile, Batman loses control of the vehicle. He also fails to rescue the pageant contestant, one of the film's archetypal 'damsels in distress'. Here, Catwoman suggests to Batman: 'Seems like every woman you've tried to save ends up dead. Maybe you should retire.'

Conversely, there are a number of scenes where Catwoman displays superhero characteristics and replicates Batman in her dialogue and exploits. For instance, when Wayne exits his date with Kyle, he instructs Alfred to come up with an explanation for his absence: 'Tell her, uh, tell her I had to go out of town, a big business deal came up or some[thing]', while Kyle similarly asks Alfred to devise an excuse for her departure: 'Would you tell him for me that I've been going through a lot of changes and, no, um … could you just make up a sonnet or something?' Furthermore, superhero narratives and adaptations generally depict the 'origin' of their title hero. That is, they show how the hero obtained their powers and also their initial experimentation with these powers via performance of minor heroic acts. These include preventing local crimes and rescuing random civilians. *Batman Returns* depicts how Kyle obtained her powers and, in her first scene as Catwoman, has her rescue a woman from rape. Catwoman emerges from the shadows and beats the man unconscious: 'I just love a big, strong man who's not afraid to show it with someone half his size. … I am Catwoman, hear me roar.'[4] This act of heroism mirrors that of Batman in the opening scene of the previous film where he confronts the two muggers robbing a family and proclaims: 'I'm Batman'. Catwoman also critiques the traditional Hollywood feminine role of victim here. Rather than accepting the woman's thanks, Catwoman chastises her for expecting a man to save the situation: 'You make it so easy, don't you? Always waiting for some Batman to save you.' Having Catwoman rescue a woman from rape again foregrounds the ongoing trauma experienced by women. Emphasising the 'ordinariness' and perhaps overlooking of women's traumatic experience, the civilian is shown walking in a crowded area when she is grabbed; we see a brief glimpse of a couple walking in close proximity to her seconds before.

Batman fails to bring the film's primary villain, Shreck, to justice, that is, to hand him over to the police, and Catwoman kills him instead. Batman thus fails to fulfil one of the fundamental functions of the superhero: to defeat the narrative's primary villain in an epic battle. Batman fights The Penguin, but this confrontation is given less weight than that between Catwoman and Shreck: the Batman/Penguin battle is brief, almost devoid of dialogue and contains relatively little physical combat. The Penguin is also represented as more of a secondary villain rather than a primary antagonist, and his fight with Batman *precedes* Catwoman's battle with Shreck, further indicating The Penguin's status as secondary villain

[4] This, of course, is also a reference to Helen Reddy's feminist 'anthem': 'I am Woman'.

(generally, the superhero's defeat of the primary villain is the *final* battle in the narrative). Batman does not kill The Penguin either. Instead, Catwoman blows up The Penguin's air conditioner in his lair, which causes him to overheat and choke as he needs a cold environment to survive. Furthermore, Batman barely partakes in the Catwoman/Shreck showdown, and is eventually relegated to watching it from the side-lines. When Catwoman begins to strangle Shreck, Batman intervenes, making a failed attempt to 'save the day'. He swoops dramatically into the scene with his grappling hook, the iconic *Batman* score swelling in the background, and pushes Shreck backwards. Declaring to Shreck 'You're going to jail', viewers again expect Batman to deliver the quintessential heroic monologue employed to threaten or placate villains in superhero narratives. However, Catwoman speaks over and disrupts Batman's dialogue, compares herself to him, pushes him into the background of the scene and kills Shreck, overtaking Batman's role as hero by killing the narrative's main antagonist. She says, 'Don't be naïve, the law doesn't apply to people like him or us'. A medium shot of Catwoman lashing her whip cuts to a reaction shot of Batman hurdling backwards. Catwoman's defeat of Shreck is another parallel to Batman in the first film. Similar to Wayne killing The Joker to avenge his parents' murder in *Batman*, Catwoman's narrative culminates in avenging her oppressor by electrocuting both herself and Shreck.

This scene inverts the gender binaries of Mulvey's original schema and subverts the notion of the male hero. According to Pheasant-Kelly, 'revisionist viewing politics not only reflects a more generalised equality between the sexes but also corresponds to an associated ongoing crisis in masculinity' that developed long before the 1990s ('Reframing' 202). Harry M. Benshoff and Sean Griffin identify 'representations of failing masculinity in several late 1960s and 1970s Hollywood films', reflecting 'failures and losses in the Vietnam War' (Pheasant-Kelly, 'Reframing' 202), as well as a category of films that they call 'dumb white guy comedies' (Benshoff and Griffin 300) which 'satirise masculine prowess' (Pheasant-Kelly, 'Reframing' 202). In having its titular protagonist fail to achieve his heroic objectives, *Batman Returns* appears to take a similar approach from within the superhero genre. Furthermore, Batman resonates with what Pheasant-Kelly calls 'the prior feminising position of the passive female character of Mulvey's model' ('Reframing' 207) as he watches the action. By contrast, the film positions Catwoman as the active agent who drives the narrative, here in the form of restoring order. The scene also has Catwoman reject traditional feminine Hollywood roles imposed on her by both the narrative and surrounding male characters. In an attempt to restore order, Wayne/

Batman pleads with Kyle/Catwoman not to kill Shreck and offers her a stereotypically romantic 'fairy-tale' ending: 'Let's just take him to the police. Then we can go home. Together, Selina.' While Wayne/Batman attempts to situate Kyle/Catwoman as his (and thereby the film's) love interest, his plea makes further apparent the parallels between the characters, and therefore Kyle's/Catwoman's role as the hero/protagonist rather than love interest. Wayne/Batman repeats that they are 'the same' and points out their similar, post-traumatic dual identities: 'We're the same. We're the same. Split right down the centre.' Kyle/Catwoman rejects Batman's offer and proclaims her role as a heroic avenger who seeks justice for the patriarchal trauma imposed upon her by Shreck. Kyle/Catwoman tells Shreck that she wants him dead and hits Wayne/Batman when he reaches out and touches her face, again literally pushing him out of the frame, while Batman fails as a hero because he is unable to 'rescue' Kyle/Catwoman from her murder and suicide. Kyle/Catwoman informs him: 'I would love to live with you in your castle forever, just like a fairy tale. I just couldn't live with myself, so don't pretend this is a happy ending.'

The final scene of *Batman Returns* fully establishes Catwoman as the protagonist. Conventionally, superhero films conclude by presenting the logo or symbol of its hero. Burton's *Batman* ends with the Dark Knight standing atop a building with the iconic Bat-Signal looming in the sky. In *Batman Returns*, Wayne briefly believes he sees Catwoman's shadow in an alleyway. He wishes Alfred a 'Merry Christmas', adding 'and goodwill to all men *and women*', the addition of the phrase '*and women*' being a possible reference to the film's concern with foregrounding women's experience and their exclusion from discourse. The camera pans out and the Bat-Signal appears in the clouds in what seems to be the final shot in *Batman Returns*. However, Catwoman once again steals the spotlight from the Dark Knight. In the manner of a photobomb, Catwoman suddenly moves into the frame before the credits roll, the silhouette of her mask drawing our eyes away from the Bat-Signal, the film effectively reminding the viewer that she is the protagonist (see images below).[5] This scene also establishes Catwoman's competition with Batman for the role of protagonist, as Catwoman's disruption of the film's presentation of the Bat-Signal, what Halfyard describes as the 'instantly recognisable signifier

[5] A photobomb is a photograph that has been humorously spoiled by the appearance of an unintended subject in the camera's field of view.

Fig. 3.1 The Bat-Signal in *Batman* (1989). 'Bat-Signal'. *Wikipedia*. 2017

of Batman' (54), literally draws the viewer's gaze from the putative protagonist towards the actual one.

If we consider the film's 'photobomb' ending in the context of Mulvey's essay, the subversiveness of *Batman Returns* becomes more apparent. Mulvey claims 'the sadistic intent of the male character (and by extension the spectator) emerges in films where women are passive in the narrative and serve as sexual objects', and 'in instances where the narrative involves resistance to such control, women fall victim to either marriage or death' (as in horror films or film noir) (Pheasant-Kelly, 'Reframing' 197). In *Batman Returns*, Catwoman rejects Wayne's/Batman's offer of a 'fairy-tale' ending and refuses to die. In the film's closing scene, the viewer is led to believe that the feminist disruption of the traditional male plot has been safely contained, with the death of the female agent, but Catwoman unexpectedly lives and, in turn, continues to disrupt Batman's narrative and traditional superhero and cinematic conventions, this time, the expected male-centred and celebratory ending (Figs. 3.1 and 3.2).[6]

[6] Catwoman's continuous 'return from the dead' can be further read in relation to the character's attempt to become the film's lead in that the character literally acts in accordance with the verb in the film's title: *Batman Returns*. Often, the narrative actions of films' protagonists are outlined in the text's title, for example, John Hughes' *Ferris Bueller's Day Off* (1986) (the protagonist takes a day off from school).

Fig. 3.2 *Batman Returns*: Final Scene. 'Special Review: *Batman Returns*—Villainy of Biblical Proportion'. *The Viewer's Commentary*. 2012

Moreover, Catwoman repeatedly asserts that she has nine lives and she is 'killed' eight times in the film: Shreck pushes her from a window, both Batman and The Penguin throw her off a building, and she 'dies' when electrocuting Shreck. Shreck also shoots Catwoman four times in the climax, to which she remarks: 'You killed me. The Penguin killed me. Batman killed me. That's three lives down. You got enough in there to finish me off?' In having Catwoman murdered by Shreck, Batman and The Penguin, the character is killed each time by the film's representative members of the patriarchy. That Catwoman is semi-immortal is also essential to the representation of the character as one attempting to break out of the narrative's subplot and become the film's lead. In continuously returning from the dead, *Batman Returns* depicts Catwoman as resisting the narrative's attempts to write her out of the film, the character repeatedly clawing her way back into the script to highlight her narrative of patriarchal trauma.[7] Catwoman is 'killed' precisely at moments when the character refuses to fulfil the traditional feminine roles assigned to her in the film (that of love interest, villain or victim). It is suggested that Kyle is murdered by Shreck not only because she attempts to become part of the patriarchy but also because she does so in favour of the more traditional feminine role as love interest or erotic object. Before she vandalises her

[7] A textual phenomenon brought to the extreme in *Twin Peaks* and its murdered female lead, Laura Palmer, and other characters that are represented as threatening narrative conventions and content.

apartment, Kyle receives another message from Shreck's department store that guarantees that wearing their perfume will attract the attention of one's boss: 'One whiff of this at the office and your boss will be asking you to stay after work for a candlelight staff meeting for two'. By contrast, Kyle pursues a professional relationship with her boss rather than a romantic one as suggested by the perfume advertisement. Batman and The Penguin also kill Catwoman for refusing traditional feminine roles. Batman pushes Catwoman off the building when she chastises him for his rescue and refuses to play his damsel in distress, while The Penguin kills Catwoman for refusing to play his love interest and rejecting his sexual advances, exclaiming: 'You lousy minx! I ought to have you spayed! You send out all the signals! And I don't think I like you anymore!' The Penguin throws Catwoman off the building they stand upon and she crash-lands on a bed of flowers in a green house, seemingly dead. Refusing to be killed off and silenced, however, Catwoman rises from the earth and screams so loudly the glass walls of the green house shatter to pieces.[8] This scene parallels Batman's murder of Catwoman in that she lands in a truck of cat litter. The image of Catwoman literally emerging from dirt- and ash-like substances (flowers in earth, cat litter) further drives home the image of the character dying and resurrecting.

Twin Peaks

Premiering on ABC in 1990, David Lynch and Mark Frost's *Twin Peaks* ran for two seasons until its cancellation in 1991. However, the initial success of the series sparked a media franchise, leading to the release of a feature film, *Twin Peaks: Fire Walk with Me* (1992), several tie-in novels including Jennifer Lynch's *The Secret Diary of Laura Palmer*, and events such as the '*Twin Peaks* Festival' in the UK and a screening of all the episodes at London Battersea Arts Centre.[9] In the years following *Twin Peaks*' release, the series has been listed amongst the greatest television series of all time, has received universal acclaim from critics and audiences alike, received three Golden Globes and two Emmys and has gained a cult

[8] The shattering of the green house evokes the concept of the 'glass ceiling': an unacknowledged and illegal barrier to career advancement for women and people of colour. The inclusion of a glass structure is significant as this scene depicts one of Catwoman's resurrections and in turn advancement in the narrative.

[9] This chapter will refer to *Twin Peaks: Fire Walk with Me* by its abbreviated title: *Fire Walk with Me*.

following. Indeed, while multiple academic works and dissertations have been written on the series, Pheasant-Kelly asserts that the cult status of *Twin Peaks* is 'uncontested' ('Strange Spaces' 96). *Twin Peaks* is frequently referred to as 'the original watercooler TV show' by fans and critics, and the series renewed interest as a cult classic resulted in it being revived as a limited event television series on Showtime in 2017, entitled *Twin Peaks: The Return*. Pheasant-Kelly observes that *Twin Peaks*' cult status is both intrinsic to the text itself and emerges through fan responses ('Strange Spaces' 95). Multiple Internet groups and weblogs continue to detail viewers' responses to *Twin Peaks*, in which individuals express opinions and share speculations, and repeat memorised lines of dialogue (such as 'the owls are not what they seem'). The Lynchian hallmarks of the series likewise promote cult spectatorship, including difficult themes such as incest and murder, ambiguous generic identity (the series incorporates mystery, horror, drama, melodrama and detective procedural), lack of closure and a fascination with space (evident in spaces such as The Black Lodge, the series' otherworldly dimension). As Pheasant-Kelly notes, these 'transgressive and paranormal qualities' provide a 'cultish appeal' ('Strange Spaces' 96).

This chapter provides new reading of *Twin Peaks* by analysing it in terms of competitive narration, specifically the second type of competitive narration.[10] As noted, this involves two narratives vying for the viewer's attention, but neither one successfully overtakes the other and emerges as the main plot, resulting in a narrative that consists of alternative and contradictory plotlines. This strategy aligns with mutually exclusive narrative possibilities, which McHale says has the effect of not only destabilising 'the ontology of the projected world', but simultaneously lay bare 'the process of world-construction' (101). Likewise, the second type of competitive narration involves two narratives that continually disrupt, contradict and distract from each other to emerge as the dominant plot in order to undermine how conventional trauma fiction represents the experiences of women. According to McHale, there is no way of processing a metaphorical expression 'without registering the two possibilities and the tug-of-war between them—without, in other words, hesitating between the literal and the metaphorical' (135). *Twin Peaks*' supernatural representation of trauma concepts similarly results in the series presenting the viewer

[10] *Twin Peaks: The Return* will be briefly discussed because the plotline of Laura Palmer's (Sheryl Lee) murder, the main focus of my analysis, is not the main focus of *The Return*.

with two competing narratives: one metaphorical and one literal, or one natural and one supernatural. I propose that *Twin Peaks* critiques these representations, specifically those centred on childhood sexual abuse and the cultural tradition of depicting such taboo topics in supernatural terms rather than realistically. *Twin Peaks* does this through its offering of both realistic and supernatural explanations for the domestic violence in the narrative, as well as through its depiction of dominant trauma concepts in supernatural terms. These representations make overt the process of mythologising women's trauma and in turn expose culture's limitations when representing it. *Twin Peaks* further foregrounds the inadequacies of trauma culture when representing family violence by having narratives concerning rape and murder victims continually disrupt and compete with the series' 'main' plot concerned with more conventional white male protagonists, and also by interrogating certain conventions of trauma representation such as the dominant aesthetic models of trauma fiction and the practice of myth-making more widely.

Trauma Concepts

Twin Peaks employs supernatural metaphors to represent a number of trauma concepts and ideas that were popular during the time the series was produced. *Twin Peaks* centres on the rape and murder of a high school student named Laura Palmer (Sheryl Lee). The series' killer is revealed to be Laura's father, Leland Palmer (Ray Wise), who is regularly possessed by a demon named BOB (Frank Silva) from another dimension called the Black Lodge. BOB feeds on human suffering and seeks to inhabit the bodies of human hosts in order to impel them to commit atrocities.[11] Because metaphors result in a *hesitation* between the metaphorical and the literal, the series participates in the cultural tradition of evading family violence and simultaneously refutes it. The literal or realist narrative in which Leland is the culprit exposes family violence, while the metaphorical or supernatural narrative more traditionally tries to cover it up, and as McHale says of mutually exclusive narrative possibilities, having such narratives compete for the viewer's attention has the effect of laying bare the process of world-construction. In depicting family violence in this way, *Twin Peaks* is in accordance with representations of rape and incest such as those of

[11] BOB is generally referred to in upper case in reviews and critical work on *Twin Peaks*, as is the character MIKE.

Morrison in *Beloved* (which was published four years before *Twin Peaks* in 1987). According to Luckhurst, while the novel incorporates supernatural elements, rather than distancing uncomfortable subject matter, 'the use of the supernatural' in such novels foregrounds the limits of discourses such as 'historiography, law or medicine' to convey them (*Trauma* 97). *Twin Peaks*' dual narrative structure, the way in which it continuously hesitates and alternates between realist and supernatural accounts of events, is particularly appropriate for depicting family violence and the traumatic experiences of women, people of colour and queer individuals. First, these experiences are often debated or dismissed as untrue and imagined (Herman, *Father* vii). Second, *Twin Peaks*' dual narrative reflects what Janet Walker describes as the 'vicissitudes of memory' ('False' 212) in regards to childhood sexual abuse, asserting that memories of childhood abuse in particular might be 'reworked in memory' and 'affected' by the victim's fantasies (Walker in Gibbs 13). Walker adds that fantasy does not belie the truth of the event but is connected to and produced by it ('False' 212).

For instance, Leland's transformation into a demon can be read as a supernatural representation of Freud's concept of 'screen memories' in that Laura sees Leland as someone else whenever he assaults her because the idea of her father as her abuser is too difficult to confront. According to Freud:

> Among our childhood memories … there are some scenes that turn out … to have been falsified. … they transfer an event to a place where it did not happen … merge two people into one, substitute one person for another … they serve to repress and replace objectionable or disagreeable impressions. ('Screen Memories' 20–21)

Screen memories are often represented in fiction by characters displacing traumatic events onto the supernatural. For instance, Billy Pilgrim in *Slaughterhouse-Five* tries to concentrate on 'pleasant moments' (96) and begins to believe that he has been abducted by aliens to a paradisiacal planet named Tralfamadore. Leland's possession can similarly be read in terms of this idea of screen memories and the displacement of 'objectionable' content onto the supernatural, but in texts such as Vonnegut's, it is made clear that the protagonists' otherworldly encounters are products of their imagination. In Laura's case it is literally true and Leland physically transforms into BOB. This is established as an actual occurrence in that

BOB is not only referred to in Laura's subjectivity but both takes possession of and is seen by other characters in the series (Stevenson 76), such as Laura's mother Sarah Palmer (Grace Zabriskie) when he materialises in her living room.

Lynch claimed that while the series is about the 'devastation of the victim of incest ... [i]t also dealt with the torment of the father—the war in him' (Rodley 185). Following Laura's murder, Leland reveals that he was a victim of childhood abuse by BOB. The language he uses to describe BOB's initial possession of him when he was a child is indicative of rape: 'I was just a boy ... he said he wanted to play. He opened me ... and came inside me' ('Arbitrary Law'). Thus, if we look at Leland's possession in terms of his traumatic experience, a number of major conceptions of trauma associated with childhood abuse can be applied to his character as well. For example, Leland's possession can be read as a supernatural representation of what Herman refers to as the 'generational cycle of abuse' (*Trauma* 114), the belief that victims of abuse become perpetrators of abuse and 're-enact their childhood experiences' (*Trauma* 113), in that Leland transforms into his abuser BOB.[12] Leland's transformation into BOB can also be interpreted as a supernatural metaphor for dissociation, which has long been a pervasive idea in trauma theory. As noted, dissociation is a symptom of trauma whereby an individual splits off a part of their consciousness from a traumatic experience and remembers it as occurring to someone else, thereby creating what Herman calls an 'alter personality' (*Trauma* 103). Pierre Janet describes dissociation as when victims 'look' at a traumatic event 'from a distance or disappear altogether, leaving other parts of their personality' to experience and 'store' the event (van der Kolk, 'Intrusive' 168). Janet's model of trauma became favoured again by the late 1980s. The oscillation between the unknowing Leland and the demonic BOB represents this shift 'between knowledge and repression' (Vickroy 8) and alter personalities symptomatic of childhood abuse. When interrogated by the police, Leland claims not to have known when BOB was controlling him: '[w]hen he was inside I didn't know and when he was gone I couldn't remember' ('Arbitrary Law'). Leland also does not accept responsibility for the murder of Laura and instead places the blame on BOB, that is, literally on another person: '[He] wanted Laura ... and

[12] While such an occurrence is rare, indeed, Herman also notes that 'the majority of victims do not become perpetrators' (*Trauma* 113), the opposite has been a pervasive idea in trauma studies, particularly during the time *Twin Peaks* was produced.

then [he] had me kill [her]' ('Arbitrary Law'). In contrast to conventional trauma fiction, then, Leland is actually subject to demonic possession as opposed to dissociating the traumatic event in his mind; Leland is literally two different people.

However, because of Leland's shifting of responsibility onto another, the Leland/BOB split also evokes perpetrator trauma. This model of trauma focuses on the traumatic experience of the perpetrator and, according to Gibbs, is both characterised by an 'inversion of perpetrator/victim status' (19) and 'linked to the notion of agency, in particular the denial of agency, as a means to slough off responsibility' (247). This 'conflation of perpetrator and victim, or transformation of one into the other' (Gibbs 178) is depicted supernaturally in *Twin Peaks* in that Leland is literally both the victim and the perpetrator. Leland raped and killed Laura when under the influence of BOB so while he committed this act of atrocity, he was at the same time stripped of agency and victim to a diabolical force over which he had no control. In the scene of his confession, there is what Randi Davenport refers to as a 'struggle between recognition and denial of the abusive father's culpability' (257) in that Leland begins to simultaneously accuse BOB of killing his daughter and express responsibility for it himself: 'I killed my daughter. I didn't know. Forgive me. … He made me do things, terrible things. … [he] made me kill [Laura]. Oh God, have mercy on me. What have I done?' ('Arbitrary Law'). While the shifts in narrative voice in Leland's confession evoke dissociative characteristics associated with victims of abuse, his alteration between first- and third-person pronouns also recalls those found in representations of perpetrator trauma in order to diminish responsibility for the narrator-protagonist's actions in that Leland can actually displace the blame onto someone else.

The alternating nature of the victim/perpetrator status is also evident in Leland's murder of Laura's cousin Maddy Ferguson (Sheryl Lee). BOB compels Leland to kill Maddy and while he strangles her, Leland metamorphoses alternately into BOB and then back to himself, thereby literally fluctuating between victim and perpetrator. Flashes of BOB alternate with Leland throughout the assault, showing BOB kissing and biting Maddy one moment and Leland crying hysterically the next (see images below) (Figs. 3.3 and 3.4).

This scene also evokes Freud's concept of *Nachträglichkeit* in a supernatural way. *Nachträglichkeit* is when a traumatic event is not fully acknowledged at the time of the event, becomes repressed and is remembered later through flashbacks when the sufferer is exposed to anything

Fig. 3.3 Leland kills Maddy. Murray, Noel. '*Twin Peaks* Season 2, Episodes 2–7: There Will Be BOB'. *NY Times*. 2017

Fig. 3.4 BOB kills Maddy. Hughes, Eric. 'TV Rewind: *Twin Peaks*'. *Box Office Prophets*. 2011

remotely associated with it: 'The time that elapsed between the [incident] and the first appearance of the symptoms is called the "incubation period", ... It is the feature one might term latency' (Freud, *Moses* 84). The term flashback was also incorporated into *DSM-III-R*, the revised version of the third edition of the *Diagnostic and Statistical Manual of Mental Disorders* (*DSM-III*), in 1987 and it moved into the literature on trauma in the 1980s (Leys 242). In *Twin Peaks*, however, the traumatic event actually returns in that Laura's murder is repeated via Maddy's murder. Another reason Maddy's murder, as Martha Nochimson says, 'recreates the original atrocity' (154) is that, aside from their hair colouring, they are identical in appearance, that is, both characters are played by Sheryl Lee, and their murders play out in a similar fashion. Leland/BOB refers to Maddy as Laura when he is strangling her and he wraps both of their bodies in plastic once he has killed them. Additionally, Christy Desmet points out that 'Lynch insists on the presence of sexual desire' in Maddy's assault in that BOB kisses and bites her; not only is Laura's murder replicated then but also the illicit desire behind it.

Mythologisation

Twin Peaks' supernatural representation of then-emerging trauma concepts can be read in relation to the series' foregrounding of the limitations of fiction when it comes to representing family violence, that is, the way in which fiction conceals and mythologises the phenomenon. For Luckhurst, *Twin Peaks* 'worked itself up to address father-daughter incest but then promptly looked away, seeking refuge in myth' (*Trauma* 204). Elizabeth Brent et al. similarly observe, 'the narrative places the blame not on the abuser (Leland) but an abstract notion of evil (BOB). … The abuser is not held responsible for his actions, because BOB made him do it' (192). In response to such arguments, Stevenson suggests,

> the reason Lynch approaches this subject "fantastically" has to do with the fact that … we still lack a settled language that would enable us to talk about these things 'realistically'. (72)

Reading *Twin Peaks* in terms of competitive narration, I propose an additional interpretation, that *Twin Peaks* presents the viewer with two competing narratives, one in which Leland is the culprit, the other where BOB is, one that exposes childhood abuse and the other that more traditionally tries to cover it up. These two narratives are depicted as competing for screen time to emerge as the dominant or 'true' narrative. However, unlike *Batman Returns*, neither successfully overtakes the other, resulting in a plot that consists of alternating and contradicting narrative events. Instead of straightforwardly displacing Leland's abuse to the supernatural, the series only *at times* suggests that Leland was subject to demonic possession when committing these atrocities, whereas other moments propose the opposite, namely, that Leland was not under BOB's influence when he harmed Laura and Maddy.

Certain scenes show Leland to be a concerned and caring father with no knowledge of the crimes he has committed or was compelled to commit, thereby suggesting that he was subject to supernatural forces beyond his control. These scenes include his genuine reaction of shock having received the news of Laura's death, his claim neither to have known nor remembered when BOB was controlling him, and his attempt to help the police with their investigation of Laura's murder. However, other moments in *Twin Peaks* contradict such scenes and suggest the opposite, showing Leland to be abusive when he is clearly *not* under BOB's influence. These include the scene where Leland grabs Laura's face at the dinner table and aggressively chastises her for not washing her hands, when Leland drugs Sarah before entering Laura's room at night, and when he informs a prostitute that she 'looks just like' his daughter (*Fire Walk with Me*).

Such contradictions also occur within the same scene. The struggle between recognition and denial of the abusive father's culpability is evident the morning after Laura discovers Leland and BOB are the same person. Leland asks a distraught Laura: 'Is something wrong this morning?' (*Fire Walk with Me*). When Laura then tells him to 'stay away' from her and leaves the house, the camera lingers on Leland's face in a close-up. At first, Leland appears confused, his expression vacant; however, seconds later, ominous music is heard and he begins to smirk. This moment suggests that Leland is both aware and oblivious as to why Laura is distressed. Similar contradictions occur in the scene of Laura's murder at the end of *Fire Walk with Me*. Leland possessed by BOB drags Laura into an abandoned train car, and binds and tortures his daughter before killing her. Leland screams 'No! Don't make me do this! No!', suggesting he was coerced by supernatural entities beyond his control when committing this act. Before this, however, a distressed Leland cries to Laura 'I always thought you knew it was me'. In this shot, Leland is standing to the right of the frame and is holding pages of Laura's diary, in which she writes about her abuse and claims to have no knowledge of BOB's identity. This shot is followed by a low-angle shot of Laura's bloodied face, but BOB is standing to the left of the frame. BOB jeers 'I never thought you knew it was me'. This scene, then, suggests that Leland was not only aware of the abuse he inflicted on Laura, but also that Leland was under the impression Laura had 'always' known it was he who had abused her.

The struggle or competition between the realist and the supernatural narrative is further visualised in scenes depicting Leland/BOB's acts of violence. As with Maddy's murder, Leland alternately metamorphoses into BOB and then back to himself, literally fluctuating or flickering between the two identities when he kills Laura. Shots of Leland interchange with BOB as he tortures and strangles her. If *Twin Peaks* were to fully participate in the tradition of representing child abuse in supernatural terms then, it is more likely that the series and prequel would only show BOB committing these acts and we would not see flashes of Leland interchanging with him throughout, whereas in these sequences it is as if the series wants to cover over its violent content with a supernatural veneer and strip it off to reveal the actual source of family violence. Indeed, Luckhurst notes: '*Twin Peaks* was striking because it refused the traditional framing of the issue [incest], disguising itself and then (arguably) working to transpose the secret had revealed into a different register entirely' (*Trauma* 201). Further underscoring culture's concealment of family violence, these scenes of violence in *Twin Peaks* overtly foreground their artifice. The scene of Maddy's murder features exaggerated melodramatic performances. BOB chases Maddy around the Palmer living room. Maddy continuously screams, waves her arms and places her hands upon her head as she runs, while BOB growls, bears his teeth and wiggles his fingers, gesturing her to come closer to him. BOB then grabs Maddy by the waist and spins her around in circles, a gesture resembling a dance. A literal spotlight also follows BOB as he assaults Maddy, emphasising this scene as a work of performance. Significantly, the spotlight is not present in the sequence that features Leland killing Maddy, rendering these shots more realistically and suggesting that the images of BOB, by contrast, are a supernatural veneer that covers up the real-world issue of domestic abuse. Further exploiting the scene's cinematic techniques, the sound changes and distorts only during the shots of BOB. Non-diegetic, monstrous roars reminiscent of B-horror monster movies can also be heard in these moments. Additionally, the shots of BOB are rendered in slow-motion, in contrast to those of Leland, which are presented in real time. The scene of Laura's murder contains similar foregrounding of cinematic techniques such as the use of television static which intercuts the scene (specifically, at the moment Laura catches a glimpse of BOB's reflection in the mirror on the floor of the train car), and references to theatrical performance, which include a shot of a monkey wearing a mask that intercuts the scene, and again, the employment of a spotlight. In keeping with the scene's contradictions regarding Leland's culpability, this time the spotlight flickers throughout the scene sporadically rather than limited to shots of BOB. The performative or staged nature of the scene of Maddy's murder is further referenced through the imagery of a literal stage at The Big Bang Bar in the scene that precedes it.[13] In this scene, The Giant (Carel Struycken), another being from the Black Lodge, appears in a vision to FBI Special Agent Dale Cooper (Kyle MacLachlan), the detective attempting to solve Laura's murder, to inform him that 'It is happening again'. We can interpret this line as referring to Leland's violence occurring again; it is also a commentary on the pervasiveness of culture's repression of family violence through supernatural content.

Competing and Experimental Scenes

Twin Peaks not only realises two mutually exclusive lines of narrative development at the same time, but also has moments where these plots, the realist one and the supernatural one, are depicted as struggling to overtake each other to the point of producing scenes that are fragmented and confusing. This occurs particularly when the series broaches taboo topics such as family violence or violence against women. In such scenes, there is a simultaneous attempt to divert the viewer's attention from the controversial content. These scenes are intercut with supernatural imagery, a supernatural scene may be superimposed over them, or the dialogue is interrupted and somewhat drowned out. In *Fire Walk with Me*, Leland and Laura are pulled over by MIKE (Al Strobel), who derives from the Black Lodge and is attempting to stop BOB. When MIKE attempts to tell Laura of Leland's crimes, his dialogue is constantly disrupted and drowned out by both diegetic and non-diegetic sources. We can hear MIKE saying: 'It's him! It's your father!' as he points to Leland and there is a brief flash-forward to the discovery of Laura's body wrapped in plastic, but the rest of his words are barely audible as they are overtaken by the sounds of loud traffic and both Leland and Laura screaming over him. The scene is also intercut with an image of a dog barking loudly. When Leland drives away and stops outside a gas station, one of the employees also tries to talk to Leland about Laura but parts of his dialogue are muted completely.

[13] The full name of the bar is The Big Bang Bar, but in the series the bar is referred to primarily by its local nickname the Roadhouse.

A similar scene occurs earlier in the film when Philip Jeffries (David Bowie) enters the FBI office. Like Cooper, Jeffries was an agent who investigated the murder of another young victim named Judy. The case was never solved because Jeffries disappeared to the Black Lodge for two years. Jeffries attempts to inform Cooper and Regional Bureau Chief Gordon Cole (David Lynch) of where he has been, but his words become fragmented and he shouts non-sensical utterances, proclaiming, 'Well now, I'm *not* gonna talk about Judy. In fact, we're not gonna talk about Judy at all. We're gonna keep her out of it.' Jeffries' dialogue is disrupted and drowned out by various loud noises to the extent that the characters within the film are unable to hear what he says (Cole exclaims: 'What the hell did he say?!'). An otherworldly scene is then superimposed over the scene, essentially blocking it out from the viewer, called the Convenience Store Scene. This otherworldly scene depicts the Black Lodge/supernatural characters in a large, dilapidated room. These include BOB, a dwarf in a red suit called The Man from Another Place (Michael J. Anderson) and the monkey wearing a mask. These figures make illegible gestures and utter random words and phrases such as 'Garmonbozia', 'convenience store' and 'Fire Walk with Me'. The bizarre sequence attempts to conceal and distract the viewer from the controversial subject matter being discussed. However, this strategy simultaneously draws our attention to it by laying bare the process of this concealment and allowing the taboo content to still remain somewhat discernible to the viewer. We can see the original scene attempting to 'break through' the supernatural scene superimposed over it, as flashes of Jeffries discussing the victim Judy intercut the Convenience Store Scene. What also intercuts both scenes are images of television static, as if to imply that the 'battle' between these two scenes for screen time and the viewer's attention is about to break our television screens. The scene appears to foreground its artifice and incorporate metafictional references to the series as a work of television as a way of critiquing culture's supernatural censorship of family violence. Indeed, this scene is additionally suggestive of someone attempting to 'switch off' the film in a further attempt to censor its abuse narrative. Television static often appears when the film broaches the topic of violence against women, such as in the scene where Laura discovers her father is her abuser.[14]

[14] Flickering lights feature throughout Lynch's oeuvre and often represent the transition and 'flickering' between different realities.

When we return to the original scene, Jeffries has disappeared. Cole says 'He's gone!' and instructs forensic analyst Albert Rosenfield (Miguel Ferrer) to call the front desk, who reports: 'I've got the front desk now, he was never here'. Not only has the film attempted to distract the viewer from its taboo content then, but explicitly *erases* it by narrating an event, rescinding it and replacing it with another event. Jeffries is literally removed from the scene and the film itself as this character does not appear in the narrative again. However, while Jeffries seems to have been 'erased' from the film, there are scenes where this character appears to be attempting to work his way back into the narrative. In the original script of *Fire Walk with Me*, Jeffries had an entire subplot which dealt with his investigation of Judy's murder. Due to time constraints, this subplot was removed and features in a series of deleted scenes in the DVD extras. Lynch nevertheless chose to include Jeffries' scene with Cooper and Cole at the FBI station. In a film concerned with fiction's limitations when representing traumatic experiences of women and taboo topics, this seems significant. It is as though *Fire Walk with Me* represents Jeffries, a character who was edited out of the film and relegated to its 'bonus content' section, as breaking out of the deleted scenes and clawing his way back into the film to tell the audience about the victim Judy. Despite the film's apparent attempts to block out this character and his subplot, there are moments in the film where Jeffries is represented as attempting to disrupt and return to the main narrative. Following Albert's announcement that Jeffries was 'never here', Cooper looks over the CCTV footage which shows Jeffries walking out of the elevator and into the station, and informs Cole: 'He *was* here'. The image of the masked monkey that recurs in the film and interrupts particular scenes can also be seen in relation to Jeffries' subplot. As noted, when Leland disposes of Laura's body, the scene is intercut with a close-up shot of the monkey and it utters the word 'Judy'. *The Return* reveals the identity of Judy (originally known as Jowday) as a mythological entity or 'negative force' that is similar to BOB. This is in keeping with the reading of Judy as representative of family violence and its associated trauma, specifically society and culture's covering up of taboo content. Like Leland, Judy possesses Sarah. This can be taken metaphorically, as Sarah being possessed/traumatised by the knowledge of Laura's abuse and murder by Leland. Furthermore, *The Return* takes the competing narrative structure evident in the above scene a step further. *The Return* contains even more plotlines than its parent series, each of which appears to struggle against one another for screen time, to the extent that the series does not form a cohesive storyline. Multiple narratives are introduced and either abruptly end or are left unresolved, such as the introduction and subsequent murder of Cooper's doppelganger/BOB, and the fate of Audrey Horne (Sherilyn Fenn), whose plotline is concluded with the character waking in a white room having danced at the Roadhouse nightclub. The closing scenes of each episode present numerous potential narratives, featuring characters that do not otherwise appear in the series discussing topics unrelated to any of the series' plotlines.

Laura's Return

Laura similarly disrupts the narrative of *Twin Peaks*. Trauma fiction's convention of focusing on male characters has the effect of silencing female characters, who are often killed off and their experiences described for them. Because *Twin Peaks* takes the form of an episodic serial detective story, the series appears to conform to this convention. *Twin Peaks* initially focuses on Cooper's investigation of Laura's murder, while Laura is murdered when the narrative begins. However, *Twin Peaks* again both conforms to and undermines this convention, by having Laura return from the dead and disrupt the 'main' narrative in order to tell her story. For instance, Lynch made *Fire Walk with Me* a prequel to the series because he wanted to see Laura 'live, move and talk' (Rodley 184). Laura also continuously 'returns' in the television series. As Brent et al. note: '[t]he earliest episodes return obsessively to Laura's image and voice. Her Homecoming Queen picture is displayed under the end titles and many times in the early episodes; her voice is replayed on tape and videotape' (184). We can also see Laura as 'resurrected' via Maddy. Not only do they suffer the same fate and are played by the same actress, but as the series progresses, Maddy in a sense 'becomes' Laura. Maddy says that in the wake of Laura's death, 'suddenly I got the chance to be Laura' ('Demons'), and increasingly resembles Laura in both her appearance and demeanour.

Laura actually returns from the dead in order to disrupt the narrative and talk about her traumatic experience in her own words. There are a number of scenes where Laura, as Desmet says, 'continues to be felt as a presence in *Twin Peaks*' (96). This is evident when the machinery lowering Laura's coffin into the ground at her funeral mysteriously malfunctions and the coffin begins moving up and down, its noisy movement literally disrupting her eulogy as though Laura refuses to be buried and spoken about. Laura's voice can also be heard at certain moments in the series. Maddy hears Laura's voice, whispering the words 'Maddy' and 'Daddy' as though warning Maddy of her fate. In the finale of *The Return*, Laura is fully resurrected when Cooper goes to either an alternate dimension or timeline to prevent her murder. The resurrected Laura has no memories of her abuse until Cooper brings her to the Palmer home, and the episode ends with Laura screaming as she recalls her past. Laura and her story of American family violence once again claws its way back into the narrative in spite of the limited series' multitude of unrelated storylines generated to distract from it. Laura's abuse was not referred to until the finale, where the series loops back to the narrative its parent series had also featured and simultaneously 'covered up'. Cooper's attempt to go back and erase the murder from happening in the first place can be seen as a furthering of the parent series' representation of the concealment of family violence in American culture, as the series ensures that Laura remains traumatised from her abuse, her scream in the concluding scene mirroring that in *Fire Walk with Me* upon discovering Leland to be her abuser/BOB.

Laura also returns in dreams. Cooper has a dream in which Laura informs him about her murder, which takes place in the Black Lodge. The Black Lodge is a large room enclosed by red drapes (the stage-like setting again recalling the idea of the performative and staged nature of family violence representations). In the dream, Laura speaks disjointedly (the effect results from them speaking backwards, and then being played in reverse) and whispers in an elderly Cooper's ear. It is revealed in a later episode that Laura identified her killer as Leland here. Because this information turns out to be factual and enables Cooper to solve the case, Laura literally returns from the dead in that she possesses the solution to her own murder and has the ability to communicate it to Cooper in his dream. Moreover, it is later revealed that dreams are accorded the same level of reality as events that take place in the real world of *Twin Peaks.* Cooper's dream does not belong to him alone. He later discovers Laura's diary in which she describes the same dream before she died and in it tried to tell him the identity of BOB:

> I had the strangest dream. I was in a red room with … an old man. … I tried to talk to him. I wanted to tell him who BOB was because I thought he

> could help me. My words came out slow and odd. It's frustrating trying to talk. Even if it was only a dream, I hope he heard me. No one in the real world would believe me. ('Arbitrary Law')[15]

However, while *Twin Peaks* represents Laura as disrupting the narrative in order to give her account of events, unlike *Batman Returns*, Laura's narrative does not successfully overtake the series' main plot. Brent et al. note that *Twin Peaks* is progressive in that it allows incest victims, an often silenced voice, to express pain and despair, but points out that the series at the same time acknowledges the convention of silencing these victims (192–193). Indeed, while *Twin Peaks* gives voice to its abuse victim by allowing Laura to return and share her experience, the series simultaneously silences this voice in that Laura (similar to Jeffries) has difficulty communicating her experience. Laura is barely understandable because of her backwards speech. While her dialogue is subtitled, however, it remains ambiguous because what she says is also opaque. When Cooper asks: 'Are you Laura Palmer?', Laura replies, 'I feel like I know her but sometimes my arms bend back'. Laura also makes enigmatic gestures such as when she touches her nose. Yet while such actions and replies appear lacking in sense, they are oblique references to details of Laura's murder that Cooper must decode. Laura touching her nose refers to her cocaine addiction and involvement in the drug trade before she died while the comment that her arms 'bend back' is a reference to her being bound on the night of her death.

Critiquing Trauma Conventions

These scenes can be read in relation to *Twin Peaks*' critique of trauma culture's limitations. While Brent et al. argue that *Twin Peaks* simultaneously works to give the incest victim a voice and silence that voice, it can also be argued that the series is dramatising and critiquing the ways in which culture silences these victims. Firstly, Cooper's dream evokes the dominant concept of trauma's unrepresentability. While Caruth's theory was written in the mid-1990s, she in part builds on the writings of Bessel

[15] Also, when Cooper physically enters the Lodge in the series finale, Laura informs him that she 'will see him in twenty-five years' ('Beyond Life and Death'). This is a reference to his original dream in which he was an older man. *Twin Peaks: The Return* also premiered twenty-five years after the original series.

van der Kolk published in 1980. Van der Kolk claimed that flashbacks and nightmares are 'dissociated from all verbal-linguistic-semantic representation' (in Leys 247) and that '[t]he essence of the trauma experience is that it leaves people in a state of "unspeakable terror"' (193). Family violence is therefore represented in both supernatural and experimental forms, further distancing the topic. This conception of trauma as incomprehensible is evoked in that the Black Lodge residents converse with Cooper in a language that is difficult to decipher. However, like the series' incorporation of the supernatural, *Twin Peaks* simultaneously acknowledges the inadequacy of this convention, exaggerating the convention to the point of parody and exposing its limitations. There are moments when Laura attempts to communicate her traumatic experience to Cooper and language loses all meaning and literally breaks down into absurd phrases and non-sensical sounds, such as when Cooper physically enters the Lodge in the original series' finale. Here, Laura utters broken sentences and random words (such as the word 'Meanwhile'), makes indecipherable gestures such as winking backwards and pointing to non-existent things and screams frantically. Such scenes suggest that this type of experimental representation is futile for conveying the trauma of abuse and a further way of silencing the victim. *Twin Peaks* then appears more in line with feminist and post-colonial trauma criticism which argues that an aesthetic model based on the insistence that trauma is unrepresentable marginalises individuals including women, people of colour, queer people and non-Western people. Gibbs says, 'an exclusive valuing of experimental forms marginalises many non-Western trauma representations' (25), where 'there is an urgent political imperative to narrate traumas in order to educate Western readers' (26). Craps and Buelens also argue that 'the Western discourse of unspeakability ... is seen as politically debilitating' (*Studies in the Novel* 5). Lowenstein, too, points out that when the valuing of an experimental high-modernist aesthetic 'reaches its extremes', 'when the traumatic experience becomes equated solely with the "unrepresentable"', in actuality 'silenc[es] ... both experience and representation' (5). *Twin Peaks* similarly appears to foreground the inadequacy of this aesthetic when representing the more gradual, insidious trauma experienced by women, such as family violence, in that it prevents Laura (and by implication women in similar situations) from directly communicating her experience. Indeed, there is an overt critique of this convention when Laura notes in her diary that it was 'frustrating trying to talk' in this manner, when her 'words came out slow and odd'.

A similar, more overt critique of culture's silencing of family violence and the practice of myth-making more broadly occur in the aftermath of Leland's confession and death. Having witnessed these events, Cooper, Sheriff Harry S. Truman (Michael Ontkean), Albert and Major Garland Briggs (Don S. Davis) decide to displace Leland's rape and murder to the supernatural:

> HARRY: [T]his is way off the map. I'm having a hard time believing.
> COOPER: Harry, is it easier to believe a man would rape and murder his own daughter? Any more comforting?
> HARRY: No.
> BRIGGS: Any evil that great in this beautiful world. Finally, does it matter what the cause? …
> ALBERT: Maybe that's all BOB is. The evil that men do. Maybe it doesn't matter what we call it.
> HARRY: Maybe not. ('Arbitrary Law')

However, the above scene is presented in such a way that the viewer is aware of the absurdity of this practice in that it depicts officers of the law more readily accepting demonic possession, a supernatural explanation for Leland's crimes, rather than the much more likely possibility of domestic paternal abuse because it is 'easier' and 'more comforting'. An analogous scene occurs when Cooper 'explains' Leland's abuse and murder of Laura to Sarah and says that Leland was not responsible for his actions: 'there are things dark and heinous in this world—things too horrible to tell our children. Your husband fell victim to one of these, long ago when he was innocent' ('Dispute Between Brothers'). According to Brent et al., Cooper's argument '[t]hat child abuse is "too horrible to tell our children" is a notion which keeps abused children from being able to tell adults of the dark and heinous things to which they have been subjected', and that there is a contradiction between rape being too horrible to tell children about and Laura being introduced to this trauma as a child (193).[16] While in the aforementioned scenes Lynch initially appears to follow the tradition of suppressing difficult subject matter such as incest and displacing it to the supernatural, the overt self-consciousness with

[16] This scene also reflects the wider American tradition of mythologisation and concealment of violence, for example, American political myth-making or mythologisation of historical episodes of extreme violence as something different, such as the mythologisation of Westward expansion as a cover up for genocide.

which he treats the convention suggests his engagement with it is sceptical. It is also significant that the characters who produce the 'socially acceptable narrative to palliate the incest in the midst' are all white males in varying positions of power (law enforcement and the military). This further foregrounds the practice of mythologising family violence and the traumatic experiences of women. As noted, trauma narratives, including those that depict child abuse and violence against women, are similar to representations of wider historical atrocities in that they are usually presented from a dominant or white male perspective, and are thereby susceptible to power relations, androcentric bias and mythic interpretations.

Conclusion

Competitive narration is a narrative technique where a text features either one plot that overtakes another or parallel plots that alternatively vie for the reader's or viewer's attention. It is a technique in which an apparent subplot overtakes and displaces what is purportedly the main plot of the narrative. We can read certain popular texts in terms of competitive narration in order to analyse how the text highlights culture's phallocentricism regarding trauma. That is, how culture often either neglects the traumatic experiences of diverse individuals in favour of looking at those of conventional straight white male characters or mythologises these experiences by representing them in supernatural terms. Analysing *Batman Returns* and *Twin Peaks* in terms of competitive narration reveals both texts to diverge from and undermine conventional trauma representation, and subvert cinematic representations of gender. Competitive narration is therefore an important and relevant framework through which to read both trauma representations and popular culture more widely. Further texts we can read in terms of competitive narration include Jonathan Nolan and Lisa Joy's *Westworld* (2016–present), which features women and characters of colour literally breaking out of a game world scripted by white men, and rewriting their sexist and violent narratives. Another example is Charlie Brooker and Toby Haynes' *Black Mirror* episode 'USS Callister' (2017).[17] This episode features a female character subverting and overtaking that of a male character, and foregrounds the sexism of pop cultural fandoms such as perceived notions of male ownership over particular franchises, toxic

[17] While *Black Mirror* has English writers, the series moved to Netflix and majority of the episodes were filmed and set in the US, in addition to featuring a predominantly American cast.

masculinity and discrimination against women found within certain fanbases, as well as the lack of diverse representation in popular culture. Competitive narration provides a new feminist trauma paradigm but can be used to analyse the representation of diverse characters more widely (as in, beyond trauma representation), such as texts in which characters are shown to break out of character archetypes. This is apparent in texts including Beau Willimon's *House of Cards* (2013–2018), Vince Gilligan's *Better Call Saul* (2015–present) and Frank Darabont's *The Walking Dead* (2010–present), in which female characters and characters of colour shift from traditional roles of love interests and racial stereotypes to getting unique narrative arcs of their own. Competitive narration can also be used to analyse Trojan Horse narratives, whereby a text initially focuses on a white or male protagonist but is gradually overshadowed by a diverse cast or character. This is evident in Jenji Kohan's *Orange is the New Black* (2013–2019) and Richard Price's *The Outsider* (2020). Ultimately, in their representation of traumatic experiences of women, *Batman Returns* and *Twin Peaks* are innovative as trauma texts both formally and thematically. As we shall see in the following chapters, analysing the representation of women's trauma in these two male-produced texts from the 1990s reveals how perceptions of trauma and feminism have changed in the past thirty years, and the differences between how straight white male writers and women, queer and American ethnic writers perceive these concepts.

CHAPTER 4

Polynarration: The Wachowskis' *Sense8*, Rebecca Sugar's *Steven Universe* and Nia DaCosta's *Candyman*

This chapter and the following examine popular trauma texts by writers diverse in terms of gender, race and sexuality. These chapters will explore two paradigms of trauma representation: polynarration and sceptical scriptotherapy. To begin with polynarration, this technique is explored in relation to *Sense8*, *Steven Universe* and *Candyman*. Polynarration features diverse groups of characters acquiring interconnectivity abilities that enable them to supernaturally share traumatic experiences and help one another recover. This produces unique narratives where a singular traumatic event is told from a range of diverse perspectives as characters' consciousnesses and/or bodies amalgamate. The characters in these texts are shapeshifting, changeable and combinable. Polynarration involves a supernatural polyphonic narrative that reworks on popular trauma concepts and techniques, in particular contemporary concepts of trauma in relation to the Internet. Polynarration combines trauma theories of communal healing and testimony; experimental techniques of earlier paradigmatic trauma texts including shifts in narrating voice, fragmented chronology and decentred subjectivity discussed by Vickroy and Gibbs; and Internet Psychology, specifically Martin Tanis' writing on online social support groups.

S. Travers, *Trauma in American Popular Culture and Cult Texts, 1980–2020*, https://doi.org/10.1007/978-3-031-13287-2_4

Contemporary Feminism

The differences between the approaches of the male-written texts (*Batman Returns* and *Twin Peaks*) and the texts produced by women, queer writers and writers of colour (*Sense8*, *Steven Universe*, *Candyman*, *The OA* and *Mr Robot*) are significant. *Batman Returns* and *Twin Peaks* feature female characters overtaking male-centred narratives, whereas *Sense8*, *Steven Universe* and *Candyman* feature diverse groups of characters sharing narratives. The later texts by women, queer writers and writers of colour appear to reflect more contemporary perceptions of feminism. According to Penny A. Weiss, modern feminism tends to reject 'the self-interested, autonomous individual of liberalism as both mythical and understandable', and finds a more social view of the self and a 'collective, interdependent and cooperative model of social relations' more favourable (Weiss and Friedman 3). It is important to note here that feminism is not a single unified agenda and has a history of different ideas in conflict, for instance, not all feminists favour communitarianism and some reject it (Weiss and Friedman n.p.). However, April Sizemore-Barber observes that 'now feminism is inherently intersectional feminism—we are in a place of multiple feminisms'. Indeed, modern feminism emphasises intersectionality as key. Kimberlé Crenshaw, who coined the term, describes intersectional feminism as 'a prism for seeing the way in which various forms of inequality often operate together and exacerbate each other', such as the distinct forms of oppression faced by women of colour and trans women. The Internet becoming commonplace and the rise of social media are further crucial factors here as they enable a range of individual voices to be heard. Jessica Valenti notes that modern feminism is conceived and propagated online, where feminist discourses and activism take place. Polynarration takes both the pluralism of modern feminism and its relationship with the Internet into account, as this framework is used to analyse texts featuring themes including shared consciousness, group abilities and diverse perspectives. The same can be said for sceptical scriptotherapy, which, as examined in the next chapter, is a type of writing that features characters consciously reworking traumatic events into fantastical alternatives rather than relaying them exactly as they happened. This technique involves a dual narrative structure. However, it is again in contrast to competitive narration explored in the previous chapter and aligns with more contemporary feminist ideologies. The dual narratives are not in competition with one another but are instead a means of working through trauma for the characters depicted. The concept of storytelling inherent to sceptical scriptotherapy also implies a listener and therefore concepts of communal healing. Further, the reworking of traumatic events is in contrast to the more political, myth-making practices evoked in texts such as *Twin Peaks*, with the revised narratives being represented as solely for the purposes of individual characters' healing.

Batman Returns and *Twin Peaks* reflect the earlier, often male perspective of feminism as a battle between the sexes or 'between two opposing sides', the concept of feminism as women 'beating men', 'putting men down' or 'being better than them' (Kellee Pratt), in addition to male fears of women taking over patriarchal society and men's loss of privilege (Creed 51). By contrast, contemporary feminism believes the movement benefits everyone and equality is gained by men and women working together (the groups of individuals in *Sense8* and *Steven Universe*, for instance, include straight white male characters alongside women, characters of colour and queer characters). Current feminism also aims to stress that the movement is anti-misandry and critiques systems of power rather than individual men. Further reflecting earlier attitudes towards feminism, *Batman* and *Twin Peaks* evoke the perspective of feminism as 'bra-burning', which was the metonym for post-war American feminism as radical, angry and 'scary' (Grady). Indeed, both texts incorporate themes of horror, violence and women taking revenge against male characters. Additional earlier perspectives of feminism evoked in *Batman Returns* and *Twin Peaks* include feminism as a white, heterosexual, cisgender and middle-class movement (the cast in either work is not diverse and neither text acknowledges how different forms of oppression intersect), and the rejection of femininity in favour of emphasising 'sameness' between men and women. Current feminism acknowledges the different lived perspectives and experiences of men and women, and embraces ideas and aesthetics of femininity. In *Sense8*, *Steven Universe* and *Candyman* the diverse characters and their unique perspectives amalgamate. *Batman Returns* and *Twin Peaks*, on the other hand, represent female characters mimicking and attempting to take on the roles of male characters. For instance, in *Batman Returns*, Kyle destroys all signifiers of femininity in her apartment when she becomes 'empowered' and transforms into Catwoman, and increasingly resembles Batman in her dialogue, role and behaviour. Laura in *Twin Peaks* resurrects and becomes a detective-like character who solves the central mystery of the series instead of Cooper. *Batman Returns* and *Twin Peaks*, then, feature female characters overtaking male-centred narratives. By contrast, *Sense8*, *Steven Universe* and *Candyman* feature diverse groups of characters sharing narratives, reflecting more contemporary perspectives of feminism as communal, plural, intersectional, online and embracing of the ideas and aesthetics of femininity.

Moreover, *Batman Returns*, *Twin Peaks*, *Sense8*, *Steven Universe* and *Candyman* each employ the supernatural to further explore rather than conceal the trauma of diverse individuals. However, further reflecting a male perspective of feminist representation, the subversive female characters in *Batman Returns* and *Twin Peaks* are sexualised and both films feature scenes of violence against women. In *Batman Returns*, Catwoman conforms to the fetishised figure Mulvey describes and there is an emphasis on bodily form. Catwoman is also subject to violence by each of the prominent male characters in the film. In *Twin Peaks*, a number of scenes contain graphic sexual violence, such as that in which Leland/BOB enters Laura's bedroom and rapes her in *Fire Walk with Me*. Conversely, *Sense8*, *Steven Universe* and *Candyman* do not feature sexualised scenes of violence. Likewise, in the texts analysed under the sceptical scriptotherapy framework in the next chapter, *The OA* and *Mr Robot*, the fantastic is employed to explore the traumatic effects of sexual violence (specifically escapism), and neither series resorts to graphic and sexualised rape scenes.

Additionally significance regarding polynarration and contemporary texts' representation of diverse character groups is the sexist and racist practice of deeming a traumatic event more credible when reported by more than one person, such as a group of women or a group of people of colour. Examples of such include the sixty women that accused Bill Cosby of sexual misconduct in 2018 and the eighty women that accused Harvey Weinstein in 2017. Similarly, Yahya Abdul-Mateen II says of Black trauma:

> Traditionally when we listen to stories of black trauma … whether it be individual or systemic … a lot of the times those stories aren't necessarily believed or they're met with further interrogation … we need supplemental evidence in order to be believed … instead of simply taking our stories and experiences for truth. (*Los Angeles Times*)

Mirroring this, the super-empowered groups of characters in *Sense8*, *Steven Universe* and *Candyman* are shown to be literally stronger together and enabled to overcome trauma.

Before analysing *Sense8*, *Steven Universe* and *Candyman* through the framework of polynarration, it is first necessary to outline the theories from which this framework stems. To reiterate, polynarration combines theories of polyphony; trauma theories of communal healing and testimony; and Internet Psychology, specifically Tanis' writing on online social support groups.

Polyphony, Trauma

To begin with polyphony, polyphony is a feature of narrative which includes a diversity of simultaneous points of view and voices. The concept was introduced by Mikhail Bakhtin. Similar to Lyotard's concept of micro-narratives, Bakhtin describes polyphony as 'a plurality of independent and unmerged voices and consciousness, a genuine polyphony of fully valid voices' (7). Bakhtin's primary example of polyphony is Fyodor Dostoevsky's prose, whose characters are 'not only objects of authorial discourse but also subjects of their own directly signifying discourse' (7). Polyphonic narratives present multiple, often fragmented voices, and may reference different registers, discourses, languages and cultures (as in James Joyce's *Finnegans Wake*). According to McHale, 'the polyphonic novel, unlike monological genres, acknowledges and embraces a plurality of discourses and the ideologies and world views associated with them' (166). An extension of polyphony is evident in Bakhtin's concept of heteroglossia, which differs from polyphony in that the multiple voices of heteroglossia are more likely to be antagonistic and competing (similar to *The Shining*, *Batman Returns* and *Twin Peaks*). In these narratives, fragments of discourses, imagery and narratives are juxtaposed without co-ordinating into an overall narrative, with ideas being presented within what Nicholas Sloboda calls a 'textual collage' which creates an open-ended text and rejects synthesis (117; 121).[1] Polynarration, then, aligns with polyphonic narrative structures, but combines this approach with trauma concepts of testimony and communal healing. Testimony involves writing or retelling a trauma narrative, while communal healing involves sharing a trauma narrative with others as a means of recovery. Critics such as Herman and Vickroy advocate this kind of healing, with Herman insisting that for healing to take place, trauma survivors must tell 'the story of the trauma' (*Trauma* 175) and that recovery is only possible within the context of relationships (*Trauma* 133). Vickroy, likewise, says that communal support and connecting with other survivors are essential for recovery (70),

[1] Similar to *The Shining*.

while Kai Erikson claims that traumatised individuals can 'develop a form of fellowship of that common tie' (187). Vickroy adds, however, that testimonial narratives such as Claude Lanzmann's film *Shoah* (1985) emphasise conflicts and dialogism in retelling traumatic events, and that Lanzmann's use of dialogism creates a narrative wherein 'many voices, emotions, and experiences intermingle to produce memory' (20–21). Aligning with this idea in particular, *Sense8*, *Steven Universe* and *Candyman* feature diverse characters literally sharing traumatic events via interconnectivity abilities such as telepathic communication, possession-like powers and body fusion. This representation also reworks a number of techniques found in foundational, twentieth-century trauma texts such as fragmented chronology, shifts in narrating voice and decentred subjectivity, as characters' perspectives and bodies shift and blend. Vickroy notes that earlier trauma texts feature radical shifts in contexts such as time and space because protagonists 'live in durational rather than chronological time' and cannot differentiate the past from the present, adding that this gives the impression that protagonists lack agency and cannot control the narrative (6). By contrast, characters in *Sense8*, *Steven Universe* and *Candyman* have control over these shifts in time, space and perspective, and these shifts are depicted as therapeutic, being presented as a form of superpower and a means of communication amongst the interconnected character groups.

Trauma and the Internet

The polyphonic narratives and interconnectivity abilities of the characters in *Sense8*, *Steven Universe* and *Candyman* relate to engaging with trauma in a secondary capacity, including not only communal healing and testimony but also secondary trauma and transmission. More uniquely, however, *Sense8*, *Steven Universe* and *Candyman* evoke these concepts in relation to the Internet. The characters' interconnectivity abilities reflect newer types of testimony and communal healing that take place online, specifically the therapeutic re-enactments related to sharing and reading about trauma in forums amongst a diverse range of fellow survivors. This mode of recovery is significant for women, people of colour and the LGBTQIA+ community in particular, because the Internet is a platform that can enable a range of individual voices to be heard, in contrast to conventional trauma theory and fiction which is often exclusionary and focuses predominantly on straight white men. While this platform still has its own inbuilt biases and barriers—such as who decides what we see on social media platforms, who gets to speak freely on the Internet and who can access it—the Internet does in some ways level the field and break down barriers to the presentation and reception of narratives. Studies have found that members of online support communities exhibit higher levels of empathic concern. For instance, according to Tanis, the ease of access to a large number of people, unrestricted by time, place or barriers, provides a sense of 'universality and communality in online groups' (148). Despite the fact that members of online communities differ in dimensions including race, gender, sexuality and class, they possess the same mental or physical condition, or have gone through similar traumatic experiences (Tanis 147). The anonymity that the Internet affords increases the perceived similarity amongst members by erasing cues that may signal individual differences and focusing solely on the issues of the members, thereby drawing increased attention to what all members of the group share, which, in turn, generates feelings of belonging and social identification. The lucidity of the narratives of *Sense8*, *Steven Universe* and *Candyman*, the blending and shifts between the diverse characters' perspectives, in addition to how these texts' characters acquire powers as a group, reflect this type of testimony and healing.

The interconnectivity of the character groups in *Sense8*, *Steven Universe* and *Candyman* also parallels possible traumatic effects associated with reading about trauma online, such as secondary trauma. Secondary trauma can result from testimony, as secondary trauma is when an individual is traumatised from listening to, reading about or learning of another's experience. Dominick LaCapra describes secondary trauma as the listener, reader or viewer appropriating the victim's experience, 'to confuse self and other, and collapse all distinctions' between them (21). This is similar to how the groups' identities and consciousnesses are blended and sometimes confused in *Sense8*, *Steven Universe* and *Candyman*. These characters experiencing the past traumas of different members of the group evoke how individuals may experience secondary trauma having read about others' experience online. Also relevant is the concept of disaster or 'doom scrolling' and the impact this has upon second-hand trauma. The flow of negative content may cause people to believe that they must act as a witness and cannot look away. Race-specific trauma and its links with social media are an additional concern. According to Monnica Williams, race-based traumatic stress injury is 'the emotional distress a person may feel after encountering racial harassment or hostility' and describes its cause in individuals as not only stemming from being 'directly targeted by racial discrimination or aggression' but also from watching it second hand on social media. Pilot Viruet notes that since the 2016 election, racist trolls and alt-right personalities have only become more 'emboldened, outspoken and confident', and that race-based stress can also be the result of witnessing racism on social media, 'from obsessively watching videos of police brutality to having racist comments flood your Twitter feed'. Conversely, Claire Diaz-Ortiz says that engaging with social media builds empathy in individuals because 'we are more informed about each other's struggles', citing the '#JeSuisCharlie' hashtag as 'an incredible example' of the power of 'mass empathy'. Certainly, through social media, different groups of people are becoming more aware and supportive of the specific issues faced by various marginalised groups. John Biggs notes that because of the Internet, we are entering a 'new age of empathy':

> Our nervous systems … have expanded on essentially a global scale and every twitch on some distant shore is felt in the grey matter between our eyes. … the Internet [is] … a way to connection to billions of people. … I tear up at … things in the news … at school shootings.

It is important to note that the Internet also has the capacity to elide empathy when people do not think of the human writing the content, and that there is an additional danger of social media bubbles whereby one surrounds themselves with like-minded people and does not come into contact with different views. However, the texts examined in this chapter align with the former, more positive view of the Internet relating to marginalised individuals. *Sense8*, for instance, has been described by Emily VanDerWerff as 'hopelessly naïve' in this regard.

Sense8

Released on Netflix in 2015 and co-created with J. Michael Straczynski, Lana and Lily Wachowski's *Sense8* is an American science fiction television series with elements of fantasy, drama and thriller. *Sense8* defies categorisation and genre, and was planned to consist of several seasons but was cancelled by Netflix after two seasons. Fan response to *Sense8*'s cancellation was intense and global. There were a number of hashtag campaigns on Twitter and Facebook, a group called 'Operation Flip Flop' contacted

Netflix CEO Reed Hastings, and a change.org petition authored by 'THE GANG *Sense8* Fans' demanded the series renewal and garnered over 500,000 signatures. Netflix responded not by renewing *Sense8* but by approving a two-hour final episode that would wrap up the series' narrative. Regarding diversity, the Wachowskis are queer and transgender cultural producers, having come out as trans women in 2008 and 2016, respectively.[2] They are known for creating some of the world's first transgender-authored mainstream film and television. The Wachowskis are most famous for their science fiction action film *The Matrix*, which has—since the sisters' coming out—been viewed through their transness (Lachenal). *Sense8*, however, is considered one of the most diverse television series to date, with the series being recognised for Outstanding Drama Series at the 2016 GLAAD awards. The series is the Wachowskis' first foray into television and marks a number of further televisual firsts (Keegan, 'Tongues' 605). For instance, *Sense8* is the first series to feature a transgender actor to play a lead transgender character, and the first to be written and directed by transgender creators. In addition, *Sense8* features characters diverse in terms of race, gender, sexuality, language and geography, the series being shot in sixteen different cities in eleven countries across the globe. *Sense8*'s multinational ensemble cast includes: Capheus Onyango (Aml Ameen; Toby Onwumere), a matatu driver in Nairobi attempting to earn money to buy AIDS medicine for his mother; Sun Bak (Bae Doona), an underground kickboxer and daughter of a Seoul business executive, that is made to take the blame for her brother's embezzlement and sent to prison; Nomi Marks (Jamie Clayton), a trans woman hacktivist living in San Francisco; Kala Dandekar (Tina Desai), a pharmacist and Hindu living in Mumbai arranged to marry a man she does not love; Riley Blue (Tuppence Middleton), an Icelandic DJ living in London, attempting to escape her tragic past involving the death of her family and now involved in the drug trade; Wolfgang Bogdanow (Max Riemelt), a Berlin locksmith and safe-cracker who participates in organised crime and has unresolved issues with his abusive late father; Lito Rodriguez (Miguel Ángel Silvestre), a closeted actor in Mexico City; and Will Gorski (Brian J. Smith), a Chicago police officer haunted by an unsolved murder from his childhood.

[2] Lana came out as a transgender woman in 2008, and Lily came out as a transgender woman in 2016.

Interconnectivity Powers

Together, the group forms a cluster of 'sensates', a species of humans telepathically connected to one another. The plot concerns the cluster's attempts to both discover the meaning of their unique connection and escape an organisation (named BPO) commanded by a sensate called Whispers (Terrence Mann), who aims to capture, and either assassinate or contain, members of his own kind. Each member of the group is born human, all on the same day at the same moment (8 August), but possesses a dormant connection to their cluster that must be activated by a sensate outside of the cluster, referred to as the clusters' parent. This process, in which each member becomes a sensate and their powers of interconnectivity awaken, is described in the series as being reborn or a 'second birth' (possibly a play on the term 'woke', an increasingly used byword for social awareness).[3] After this birthing, the psycellium, a psychic nervous system present within all sensates, becomes active and allows the members to telepathically, telekinetically and sympathetically connect to their cluster. This connection grants the individuals within the cluster three main abilities, which include visiting, sharing and their psychic link.

The psychic link is the mental and emotional connection between the group's members, which begins as a sensory input, in which one sensate experiences something another sensate within their cluster is experiencing at the same moment. For instance, one sensate living in Mumbai can feel the rain and snow another member of the group feels in Berlin. Eventually, this link strengthens to the point that the sensates can feel each other's thoughts, emotions and memories. As for visiting, this ability allows sensates to mentally communicate with each other, and mentally transport to one another's locations, where they see and experience everything the other feels within that environment. This is often done instinctively, such as when one member is distressed or in need of help.[4] Lastly, sharing is the ability of the cluster to access each other's knowledge, skills and strengths. In the case of skills, sharing allows the members to physically control fellow sensates as they watch, and literally experience each other's perspectives. For instance, Lito literally experiences Sun's sexual harassment in Korea by a prison doctor while he is in the midst of an interview on his

[3] Woke is a political term of Black origin refers in particular to issues concerning racial justice, and its widespread use since 2014 is a result of the Black Lives Matter Movement.

[4] Visiting can also be done with other sensates outside of the cluster, but only after physical first-hand, eye-to-eye contact has been made.

upcoming film in New Mexico, shouting 'No! I'm not going to do that!' ('Demons') to the doctor and interviewer simultaneously. The doctor is questioning Sun on her sexual history in an inappropriate manner and attempts to perform an unnecessary examination on her. Likewise, Lito is being pressed by the interviewer on his personal life, which thematically links the two scenarios. Both characters are also shown to physically switch bodies, locations and perspectives throughout the scene, and their shared consciousness and replies enable them to divert their respective situations. An analogous scene is where Will, a straight, white and cisgender male, directly experiences the transphobia and transphobic violence inflicted upon Nomi by her family and doctors. He shares her frustration when they misgender Nomi and refer to her by her assigned male birth name 'Michael' ('Her name is Nomi!' ('I Am Also A We') he says angrily), and takes on Nomi's perspective when the doctors strap her to a hospital bed to forcibly lobotomise her. Will wakes in his apartment to find his hands chained to the couch he is resting on and anaesthesia placed in his arm. Seconds later, he finds himself on the operating table in place of Nomi, in which they then work together to escape the hospital, with Will lending Nomi his police work skills so she can unlock the handcuffs confining her.

The sensates are continually shown in the series to overcome personal traumas by literally experiencing those of each other. There are a number of scenes in which the group shares traumatic past encounters with discrimination, such as when Nomi is mentally teleported to New Mexico to comfort Lito in the aftermath of his breakup. David Levesley in *Outward* describes this scene as 'a display of raw heartbreak and queer solidarity quite unlike anything else you'll experience on screen'. Here, the two discuss coming to terms with their identities with regards to sexuality and the societal reaction to coming out, and Nomi 'shows' Lito a memory from early childhood in which she refused to shower with her male swimming teammates due to insecurity over gender dysphoria, and her subsequent subjection to a scalding hot shower by these boys. Inspired by Nomi overcoming her childhood assault, Lito gains the courage to both come out as gay and rescue his friend from her abusive boyfriend. This incident in particular demonstrates how the cluster is interconnected in terms of sharing and overcoming personal traumas. Wolfgang, having aided Lito in his physical confrontation by lending him his strength and combat skills, appears to overcome his trauma produced by the physical violence inflicted upon him by his late father. Throughout the first season, Wolfgang has frequent flashbacks of his father's abuse, whereas in Season Two, he is shown to dwell substantially less on his childhood. What also appears to help Wolfgang's recovery is sharing ('Demons') these memories with Kala and Sun, as well as empathising with Sun's imprisonment and brother's attempt on her life while in prison. Wolfgang feels similarly entrapped in the criminal underworld of Berlin, and family members have made attempts on his life. By turns, Sun's and Wolfgang's confrontations with their families and long held beliefs regarding concepts of family inspire Kala to resolve her inner conflict between cultural sensibilities with her own parents and personal desires regarding her relationships and career.

Emotional and physical pain are also physically felt amongst the cluster. In the Season One finale, each member of the cluster experiences their fellow sensate Riley's memories of her family's death. When Riley went into labour with her first child, her husband attempted to drive her to hospital through the Icelandic snow. As a result of the icy conditions and low visibility, the car crashed and toppled off the road, killing Riley's husband instantly. Riley gave birth to her daughter and attempted to leave the car, but became trapped in the mountain winter and her baby froze to death in her arms. The sensates not only remember these memories as if their own, but members such as Will experience the physical sensations of this event, such as when he is momentarily pregnant and in physical pain. Indeed, when one sensate is presently in extreme physical danger, the rest of the cluster is also at risk of dying. This is evident earlier in the first season in Riley's attempted murder via suffocation by members of the drug trade with which she is involved in London. Here, shots of Will are shown intercut with Riley as a bag is placed forcibly over her/their head/s. A similar sequence occurs during Sun's attempted hanging in prison at the beginning of Season Two. This time, all of the cluster are shown grasping their necks and unable to breathe in their own locations, and intercutting shots of each of them are also shown in place of Sun in the noose.

Sense8: Polynarration

I argue that *Sense8* is suitable for analysing in terms of polynarration. The sensates' interconnectivity powers not only reflect traditional means of testimony and communal healing but also relate to newer perspectives on these concepts in relation to the Internet, in addition to further concepts related to engaging with trauma in a secondary capacity online including secondary trauma, transmission and diversity. Indeed, when planning to create a television series, the Wachowskis decided to create a series that would explore the relationship between empathy and evolution in the human race (Grey Ellis). There are scenes in Season Two in which the sensates explicitly talk about how, for non-sensates, the Internet stands in for their shared consciousness, while VanDerWerff compares the sensates' abilities to social media, noting, 'I can't know what it's like to be a wrongly imprisoned Korean woman, but if she has access to Twitter, I can read about her travails and get a sort of second-hand feel for what it's like to be in her situation. But for the sensates themselves, they can actually live their fellow sensates' experiences.' The sensates' interconnectivity powers, then, can be read as supernatural interpretations of ideas of communal support, empathy and the kind of therapeutic re-enactment of traumatic events involved in sharing and retelling experiences online. For instance, how the sensates share the perspectives and traumatic experiences of each other evokes the increased empathy apparently enabled by the Internet and the possible related traumatic effects. This is evident in how Lito and Will experience Nomi's subjection to transphobia and re-enact her childhood assault (Lito is shown in place of child Nomi walking into the boys' shower room in Nomi's flashback). The conflation of the different sensates' consciousness and bodies here parallels transmission, as Lito and Will literally appropriate Nomi's experiences, confuse themselves with her, and the distinctions between these characters collapse. The way in which emotional and physical pain is felt amongst the cluster can also be taken as evocative of empathy enabled by the Internet and transmission, in addition to secondary trauma, how trauma survivors get a second-hand 'feel' for others' experiences online. The sensates' experience of one another's trauma reflects how individuals may suffer nightmares having read about a stranger's traumatic experience online. According to Noreen Tehrani, for instance, some Internet child abuse investigators (ICAIs) experience PTSD.

The sensates' supernatural linkage also reflects communal healing. There are a number of scenes that show the entire cluster appearing to one of their fellow sensates in times of despair, such as when Sun visits her parents' graves, what the online critic A.X.S. describes as a scene of 'countless cuddles and declarations of unity'. Sun's father regretted sending her to prison in place of her brother and was about to confess the crimes of his son to the police. To prevent him from doing so, Sun's brother killed their father. This leaves Sun feeling responsible for her father's death and alone: 'everything I considered my home is gone ... my brother killed my father because of me' ('I Have No Room in My Heart for Hate'). Here, all seven of Sun's sensate siblings arrive to comfort her, and their advice and encouragement are not unlike the type of reassuring comments commonly found in online message boards for trauma survivors. For instance, Riley assures Sun that 'what happened was not [her] fault'; Nomi and Kala warn Sun against taking revenge on her brother; and Capheus shares his mother's advice on finding peace in the wake of his father's murder. Wolfgang, on the other hand, compares Sun's brother to his father, and tells her that his death would be for the best: 'My father was like your brother. The world is better off without them.' Will and Lito assure Sun that the cluster will support her decision regardless, and emphasise the unity of the group. Will reminds Sun 'you have us', and Lito notes: 'There's no easy answer, Sun. Whatever you decide to do, just know that you don't have to do it alone.'

This scene, and the sensates' abilities more generally, evokes an online community in a number of further ways. As noted, a sensate cluster requires eight people to activate it. That the sensates' powers only work successfully with a group of people who are seemingly worlds apart, secondarily and literally experiencing each other's traumas, suggests online communal healing. Online communities are also usually built up of multiple diverse people. That the sensates are diverse individuals who share similar traumatic experiences evokes Tanis' observation that the anonymity of the Internet and the focus on what the members of social support groups have in common such as a particular traumatic experience increase perceived similarity. This generates feelings of belonging and social identification regardless of race, gender, sexuality and class, and time and place barriers. As Tanis says, perceived similarity can be an important motivation for joining an online community because it provides 'the feeling that one is a part of a larger group' (299). The above scene ends with the cluster embracing in what David Goldberg calls a 'magical eight-way hug', which can likewise be described as a visual representation for the kind of global support found in online communities. There are a number of similar grand interconnected montages in which each of the sensates revels in each other's connection, such as scenes in which one sensate listens to music and the cluster sings along, which have been read as forms of 'communal ritual and festivity' (Deborah and Rob). These scenes also evoke how creative expression is sometimes a feature of online therapy groups, whereby users may be encouraged to express their trauma via activities such as storytelling, and sharing poetry and art postings for the group to enjoy.

The Wachowskis' work has been described by Cael M. Keegan as employing a trans aesthetic. According to Keegan, this aesthetic 'treats cinema as if it were gender itself—disrupting, rearranging, and evolving the cinematic sensorium in the same manner that trans disrupts, rearranges, and evolves discrete genders and sexes' ('Sensing'). For Keegan, this effect is resonant with the experience of gender transition and its multiple embodiments across time and spaces, evident in how the sensates jump back and forth between each other's worlds. Keegan says that *Sense8* represents and replicates 'hypermodern globality' and 'seeks to aesthetically translate transgender as a form of consciousness—a way of perceiving or knowing that occurs between and across bodies, cultures, and geographies' ('Tongues' 606). The multiplication of subjectivity in *Sense8*, the mutation of the sensates into a merged consciousness and the way in which their brains morphologically shift and the borders of their bodies fall away, is for Keegan evocative of the 'plural selves of gender transition' ('Tongues' 607). Keegan says: '[t]his is not an 'arrival at a "real" gender but a constant negotiation of multiple gendered selves across the spectra of perceivable gendered embodiments, which are traversed temporally and carried internally' ('Tongues' 607). The camera and musical scoring work in particular ways to represent this phenomenon, which attempts to decentre the viewer's notions of discrete embodiment, linear spatiality and temporal causality, attempting to pluralise viewers' 'perception of how a narrative or self can take place' (Keegan, 'Tongues' 608). For instance, Nomi, her past male-assigned self and Lito all intercut in the flashback scene of Nomi's childhood assault.

Moreover, the sensates' supernatural means of communication evokes how the anonymity of the Internet often makes it easier for people to talk about their trauma. For Tanis, 'features of computer-mediated communication (CMC) offer possibilities for social support in a manner that would be less easy or even impossible in a face-to-face context'. This is significant in terms of representing trauma and diversity in particular. The diverse group in *Sense8* gains abilities to more easily communicate their traumas to each other, which includes ostensibly taboo experiences of marginalised individuals that are frequently excluded from trauma criticism but discussed widely online such as transphobia, sexism in East Asian culture and AIDS. As with the texts examined in the previous chapter, this representation reworks the conventional employment of transmission and experimental formal techniques in trauma narratives, with *Sense8* employing both the supernatural and experimental filming techniques for representing the traumatic experiences of diverse characters rather than repressing them. That the series embeds certain sensates in culturally specific narratives further suggests online communication. Each of the sensates speaks English and notices how they can understand each other's languages, suggesting how Internet discourse can be translated to enable transcultural interaction and removes language barriers between users. In addition, what Keegan calls the recognisably '"ethnic" narratives' ('Tongues' 608) that the series depicts its characters within suggests not only how Internet users come from other worlds in terms of culture and place but also how individuals may perceive users from particular cultures and their ingrained stereotypes about these cultures. Clare Light says that '*Sense8*'s depiction of life in non-Western countries is built out of stereotypes … suffused with tourist-board clichés'. For example, Keegan observes that Lito inhabits a telenovela, Sun a martial-arts film, and Kala a Bollywood musical ('Tongues' 608). However, Keegan notes that the series 'resists these forms as limiting the kinds of stories that can be told' ('Tongues' 609), such as how Lito's 'telenovela narrative' unconventionally centres on a gay man, and how Kala's 'Bollywood musical' uniquely concerns the dichotomy between faith and science, and concludes with a polyamorous union. These shifts between ethnic narrative tropes and more realist, nuanced plots suggest the fluctuating perspectives of the cluster and the varying perspectives found in online communities (for instance, one user from the US may have a very stereotypical perception of life in India, which will differ greatly to that of a user actually living in India).

In addition, this mixing of genres and styles in *Sense8* evokes McHale's description of the polyphony of worlds and different world views of polyphonic narratives, which, in turn, further reflects the dialogism of the Internet, with Nomi's narrative paralleling a hacker film, Capheus' an action film, Wolfgang's a heist film, Will's a cop procedural and Riley's a melodrama. As noted, *Sense8* is somewhat unclassifiable in terms of genre, being a science fiction television series with elements of fantasy, drama and thriller. *Sense8* represents the dialogism of the Internet in a number of further ways. First, the polyphonic narrative told from a range of perspectives described above mirrors how multiple diverse individuals respond to traumatic experiences posted online and have different responses to and interpretations of them, evident in the blending of different characters' perspectives. Second, when discussing polyphony, McHale says that certain postmodernist fiction achieves 'a polyphony of worlds', likening the different world views in polyphonic narratives as projecting worlds (166). The characters in the series literally encounter new worlds and new world views as they telepathically travel the globe, which gives them a unique perspective on their respective traumas from different cultures. For example, Sun's decision on what form her quest for justice against her brother for her father's murder might take is informed by Capheus' desire for social justice via running for regional office, taking up the position of his late father who was also murdered during a riot in Nairobi. Internet users can be described as coming from other worlds in terms of factors such as culture, place, time and socio-economic background, and their advice and support to traumatised individuals may provide choices, chances and a new life to those in need.

Steven Universe

Released in 2013, *Steven Universe* is an American animated television series created by Rebecca Sugar for Cartoon Network. The series has developed a broad fanbase and has been critically acclaimed for its design, characterisation and the prominence of LGBTQIA+ themes. Indeed, *Steven Universe* is Cartoon Network's first animated series to be created solely by a woman, Rebecca Sugar, who also identifies as a bisexual and non-binary woman. The series has amassed accolades for its progressive portrayals of intersectional feminism, and queer desire and ways of being including queer-coded relationships and non-traditional family structures. Jake Pitre, for instance, describes *Steven Universe* as a 'series predicated on inclusivity, liberation and understanding' (24). The series won a GLAAD Media Award for Outstanding Kids & Family programme in 2019, becoming the first animated series to win the award. *Steven Universe* also deals with issues including trauma, sexual abuse, racism and imperialism. These thematic engagements, and the nuance and inclusivity of their implementation, are unusual in an American animated children's television series (Ziegler and Richards 1). Influenced by science fiction, fantasy and animé, *Steven Universe* follows the adventures of a half-human, half-alien boy, Steven Universe (Zach Callison), and the aliens and humans who surround him. Steven lives with the Crystal Gems, three magical humanoid aliens named Garnet (Estelle), Amethyst (Michaela Dietz) and Pearl (Deedee Magno Hall). The Gems are ageless alien warriors who project female humanoid forms from magical gemstones at the core of their being. Steven inherited his gemstone from his late mother, the Crystal Gems' former leader Rose Quartz (Susan Egan). The series centres on the group's work to protect humanity from monsters and other threats, and Steven's acquisition of knowledge about his powers and the Crystal Gem Homeworld, the capital of the Gems' intergalactic Empire where his mother hailed from.

Regarding the series' diversity, key to the conception of the Gem species is that their bodies, and thus their gender, sex and race, are just projections of the gemstones from which the characters take their names (Ziegler and Richards 2). Sugar stresses the 'representational significance of this conception for denaturalising dominant ideas of gender and for providing points of identification for those who exist outside of those ideas' (Ziegler and Richards 2). The Gems, then, are all non-binary women and independent of normative structures of gender and sex. The constructed nature of gender is underscored throughout the series, such as how the Gems' physical bodies are not only able to shapeshift but are defined as ultimately 'only an illusion' ('Fusion Cuisine'). The Gems are also diverse in terms of race, class and body type. Pearl is coded as white. The character is voiced by a white actor; her complexion is ivory, her eyes are light cyan and her nose is pointed. Garnet and Amethyst are coded as people of colour. Garnet is voiced by a Black actor. She has a deep violet, cube-shaped afro, a magenta skin tone and full lips. Amethyst is voiced by a Korean-American actor. Her skin is lilac, her eyes are dark indigo and her hair is thick and lavender in colour. Pearl has a slender build, Garnet is tall and muscular, while Amethyst is depicted as a short, plus-sized individual, a body type rarely seen in the superhero genre. In terms of class, the Crystal Gem Homeworld is a hierarchically stratified and instrumentally organised totalitarian society (Ziegler and Richards 4). Each Gem is born into a particular labouring class and must remain indefinitely within this caste system, a system which instigated Steven's mother to start a rebellion and relocate to Earth (Ziegler and Richards 4). The Gems' lives are scripted and pre-scripted, and 'lower' and 'mid-tier' Gems are frequently treated as having no value (Cooley 55). Amethyst's life was mapped out by the higher-ranking Gems. She was created to be a soldier and exploit Earth's resources, and was grown on Earth in a location called the Prime Kindergarten. Kindergartens breed soldiers, servants and skilled and unskilled labourers depending on the category of their gemstone. In addition, Amethyst emerged 500 years later than she was supposed to, making her an ostensibly 'defective' Gem who is smaller and less powerful than the Gems such as the more privileged Pearl. Pearl was born on the Gem Homeworld, and who thus had more time to hone her Gem skillset. Gems like Pearl were servants to higher-ranking Gems but are not for building or fighting; instead they are for 'standing around and looking nice and holding your stuff for you' ('Back to the Barn'). The histories of Amethyst and Pearl therefore reflect not only class but also what Olivia Zolciak describes as a 'dismal example of the way that systems of oppression function' (74).

The medium of animation is also significant to the series' diverse representation. According to Pitre, animation is 'unfixed and endlessly malleable' (23), and this fluidity of the cartoon as a medium is suitable for exploring the 'fluidity of identity' (24). For Pitre, animation is 'inherently artificial' and wholly diegetic worlds are 'only as representative as the artists choose them to be' (24). Animation is attuned to handling these signifiers; for instance, animators can 'introject' and audiences can 'decode' overt signs of same-sex desire and gay-identified characters (Dennis 132–133). Animation is likewise significant in relation to trauma representation, as the medium has the capacity for a visual style that can fluctuate to express changes in mood or state of mind (Bradley). Indeed, animated characters have the ability to contort their bodies in ways that live actors cannot, such as how eyes may bulge out of faces to express interest or hearts burst from torsos to represent desire (Pitre 24). These two points, animation's ability to represent diversity and trauma, are important to take into consideration for this chapter's reading of *Steven Universe* in terms of polynarration. Sugar explains that *Steven Universe* deliberately employs 'simple' character models to enable this flexibility and inconsistency, and represent the fluidity of sexuality and gender (McDonnell 81). I argue that this design at the same time enables the series' effective representation of trauma and online communal healing specifically. *Steven Universe* represents trauma in a number of innovative ways and PTSD as a condition is explicitly acknowledged in the series. Sugar has noted that the series deals with trauma and that she has attempted to express this theme through 'some of the metaphorical language that we built up on the show and the heightened reality that we get to work with on the show' (Lewis and Watanabe). For example, in *Steven Universe Future* (Sugar 2019–2020), the limited series that continued the parent series, and the film *Steven Universe: The Movie* (Sugar 2019), Steven is diagnosed with PTSD having fought in the interstellar war between the Crystal Gems and the Homeworld. The limited series shows Steven glowing pink when he becomes frustrated, a visual representation of how traumatised individuals react strongly to relatively minor stressors. Later, when Steven is overcome by his trauma and guilt over his violent actions during the war, he transforms into a giant monster. As with the previous section on *Sense8*, the following will examine trauma in *Steven Universe* through the framework of polynarration. I will focus on how the characters in the series overcome trauma by amalgamating their bodies and consciousness through an interconnectivity power called fusion, creating a polyphonic narrative which mirrors online communal healing.

Fusion

As noted, a central theme of *Steven Universe* is the titular protagonist's attempts to understand his gradually expanding range of powers inherited from his mother, the most significant of which includes fusion. Fusion is the ability of Gems to merge their bodies and abilities to form new, more powerful and larger beings. Fusion involves two or more diverse bodies physically combining into a single being. Fusion is employed for work or battle, or for affective purposes. Fusion usually occurs between Gems but also occurs between the Gem-human hybrid Steven and Gems, and between Steven and other humans such as his friend and love-interest Connie Maheswaran (Grace Rolek). For example, together Steven and Connie form Stevonnie (AJ Michalka). Stevonnie possesses a blend of both Steven and Connie's mind, carrying the relaxed attitude of Steven and the intelligence of Connie. Similarly, Garnet is a being made up of two Crystal Gems who have married and live together as a fusion: Ruby (Charlyne Yi) and Sapphire (Erica Shukrani Luttrell). According to Ziegler and Richards, fusion, this type of embodiment, 'unsettles the boundaries of self' because 'an individual self and body are not coterminous' (3). For Ziegler and Richards, fusion also unsettles boundaries of biological sex, gender and species; Stevonnie, for instance, is both genders and neither, and both human and alien (3). Stevonnie can be described as non-binary, agender or genderfluid. The character uses they/them pronouns, possesses male and female physical characteristics such as body curves and facial hair and shifts between masculine and feminine gender presentation via the different outfits they wear throughout the series. Stevonnie also blends Steven and Connie's races (Steven is white and Connie is Indian-American) and ages (Connie is biologically older than Steven by a number of years because Steven's alien DNA makes him age slower than humans). Similarly, the fusion between Pearl, Amethyst and Garnet (and by extension Ruby and Sapphire), named Alexandrite (Rita Rani Ahuja), combines a variety of races. Alexandrite possesses a bright magenta skin tone, Pearl's face shape, plump lips like Amethyst and Garnet and thick turquoise hair that is a collision of each of the Gems' hairstyles (the length of Amethyst's, the top tuft of Pearl's, the fullness of Ruby's and the colour of Sapphire's). Steven describes Alexandrite as his 'moms' and 'my family'. … 'It's all the Gems fused together into a six-armed giant woman' ('Fusion Cuisine').

Fusion is achieved through a dance called Fusion Dance, which appears like a form of improvised partner dancing that combines elements of different dance styles. Fusion Dance must be synchronised by the two or more Gems in order to successfully fuse into a new fusion Gem. While fusion is synchronised, it is also important to note that 'each Fusion Dance is slightly modified to take into account the specific personalities of those participating in it' (Zolciak 72). Fusion Dances are only required for Gems of differing gemstones; Gems of the same type of gemstone can fuse at will (such as two Pearls). A dance is not entirely necessary for fusion to occur, however, as fusion can also occur when the two or more participants share a moment of profound emotional unity, such as successfully overcoming an enemy together or bonding over similarities. Pitre observes that the new being created by the fusion is not two or more minds sharing one body, but is instead a single body and mind that is the expression and physical manifestation of the love and/or mutual understanding between the two or more Gems (26). Not only is physical synchronicity required for fusion to work successfully, then, but all participants must also be mentally synched. If the two or more parties have conflicting views while fused, the singular being will revert to their constituent individual Gems, with a dissonance between parties running the risk of involuntary de-fusion. This poses a danger when faced with an enemy or 'deadly situation' ('Giant Woman'), for example, as Gems are literally stronger when merged together.

This scenario is evident in Pearl and Amethyst's failed attempt at fusing. These two characters do not get along. Amethyst says that she and Pearl no longer form Opal because Pearl is 'no fun anymore' and 'uptight', while Peal argues that Amethyst is 'difficult and a mess' ('Giant Woman'). Pearl disapproves of Amethyst's passivity ('slouching over here doing nothing'), while Amethyst detests Pearl's beratement of her ('why do you have to make things worse by squawking at me?') ('Giant Woman'). Pearl also evidences an aversion to Amethyst's form of dance, reflecting the race and class differences between them. Jane Desmond says that movement 'serves as a marker for the production of gender, racial, ethnic, class, and national identities' (36). Pearl's dance evokes ballet, 'the most highly codified, highly funded, and perhaps most elite symbol of European derived theatrical dance in the United States' (Desmond 44), while Amethyst's dance resembles hip-hop which is rooted in Black culture. As noted, both Pearl and Amethyst were subjected to oppressive and therefore traumatic forces. Pearl, at times in the series, imposes her will over Amethyst as a woman of privilege and power. For example, Pearl describes Amethyst's dance moves as 'erratic and formless', to which Amethyst replies 'you should know how I dance by now' ('Giant Woman'). However, Pearl's past is also rooted in oppression. Amethyst suffers feelings of abandonment and self-doubt while Pearl's past as a submissive servant left her with no sense of agency. When Pearl and Amethyst finally fuse successfully, they become Opal (Aimee Mann). Opal possesses the physical features of both Pearl and Amethyst, their trademark features being spliced into a composite being. As Pearl informs Steven, 'Opal is an amalgam of our combined magical and physical attributes fused into a single entity' ('Giant Woman'). Opal combines the physical features of a white woman and a woman of colour. Like Pearl, Opal has a thin rounded face with a pointed nose, and like Amethyst, Opal has plump lips, wavy hair and rounded hips. Opal's skin tone is periwinkle in colour; she is extremely tall and has four arms. Opal combines the positive personality traits of both characters: Pearl's precision and Amethyst's carefree personality. Pearl's obsessive single-mindedness and Amethyst's ability to live in the moment result in a stable fusion, with Opal achieving a sense of peace in this balance that Pearl and Amethyst rarely experience on their own. Opal also possesses a number of abilities that Pearl or Amethyst could not achieve individually. These include extraordinary agility, acrobatic reflexes and the abilities to walk on water and summon either Pearl's spear or Amethyst's whip at will, or combining these two weapons into a stronger, opalescent recurve bow.

Steven Universe: Polynarration

Fusion is a science fiction creation that acts as a narrative tool to explore a number of themes, including consent and LGBTQIA+ themes such as polyamory, queer relationships and transgenderism. As with *Sense8*, however, this ability also is suitable for reading in terms of polynarration. The concept of two or more individuals combining to form a new, stronger being so as to overcome obstacles can be read as representative of online methods of communal recovery from trauma. That fusion involves and indeed requires two or more parties to perform it successfully suggests communal healing. This ability evokes the effectiveness of sharing trauma amongst a group as suggested by critics such as Herman and Vickroy, as well as Tanis' observation that sharing trauma via the Internet enables perceived similarity, and, in turn, feelings of belonging and that one is part of a larger group. Like the sensates, when characters in *Steven Universe* fuse, they become one entity/the same person. The concept of a survivor feeling that they are part of a larger group appears dramatised in *Steven Universe* in particular, as fusion amongst the characters literally creates a bigger being. For example, Garnet is much larger than Pearl and Amethyst, Steven describes Opal as a 'giant woman' ('Giant Woman'), while Alexandrite is a six-armed giant. As noted, increased strength and stronger weaponry are also enabled by fusion, and fusion allows characters to overcome specific challenges. For example, like Wolfgang aiding Lito in his physical confrontation, Opal successfully rescues Steven when he gets consumed by a corrupted Gem. Similarly, Stevonnie's superhuman strength allows Steven and Connie to rescue Amethyst from Jasper (Kimberly Brooks), a Homeworld Gem and former antagonist, while Pearl, Amethyst and Garnet call Alexandrite 'unstoppable' when they 'fuse together with a singular goal' ('Super Watermelon Island'). The latter is evident when Alexandrite is formed to defeat the colossal fusion Malachite in 'Super Watermelon Island'.

In an interview with *Paste*, Sugar explained that *Steven Universe* is not only a 'story about how love conquers all', but also how 'support is necessary' in difficult times (Blumenfeld). As noted, mental synchronicity is additionally required for fusion to work. Similar to *Sense8*, this suggests both the dialogism and the increased empathy enabled by the Internet.[5] According to Sugar, fusion is about open communication and taking the time to understand what the other person/people in the partnership is/are feeling (Pitre 27). Sugar notes that fusion can be taken as metaphorical for healthy relationships, asserting that the bonds between individuals 'could be stronger, or weaker, depending on whether or not I care about what's going on and respect what's going on with my partner' (Pitre 27). However, this is likewise analogous to online recovery forums, how users

[5] Empathy is a recurring theme in *Steven Universe*. Steven is frequently shown to consider his enemies' perspective and give them the benefit of the doubt before engaging in physical combat with them ('why don't you try thinking about this from her point of view' he tells the Gem Peridot (Shelby Rabara) when they are faced with a monster in 'The Kindergarten Kid').

encounter a diverse range of survivors with world views that may differ from their own and must attempt to empathise with these different perspectives in order to effectively offer and receive advice. The fusion between Pearl and Amethyst reflects this, because merging into the stronger Opal requires them to look past their differences and consider each other's viewpoints. The sense of peace eventually achieved by Pearl and Amethyst's fusion into Opal that they cannot acquire individually mirrors group recovery. Similarly, fusions such as Stevonnie and Garnet are more stable fusions than Opal because the individual characters more easily cooperate and empathise with each other. Stevonnie in 'Jungle Moon' remains fused for a number of days while Garnet lives as a fusion. By contrast, the balance that holds Opal together is the thinnest of the fusions in the series, the ease with which Opal can separate highlighting the conflicting views of Pearl and Amethyst while fused. Also like the Internet is how Garnet describes her existence as a fusion as an ongoing activity that does not aspire to an endpoint. The Internet has been described by Nicol as a rhizomatic structure: '[t]he Internet "starts" and "ends" nowhere, or rather you can exit from anywhere and go from any one place to any other' (48). The rhizome according to this model 'means that connections can be made between things which are otherwise unconnected' (Nicol 48). This latter point relates to all the fusions in the series as the different characters' bodies and consciousnesses amalgamate. That fusion is generated by a dance likewise mirrors the Internet, specifically the transglobal nature of online communication and the creative activities incorporated in therapy forums. Regarding trauma representation more broadly, the Fusion Dance reworks the conventional employment of transmission in trauma fiction. This representation employs both the supernatural and experimental language (dance) for further exploring the traumatic experiences of diverse characters rather than repressing them.

That fusion in *Steven Universe* shows diverse, traumatised characters who perform a synchronised ritual with therapeutic benefits further likens the superpower to the dialogism of the Internet and the notion of perceived similarity found online. To recall, the Internet provides a platform and a sense of communality/universality for trauma survivors regardless of race, gender, sex, sexuality and class. Similarly, Eli Dunn observes that fusion signifies 'free and familiar contact between people' who would usually be separated hierarchically for 'unusual combinations' (48). The varying fusions seen throughout the series combine different genders, races and classes, as noted. They also create a polyphonic narrative as the diverse characters fused together converse within the one body and the viewer is presented with shifting perspectives. For example, Stevonnie can be read as an embodiment of an online forum, an individual made up of multiple perspectives diverse in sex, gender, race and age. Stevonnie expresses the viewpoints of both Steven and Connie at once, such as the scene in which they discuss if both parties consent to the fusion. This scene can be read as both Stevonnie asking themselves this question and a conversation between Steven and Connie. Stevonnie says aloud: 'Sweet, two donuts. One for me and one for me. Are you okay? We can stop it if you—No, no, don't worry' ('Alone Together'). In certain scenes it is unclear which party is speaking, such as when Stevonnie is sexually harassed by a man at a local gathering, who tries to coerce Stevonnie into dancing with him. Hiding in a corner of the room, Stevonnie/Steven and Connie say/s: 'I don't understand what's wrong. You have fun dancing, but this dancing isn't fun. You're supposed to like this, but why don't you like this?' ('Alone Together'). A similar scene occurs when Alexandrite alternates between displaying the distinct personalities of Pearl, Amethyst and Garnet. In 'Fusion Cuisine', Alexandrite expresses Pearl's aversion of food and cautious personality, Amethyst's love of food and argumentative personality and Garnet's social awkwardness and leadership:

> Amethyst: 'I'm hungry.'
> Pearl: 'I don't think so.'
> Garnet: 'Cut it out, you two.'

Fusion also parallels the possible dangers and traumatic side-effects of online trauma discourse. The blending and conflation of the different characters' consciousnesses and bodies via fusion evoke transmission (to appropriate a victim's experience, confuse self and other and collapse all distinctions between them) and secondary trauma. As with the sensates' feeling one another's pain, when fused together, characters in *Steven Universe* experience one another's trauma. This is evident in the scene where both Steven and Connie experience sexual harassment as Stevonnie. This scene also evokes the potential feelings of isolation from communicating only second-handedly online, as Stevonnie says: 'I wish you were here. If we were together, it would be okay. But we are together. And we're not. I'm alone' ('Alone Together').

Steven and Connie also experience each other's trauma as Stevonnie in 'Mindful Education'. Connie feels guilty having accidentally injured a classmate at school, while Steven is experiencing perpetrator trauma having fought the fusions Jasper, Bismuth (Uzo Aduba; Miriam Hyman) and Eyeball (Charlyne Yi), whom he previously failed to reason with. Steven feels further guilt because his mother died while birthing him ('my mom gave up her physical form to make me' ('Fusion Cuisine')). When fused as Stevonnie, Steven and Connie experience flashbacks of Connie's classmate, Bismuth, Jasper, Eyeball and Rose. Connie's classmate and Bismuth appear in the form of holograms stemming from both Steven's and Connie's consciousness. These figures evaporate into swarms of butterflies and form Rose's face, who looks down upon them with a disappointed expression. Stevonnie panics and at certain points it is again unclear who is speaking: 'Oh no, it's happening again. Who was that? Bismuth. Steven! Oh no, it's coming from me now!' ('Mindful Education'). These flashbacks cause Stevonnie to un-fuse. However, the therapeutic benefits of fusion are ultimately emphasised. Garnet informs Steven and Connie that for fusion to function, all parties must work together to overcome trauma:

> For a fusion to work there needs to be balance. An imbalance can cause your fusion to lose touch with reality, see things that aren't there and eventually fall apart. That is to say, if one of you is falling apart, your fusion will as well. To find balance you must understand your feelings. To understand your feelings you must see them clearly without running from them. … I'll show you but first we need Stevonnie. ('Mindful Education')

Garnet's reference to losing touch with reality, seeing things that are not there and falling apart suggests traumatic symptoms such as flashbacks and dissociation, while understanding one's feelings evokes theories of communal healing whereby individuals must confront and talk through traumatic incidents with others. Similar to *Sense8*, Steven and Connie relate to each another regarding the emotional difficulties of unintentionally harming another individual, thematically linking the two scenarios. Steven reassures Connie that she did not mean to hurt her classmate: 'but you didn't mean to hurt him. I know what it's like sometimes. You hurt people by accident' ('Mindful Education'). Later, Connie informs Steven that she feels better and stronger having spoken to Garnet and processed accidentally injuring her classmate: 'I was trying not to think about it and just made it worse. Now that I've got a clear head, we'll do so much better as Stevonnie' ('Mindful Education'). When Stevonnie un-fuses, having experienced Steven's flashbacks of Bismuth, Jasper and Rose, and begin falling from a great height, Connie suggests to Steven that they can 'fuse' and 'hover' so they will 'be okay' ('Mindful Education'). Similar to Connie's experience with her classmate, Steven says of Bismuth and Jasper that 'I didn't want to hurt anyone. I'm sorry. None of them would let me help them. I had no choice', that 'it feels so bad' and that he does not 'want to feel this way' ('Mindful Education'). Connie replies that 'there was nothing else [Steven] could've done' and that thinking about the incident and feeling bad about it is essential; Steven has 'to be honest about how bad it feels so you can move on, that's how it was for me' ('Mindful Education'). When Steven agrees, he and Connie fuse back into Stevonnie, land safely and lie on a patch of grass. Stevonnie laughs, expresses a sigh of relief and says 'I'm here', which can again be taken as a powerful metaphor for online communal healing and its effectiveness.

Candyman

Released in 2021, Nia DaCosta's *Candyman* is a supernatural horror film. DaCosta's *Candyman* is the fourth film in the *Candyman* franchise, but is a direct sequel to the 1992 film of the same name and largely bypasses the earlier sequels (Bill Condon's *Candyman: Farewell to the Flesh* (1995) and Turi Meyer's *Candyman: Day of the Dead* (1999)). Plans for a fourth *Candyman* film began in the early 2000s, with the director of the 1992 *Candyman*, Bernard Rose, wanting to make a prequel to his 1992 film. This pitch was rejected, however, and the project remained in development for over a decade. By 2018, Jordan Peele, director of landmark Black horror films *Get Out* and *Us*, signed on as producer for the 2021 *Candyman* while DaCosta signed on as director. DaCosta's *Candyman* debuted at number one at the North American box office, earning $22.4 million in its opening weekend, against a budget of $25 million, with Da Costa becoming the first Black female director to have a debut at the top. DaCosta's *Candyman* continues the story first established in Rose's *Candyman*, while expanding upon it in terms of plot and theme.

Candyman 1992 and 2021

Based on Clive Barker's short story 'The Forbidden' from the anthology *Books of Blood* (1986), Rose's *Candyman* focused on themes of race and social class in the inner-city United States. While written and directed by a white man and featuring a white protagonist, Rose's *Candyman* is often described as a pioneering 'Black horror' for the way in which it focused on anti-Black violence, and was the first film to centre on a Black supernatural killer. Peele, for instance, notes that 'though the original has some fascinatingly problematic notes (like everything ever), it changed my perspective of what was possible in film by daring to represent Blackness for what was, for me as a genre fan, the ultimate position of power' (*Los Angeles Times*). Rose's film follows a Chicago graduate student, Helen Lyle (Virginia Madsen), completing a thesis on urban legends and folklore. This research leads her to the legend of Candyman. Candyman (Tony Todd) is the vengeful ghost of Daniel Robitaille, an African-American artist and son of a slave who was murdered in the late nineteenth century for falling in love with and impregnating the daughter of a wealthy white man whom he was hired to paint. The artist was lynched by a white mob who severed his hand, covered him in honey and bees and set him on fire. Candyman returns as an urban legend, a ghost with a hook inserted into his arm, and kills anyone that says his name five times in front of a mirror. Helen investigates the Candyman legend in connection to a series of murders at the Cabrini-Green Homes, a vast public housing project on the Near North Side of Chicago, Illinois, the same location where Robitaille was murdered centuries before. Candyman eventually attempts to murder Helen because he believes her research, which claims that the Cabrini-Green residents use the Candyman legend to cope with the hardships of living there, sows disbelief in his legend and is therefore an act of violence against him (Livingstone). Candyman commits a number of violent acts and kidnaps the infant son of a Cabrini-Green resident, claiming that he must 'shed innocent blood' to perpetuate the belief in himself and continue his existence: 'Your disbelief destroyed the faith of my congregation. Without them, I am nothing, so I was obliged to come. And now I must kill you.' Candyman promises to release the baby (named Anthony) if Helen helps him to incite fear among the Cabrini-Green residents. In order to feed his own legend, however, Candyman tries to isolate the residents in a community bonfire, attempting to sacrifice Anthony by placing him in the fire. Killing Helen and Anthony would be an unforgettable event that would ensure the residents would continue to talk about Candyman, keeping the character's myth alive for many years to come. Despite this, Helen manages to remove Anthony from the fire but dies from the burns she sustained.

DaCosta's *Candyman* is set in the present day, but returns to Cabrini-Green, the location of the horrific events that took place in the original film. Whereas the 1992 film centred on a white woman, DaCosta's film features Black protagonists. DaCosta notes that the 'biggest thing for me was the shift in point of view', that the 'first film is very much from an outsider perspective, from a white point of view, and this movie is from the Black perspective and even more specifically from the perspective of Candyman' (Kelley). DaCosta adds that she has 'always wanted to see Candyman through the eyes of Black characters' (Kelley). DaCosta's film takes place one decade after the last of the Cabrini towers were torn down, and centres on a visual artist named Anthony McCoy (Yahya Abdul-Mateen II) and his partner and art gallery director, Brianna Cartwright (Teyonah Parris). Anthony and Brianna move into a loft of the now gentrified Cabrini. Having heard the Candyman legend from Brianna's brother Tony Cartwright (Nathan Stewart-Jarrett), Anthony wants to use the story as an inspiration for his artwork but unknowingly reawakens the Candyman spirit. Anthony is revealed to be the baby kidnapped in Rose's film thirty years later, and Candyman returns to complete the sacrifice of Anthony he attempted in the 1992 film. DaCosta's film takes the foundation of its predecessor and builds upon its mythology. DaCosta advances the story of Anthony and the effects of the mythology on Cabrini-Green in the present, and introduces additional themes. These themes include police brutality, gentrification, the Black Lives Matter Movement, the commodification of Black trauma and, I argue, online communal healing in the Black community.

Black Communal Trauma

Most significantly to this chapter, DaCosta broadens the Candyman legend by creating a shared mythology and expanding the Candyman character's backstory, incorporating the many different kinds of oppression and degradation faced by African-American people. Specifically, DaCosta introduces other iterations of Candyman that have come after Robitaille. Instead of solely being the ghost of Robitaille, Candyman in DaCosta's film is an amalgamation of multiple Black men who were the victims of racist brutality, the different iterations of the character existing as one entity collectively referred to as The Hive. According to Ian Cooper, one of the major things DaCosta set out to do 'was disrupt the notion that Candyman was a singularity', to honour and acknowledge 'the notion that there isn't just one story of a Black man in America wronged at the hands of whiteness' (Kelley). For this reason, I argue that *Candyman* is suitable for analysing in terms of polynarration. Similar to *Sense8* and *Steven Universe*, the concept of a number of traumatised individuals amalgamating into one body and consciousness can be read as a supernatural interpretation of online methods of communal healing from trauma. However, unlike *Sense8* and *Steven Universe*, whereby the super-empowered groups are made up of individuals diverse in terms of gender and race, in *Candyman*, The Hive is made up of a group of Black men who have wrongfully died at the hands of racist white people. These men are diverse in terms of other factors, however, such as class, age, disability and time/environment, but have all been subjected to racial trauma. This diversity within The Hive reflects communal healing but within the Black community specifically. Indeed, the different Candymen are also diverse in terms of the types of racism each were subjected to before they died, which range from microaggressions to police brutality to lynchings, mirroring how a wide range of racial traumatic experiences are frequently shared amongst groups of Black individuals online.

Black communal healing is similar to the concepts of communal healing examined above but has a particular focus on Black issues including racialised violence, systemic racism and oppression, the trauma form which is frequently inter-generational (Chioneso et al.). Instead of the traditional means of communal healing, which is individualistic and places the onus of healing on individual people, Black communal healing challenges systemic inequality, the societal circumstances and structures that cause racial trauma in the first place, and aims to dismantle white supremacist structures (Okoya). According to Wenimo Okoya, Black communal healing aims to 'shift from a society that aims to fix people to one that engages with communities to embed justice and equity into the fabric of our institutions'. Black communal healing aims to restructure conditions that create wellness and health in communities of colour, such as safe and affordable housing, food security, liveable wages, clean air and water and affordable and high-quality healthcare and schooling (Okoya). Also significant is how Black individuals seek to share their trauma specifically with Black therapists and communities of colour online, so as to ensure the listener is 'more culturally sensitive and less Euro-Western-centric' (BAATN).

The Hive

When Anthony wanders the ruins of Cabrini-Green for inspiration for his upcoming art exhibition, he meets William Burke (Colman Domingo), a laundrette owner who recounts the story of Candyman. When Burke was a child, he encountered a man named Sherman Fields (Michael Hargrove), who used to hand out sweets to the local children and was falsely accused of placing razor blades in Halloween candy. According to Burke, a razor blade was found in a 'little white girl's candy', mirroring the white privilege and societal double-standards regarding police intervention emphasised in Rose's film, whereby 'two [Black] people get murdered, the cops do nothing. … A white woman gets attacked, and they lock the place down.' Burke as a child screamed when Sherman emerged from the wall of the laundromat in Cabrini-Green and alerted the attention of the police stationed outside the houses. By the time Burke realised that Fields was harmless, it was too late, as the police arrived upon the scene and beat Fields to death (whereafter Fields was retroactively exonerated for the razor blade crimes when they still appeared in children's candy after he was murdered). Burke recounts a number of further men who were murdered by racist white people, which include 'William Samuel Evans. Run down during the white housing riots of the '50s. William Bell, lynched in the '20s'.' The film's ending credits show the stories of each Candyman manifestation after the original Robitaille. These include George Stinney, a fourteen-year-old boy who was wrongly convicted by an all-white jury of murdering two white girls in 1944 and was later executed via electric chair; Emmett Till, a fourteen-year-old boy who was falsely accused of harassing a white woman in 1955 and subsequently beaten and lynched by white men in the town; and James Byrd, Jr., who was murdered by three white supremacists in Texas in 1998, before which they beat and spray-painted him, and chained his legs to a pickup truck and dragged him on an asphalt road for three miles. Burke informs Anthony that 'Candyman ain't a he. Candyman's the whole damn hive'. When asked by Anthony if Candyman is real, Burke insists that he exists, that Candyman is made up of each of the victims Burke recounted, and is the embodiment of the trauma faced by the Black community: 'a story like that, a pain like that, lasts forever. That's Candyman … Bell is real. Samuel, Sherman, Daniel Robitaille. They're all real.'

Burke devises that Anthony become the next iteration of Candyman so as to rejuvenate the legend. Burke is angry about the gentrification of his neighbourhood and the city's building of the new high-rises, which has driven out much of Cabrini-Green's Black community. Anthony is entranced with the lore of Candyman having spoken with Burke and begins to physically transform after receiving a bee sting when he visits Cabrini-Green, which develops into a huge scab that spreads across his entire body. Burke, who is aware of Anthony's identity as the baby Candyman attempted to kidnap, later captures Anthony, saws off his right hand and replaces it with a hook. Burke also kidnaps Brianna as a witness to the 'baptism', that is, Anthony's transformation into Candyman, so she can share the legend with others. Burke plans to have the police gun Anthony down to create a new legend with the Candyman as an instrument of vengeance rather than a symbol of Black pain and suffering. When Brianna escapes the church, Anthony appears but is shot dead by the police whom Burke had called. Brianna is arrested and a police officer attempts to coerce her into agreeing that Anthony was violent and provoked the police into shooting him:

> Saying what you saw when he came at Jones … and Jones, obviously knowing what he'd done before, seeing his hook, knowing you were in danger, had no choice but to discharge his weapon. Doesn't that sound right to you? Or she's an accomplice. She held the victims down, he cut 'em up. He died coming at a cop. She goes to jail for the rest of her life. Which story is it?

However, Brianna summons Candyman by saying his name five times in the police car's rear-view mirror. Candyman appears, now taking on the appearance of Anthony, and murders all of the police officers with his hook.

Candyman: Polynarration

DaCosta's reworking of the Candyman character into The Hive, a group of people and their traumatic events merged together to create a stronger being so as to overcome trauma, can be read in terms of polynarration because it reflects online methods of communal healing and its related effects. Similar to *Sense8* and *Steven Universe*, Anthony becoming Candyman does not replace Todd's iteration of Candyman, rather it strengthens it, and therefore emphasises the effectiveness of sharing trauma amongst a group. Robitaille aims to bring other Black men into The Hive to work together to carry on his legend/share his traumatic experience, as well as to add their own experiences. According to Jordan

Williams, '[a]s each generation of Black people moves into different versions of the same old story, Candyman is reinvented accordingly'. DaCosta's representation of Candyman, then, can be read as a human embodiment of an online recovery forum as this entity is literally made up of multiple traumatic experiences and is an ongoing process. Indeed, Richard Newby's discussion of DaCosta's *Candyman* likewise stresses the cruciality of testimony to the film: 'people are stories. We are made up of the things we say about ourselves' and 'myths live and die through the power of storytelling'.

Furthermore, for this reason, The Hive reflects Black communal healing in particular. To recall, Gibbs notes the political imperative to narrate traumas of non-Western, marginalised individuals so as to educate Western readers (26). Similarly, Black communal healing aims to heal communities of colour specifically via challenging and dismantling the external, white-centred societal structures, institutions and systems. This is suggested in *Candyman* via Burke's belief that Black trauma should not be kept within the community but should be directed outwards. Having killed the police, Candyman instructs Brianna to '[t]ell everyone'. Brianna is spared by Candyman for the same reason she was kidnapped by Burke to witness Anthony's transformation: because she can inform others about the events that transpired. This will continue the legacy of Candyman/spread the story of the systemic racism and brutalities Black people have experienced throughout the generations. Candyman's refrain of 'Say My Name' throughout the film serves a similar function and further evokes a recovery forum and Black communal healing via the Internet in particular. Black individuals not only share their traumas amongst one group or the Black community but frequently through wider social media movements in order to reach other communities. Examples of such include: #BlackLivesMatter, which protested incidents of police brutality and all racially motivated violence against Black people, going viral; and the #SayHerName campaign, which remembers Black women killed by police in the US. Anthony's and Brianna's occupations as artist and gallery curator likewise suggest this kind of testimony. Anthony's work has achieved acclaim for exploring Black trauma and racist violence while Brianna's occupation involves organising stories concerning such themes and opening them up to the public (Livingstone).

Also significant is that Anthony must sacrifice his life and die in order to achieve his transformation into Candyman and fuel the character's mythology/raise awareness of systemic racism. This reflects Newby's observation of how a Black person must die in order for the community to achieve a platform, to 'tell our own stories and control our own narrative'. An example of such is how the murder of George Floyd raised further awareness of police brutality, and resulted in 'laws being changed to benefit' other Black people and the Black Lives Matter Movement (Newby). Newby says:

> sometimes terrible things must happen to someone like you in order for you to be recognised and seen. ... It's unfortunate that the only means to register empathy so often seems to be through the cyclical process of our own deaths ... it's absurd that we should have to experience that, but it's the truth.

Newby adds the significance of Candyman's transformation by Burke taking place in a church: 'Anthony is made into a martyr who dies for the sins of America. ... The Christ metaphor is apparent.' DaCosta was conscious of this tradition when making the film, noting that 'one of the most important things about Candyman is [that] he illustrates how we use stories to process trauma' and 'also how to try to transmute trauma into something useful, whether it's for a movement or to enact the law' (Kelley). This phenomenon is further reflected in DaCosta's film when the white art dealer Clive Privler (Brian King) and white art critic, Finley Stephens, only become interested in Anthony's work when it depicts Candyman, that is, when it depicts and potentially exploits racialised trauma and Black pain. Their interest grows when two individuals are murdered by Candyman at the gallery where Anthony exhibited. Finley tells Anthony: 'Your work is so macabre, and that's ... pretty interesting, considering what happened ... all of a sudden, your work seems ... eternal'. Anthony responds to Finley: 'I'm surprised at how positive your take on my piece seems to be now'.

Moreover, in contrast to the 1992 *Candyman*, DaCosta's *Candyman* is purportedly more of a community protector rather than a conventional horror villain, killing those who have wronged, harmed or threaten the Black community in and around Cabrini-Green. In Rose's *Candyman*, Black characters are predominantly subject to Candyman's violence, whereas the majority of the victims in DaCosta's film are white characters. When racist white people summon Candyman, they are figured as the monster and their deaths are a result of the trauma they inflict (Alemoru). For instance, Candyman's first victims, the couple whose bodies were uncovered at Anthony's exhibition, are a white couple 'so tantalized by Black pain' that they have sex in front of Anthony's artwork after the exhibition (Alemoru). Candyman also murders: white students who summon him in a college bathroom, before which they are shown to bully a Black student; and Finley who, as noted, is initially dismissive of Anthony's work only to eagerly embrace it when it is connected to a gruesome murder. As Kemi Alemoru notes, 'if you're mean to Black people in this film, you die'. This is in contrast to when a Black character calls upon Candyman, because the purpose is (for the most part) to alleviate their own trauma. As with an online recovery forum for Black people, the Black characters in the film employ Candyman as a weapon so as to protect them from violence and racism inflicted upon them by white people. Burke informs Anthony 'Candyman is how we deal with the fact that these things happened. That they're still happening.' This is evident, for example, when Brianna summons Candyman to protect her from the police's threats. DaCosta's *Candyman*, then, reflects both the benefits and drawbacks of online communal healing. Indeed, that the incantation to summon the potentially therapeutic Candyman figure simply consists of repeating the name Candyman suggests the transglobal nature of online communication, similar to the language translations in *Sense8* and how the Fusion Dance in *Steven Universe* enables the diverse characters to communicate their traumas to one another. However, the summoning of Candyman and the spread of the character's myth not only communicate Black trauma and protect the Black characters in the film, but also reflect secondary trauma and transmission symptomatic of reading about other's traumatic events online. The story of Candyman is not only about a traumatic event but literally inflicts trauma in its telling in how repeating Candyman's name in front of a mirror summons the character, who then inflicts trauma on the person who summoned him. This contrast appears to point to the difference in reaction between Black and white Internet users, specifically how white people frequently focus on their own distress having read about racist violence instead of the real-life implications of this violence on the Black community, effectively centring the narrative on themselves.

The Hive also reflects how the Internet enables the Black community to discuss their trauma in their own words, as opposed to more conventionally presenting these narratives from a white perspective, as in mainstream academic trauma criticism, fiction and cinema (a tradition underscored in Rose's *Candyman* via the film's white academic protagonist). As noted, the Internet is a platform that enables a plethora of voices to be heard, while Darren Mooney observes that '[t]he *Candyman* franchise has always been about narratives. In particular, the franchise is about who gets to control these stories' and that 'the story at the centre of the narrative has always been one of trauma'. This idea is likewise evoked via the film's use of puppetry when portraying the murders of the different Hive members and DaCosta's avoidance of brutalising Black characters during the film's present day sequences. Indeed, as with works that glorify the visuals of sexual violence towards women such as *Twin Peaks*, depictions of Black trauma by white writers are frequently graphic and lead to the exploitation of communities that have already suffered the original trauma. Sarah-Tai Black, for instance, confesses exhaustion at 'seeing this historical trauma continually played as entertainment'. This again connects to the associated dangers of online discourse such as secondary trauma and transmission, with Hannah Giorgis adding that depictions of Black trauma conceived and directed through a white gaze run the risk of re-traumatising Black viewers: 'productions that engage with that real-life terror can, at times, feel more like brutal re-enactments of senselessness than purposeful works of art, unintentionally compounding some Black viewers' traumas'.

That The Hive consists of Black men of varying backgrounds further evokes online communal healing, again Tanis' observation specifically that the platform erases cues that signal differences and focuses solely on the trauma the members all share, generating feelings of belonging and social identification. As with *Sense8* and *Steven Universe*, The Hive in this way also evokes the dialogism of the Internet and online recovery forums. When Anthony is resurrected as Candyman, his face is shrouded in bees, The Hive representing the collective community who has been harmed. His face shifts from Anthony's to Robitaille, and a number of voices who possess different world views all to speak at once, creating a polyphonic narrative. Like Robitaille but in contrast to a number of men in The Hive, Anthony (while born in Cabrini-Green) is a bohemian upper-middle class individual that lives in the gentrified Cabrini-Green. He is described by an art critic as an artist who 'descends upon disenfranchised neighbourhoods divining cheap rent, so they can dick around in their studios without the crushing burden of a day job'. Nevertheless, Anthony is subject to racist microaggressions, such as Clive's and Finley's exploitation and fetishisation of Anthony's Blackness via his artwork and, at the end of the film, police brutality. Mooney also observes that Anthony sells his 'ideas to a critical and commercial establishment that is largely white and built around fetishising these depictions of racialised trauma'. In addition, the term hive refers to Internet discourse in the concept of the hivemind. Analogous to the behaviour of social insects, groups of people online such as in forums become aware of commonality and think and act as a community. Individuals share their knowledge, thoughts and resources. Examples of the global hivemind are social media websites such as Facebook and Twitter, and political and social movements that began on social media such as the Black Lives Matter Movement in 2013. This links back to Tanis' observation of perceived similarity. While hive mentality runs the risk of dependency and indecision for certain individuals, it nevertheless makes people feel less alone, invulnerable and, like the Candyman character, stronger when they are part of a certain group (*WebMD*). Also significant in terms of *Candyman* and the Internet is that the film was criticised for containing too many themes including police brutality, gentrification, the Black Lives Matter Movement and the commodification of Black trauma. However, not only does this demonstrate that racism is multifarious, but like the Hive, I argue that this proliferation of themes creates a polyphonic narrative, further reflecting the dialogism of the Internet and the varying types of racism discussed in online forums.

Conclusion

This chapter examined a narrative technique that I term polynarration in *Sense8*, *Steven Universe* and *Candyman*. Polynarration features diverse groups of characters acquiring interconnectivity abilities that enable them to supernaturally share traumatic experiences and help one another recover, producing unique narratives where a singular traumatic event is told from a range of diverse perspectives as characters' consciousnesses and/or bodies amalgamate. As with the previous paradigms examined, polynarration can be employed to a range of texts to analyse trauma, intersectionality and diversity, and the connection between these three concepts. For instance, *The OA*, examined in the next section in terms of sceptical scriptotherapy, can also be read in terms of polynarration. The characters in *The OA* develop interconnectivity abilities called the Movements. As with the texts examined above, these superpowers reflect traditional means of testimony and communal healing as well as perspectives on these concepts in relation to the Internet including increased empathy, secondary trauma, transmission and diversity. *The OA* features a diverse group of people literally sharing one another's perspectives and traumatic experiences telepathically. As with the Fusion Dance in *Steven Universe*, the interconnectivity abilities in *The OA* involve the performance of a magical dance that when executed by five people in unison enables feats including the reanimation of the dead and interdimensional travel. Mike Flanagan's *Doctor Sleep* (2019) can likewise be read in terms of polynarration. The film again features traumatised characters diverse in terms of gender, race and age, who telepathically connect to protect one another from a dangerous cult that preys upon children who possess the Shining ability. Ultimately, this chapter on polynarration explored trauma narratives unique both formally and thematically. Formally, popular texts such as *Sense8*, *Steven Universe* and *Candyman* present innovative reworkings of dominant trauma theories and techniques. Further subverting convention, these texts formulate unique, fantastical metaphors to depict trauma experienced by diverse characters specifically. Thematically, these texts' diversity establishes the relevance and necessity of popular culture when examining trauma. These texts' diversity expands our knowledge of trauma representation and real-life cases of trauma, opening up avenues for a range of frequently overlooked voices to be heard.

CHAPTER 5

Sceptical Scriptotherapy: Brit Marling and Zal Batmanglij's *The OA* and Sam Esmai's *Mr Robot*

This chapter examines the representation of trauma in two texts by diverse writers: Brit Marling and Zal Batmanglij's *The OA* (2016–2019) and Sam Esmail's *Mr Robot* (2015–2019). I will read these texts through a technique that I term sceptical scriptotherapy. Before conducting this study, it is necessary to address the following: my definition of sceptical scriptotherapy and how this concept differs from traditional notions of scriptotherapy; why sceptical scriptotherapy is an important and relevant framework through which to read the trauma of diverse characters; and the theories I draw upon in formulating my concept of sceptical scriptotherapy.

Scriptotherapy

A dominant critical conception regarding trauma recovery is that healing can only take place when survivors tell what Herman calls 'the story of the trauma' (*Trauma* 175). That is, sharing and narrating traumatic events exactly as they happened are essential for recovery. Vickroy also advocates the 'healing function of literature' (8), while Shoshana Felman insists that the act of writing about trauma is 'an essential element of working through [the] experience' (54). Most significantly, Suzette Henke has coined the term 'scriptotherapy', which refers to writing about a traumatic experience for the purposes of healing, 'the process of writing out and writing through

S. Travers, *Trauma in American Popular Culture and Cult Texts, 1980–2020*, https://doi.org/10.1007/978-3-031-13287-2_5

traumatic experience in the mode of therapeutic re-enactment' (xii–xiii). Sceptical scriptotherapy, then, is a type of writing that features characters consciously reworking traumatic events into fantastical alternatives rather than relaying them exactly as they happened. Sceptical scriptotherapy differs from more traditional methods of scriptotherapy and canonical trauma fiction in a number of ways. First, fantastical narratives are represented as therapeutic and successful means of healing rather than being futile, as per convention in trauma fiction. In stereotypical trauma fiction, characters' imaginings of alternate and supernatural scenarios are conventionally represented and read as unhelpful responses to trauma and as a way of denying agency for perpetrator-protagonists. Second, sceptical scriptotherapy uniquely employs a dual narrative structure and is at times ambiguous in terms of the veracity of its supernatural content. Third, sceptical scriptotherapy is suitable for characters diverse in terms of gender and race, and individuals potentially subject to gender or racially based oppression. For these individuals, imagination is presented as the only means at their disposal that is not subject to such traumas.[1]

Conversely, the concept of sharing and narrating traumatic events has been disputed, with Gibbs noting that testimony is not always shown to heal trauma in fiction; that in specific texts characters are represented as either further traumatised having narrated past events, as in *House of Leaves*, or as preferring to forget traumatic events over therapeutic remembering—such as Lorrie Moore's *A Gate at the Stairs* (37). Indeed, Johnny Truant says in *House of Leaves*: '[w]e all create stories to protect ourselves' (20), which likewise suggests reimagining traumatic events to be more favourable than remembering them. Certain psychological studies of trauma take a similar approach, specifically by incorporating Nietzsche's concept of 'active forgetting' whereby an individual, society or culture heals by forgetting a traumatic memory (Aydin 125; Ramadanovic). Gibbs also highlights works of traumatic metafiction (*House of Leaves*) whereby a text 'interrogates the possibility about writing trauma' and dramatises the 'difficulties of constructing' a trauma narrative, thus challenging 'accepted theories regarding the representation of trauma' (87, 89, 90). Trauma texts that incorporate Henke's concept of scriptotherapy, then, will feature a character who experiences a trauma, narrates the traumatic event and

[1] This is in contrast to the texts examined under the framework of polynarration (*Sense8*, *Steven Universe* and *Candyman*), which appear to stress the importance of confronting and talking through traumatic events with others.

shares it with others and heals as a result. Sceptical scriptotherapy therefore straddles these two approaches: representations of therapeutic remembering and representations that interrogate this practice.

Trauma Culture, Phallocentricism and Feminism

As noted in Chap. 3, stereotypical trauma texts are frequently phallocentric and centre on straight white male protagonists. Traditional methods of scriptotherapy and a negative view of escapism (whereby it is considered futile and a means of denying agency for trauma perpetrators) are pertinent for reading more traditional, phallocentric trauma fiction. This is evident in *Slaughterhouse-Five*, for instance, which describes in detail the nightmares and hallucinations suffered by Billy Pilgrim, such as his imaginings of alien abduction. By contrast, I argue that sceptical scriptotherapy is more suitable for analysing contemporary popular trauma representations that feature more diverse characters, individuals normally left behind by stereotypical trauma narratives including women, ethnic minorities and the LGBTQIA+ community. In works of sceptical scriptotherapy, escapist fantasies are significantly depicted as the only way victim-protagonists can take agency over their recovery and are particularly pertinent to diverse groups as the types of trauma experienced by such individuals are often structurally beyond their control, primarily involving 'everyday' experiences of inequality and oppression. To recall, the types of trauma frequently experienced by diverse individuals tend to be the more insidious traumas resulting from ongoing situations of distress such as domestic violence, child abuse, poverty and 'repeated forms of traumatising violence such as sexism, racism and colonialism' (Rothberg, *Memory* 89). Sceptical scriptotherapy, then, provides a new framework for reading these types of experiences in contemporary popular culture.

As with competitive narration, sceptical scriptotherapy equally uncovers how texts uniquely employ the supernatural, which is significant to wider feminist trauma theory. As noted, there is a long-standing and problematic tradition in American culture to repress ostensibly 'taboo' topics by representing them in supernatural terms as a means of repression. Further, when characters displace traumatic events onto the supernatural in canonical trauma literature, the protagonists' otherworldly encounters are frequently products of their imagination, as in *Slaughterhouse-Five*. In popular culture, by contrast, the supernatural depictions of trauma experienced by diverse protagonists are generally represented as literally true (*Jessica Jones*,

Captain Marvel). Works of sceptical scriptotherapy do not conform to either of these approaches. Victim-protagonists are strongly implied to imagine alternate scenarios, but there is more of a hesitation between the realist and supernatural explanations of events than we would normally see in trauma narratives. The supernatural is presented in a more ambiguous manner. Viewers are presented with two versions of events, which can take the form of a dual narrative: a realist, tragic version of events and a more palatable, supernatural alternative. The idea of taking agency over one's recovery via escapism is significant in relation to diverse trauma protagonists. For instance, Marling and Batmanglij, the writers of *The OA*, aimed to base the series on an 'active' attempt at trauma recovery. Marling and Batmanglij describe the protagonist's actions as 'a victim taking agency and ownership over her recovery, with a sense of a mission', rather than keeping her in what they call 'the realm of passive victimhood' (Birnbaum, *The OA*). Marling adds that this is because in stories about abductions and captivity, the focus is usually on the 'team of white male law enforcement officers, once again tasked with saving the day', rather than the survivor. Moreover, while traumas such as sexual violence are often represented obliquely in supernatural terms, rape scenes nevertheless tend to be depicted graphically and glorify the visuals of sexual violence. Instead, sceptical scriptotherapy is used to explore the traumatic *effects* of such experiences (specifically escapism), which is a focus of more recent, diverse trauma representations in popular culture.

Trauma and Naturalism

Sceptical scriptotherapy is also significant to recent criticism on the relationship between trauma and naturalism. Naturalism is a form of writing that encourages a view of humankind controlled by deterministic forces including social, hereditary, biological and environmental, and features characters lacking in free will. According to Gibbs, American cultural production since 9/11 has witnessed a resurgence of naturalism, called 'new' or 'neo-naturalism', in particular contemporary American trauma literature such as that by Paul Auster and Philip Roth. This shift towards naturalist narratives is also evident in popular trauma narratives. However, in contrast to writers such as Auster and Roth, whom critics such as Gibbs consider canonical naturalist writers, naturalism in popular forms such as film and television employs experimental formal techniques and incorporates supernatural themes, transcending the limits of naturalism as a mode of representation regarding its extreme realism and 'the self-imposed limits of writers working within the laws of probability' (Campbell 504). Heidi Strengell observes this approach in Stephen King's fiction, for instance, which combines genres including science fiction and horror with naturalism to represent themes such as trauma. Strengell says that King 'examines naturalistic themes by means of ... supernatural elements' (12–13), with the supernatural providing the 'background' of the narrative and literary naturalism lending the 'worldview' (23). I argue that this approach to naturalism can be linked with sceptical scriptotherapy. Texts analysed in this chapter represent deterministic forces as traumatic and employ the neo-naturalist counterfactual form, whereby characters are shown to imagine alternative scenarios as a means of coping with these traumas via escapism. The counterfactual form is similar to the naturalist writing of Émile Zola, whereby the novelist is 'a scientist or "experimental moralist"' and develops characters 'as figures in a grand experiment to test [their] physical and emotional responses' (Campbell 501). In contemporary literature, the counterfactual form is increasingly used to represent trauma, with Gibbs noting that Auster's *Man in the Dark*, Roth's *The Plot Against America* and Michael Chabon's *The Yiddish Policemen's Union* consider 'alternative histories' as 'a form of neo-naturalist experiment', with the naturalist writer constructing 'scenarios and characters and ... let[ting] them play out at will' (207–208). For Gibbs, such texts 'apply variations to history and existing historical traumas as we recognise them', and 'these counterfactual narratives are ... used ... as a means of isolating the ways in which traumas, both structural and historical, are experienced by individuals' (208).

The type of naturalism linked to sceptical scriptotherapy finds precedence in Vonnegut, who, as noted, perceives discourses such as religion as provisional truths or 'comforting lies' to make sense of life and make its traumas more tolerable (*Conversations* 78). Billy's escapist strategies in *Slaughterhouse-Five* are an example of such, as his alien captive's advice is to concentrate on the happy moments of life and ignore the unhappy ones. One of the major works on trauma in *Slaughterhouse-Five* is Susanne Vees-Gulani's essay 'Diagnosing Billy Pilgrim: A Psychiatric Approach to Kurt Vonnegut's *Slaughterhouse-Five*', which argues that the 'Tralfamadorian philosophy, which opposes trying to make sense out of occurrences, helps Billy deal with the horrible events and their consequences by reinterpreting their meaning' (179–180). Vees-Gulani extends this reading to Vonnegut the author, arguing that the process of writing

Slaughterhouse-Five was 'a therapeutic process that allows him to uncover and deal with his trauma' (176). This interpretation has sparked varying critical responses, with Gibbs in particular critiquing Vees-Gulani's interpretation on the basis that Billy's escapism does not fully heal the character by the end of the narrative, and that Vonnegut writes this novel instead with a sense of ironic detachment:

> Billy … almost entirely withdraws from quotidian existence, and denies himself choice, agency, and responsibility … refusing agency is therefore just another form of escape that the narrative of *Slaughterhouse-Five* demonstrates to be an ultimately futile response to trauma. (61)

Gibbs' critique stems from naturalism, drawing a comparison between *Slaughterhouse-Five* and *Man in the Dark*. He argues that both texts show such philosophies to be dangerous rather than reassuring in the implication that they relieve humankind of its moral responsibilities towards human harm (61). However, Gibbs reads Vees-Gulani's essay solely in relation to naturalism and trauma in more canonical literary forms. I argue that if we read this essay in relation to *popular* naturalist representations of trauma which incorporate the supernatural, Vees-Gulani's analysis of Vonnegut's novel is in line with sceptical scriptotherapy. Certainly, *Slaughterhouse-Five* is told with a sense of ironic detachment, but this parallels the sceptical scriptotherapical reading, in which characters create overtly escapist narratives and gain temporary comfort by knowingly suspending disbelief rather than unequivocally believing. Likewise, Vees-Gulani describes Billy's fantasies as enabling him 'to avoid *some* of the distress he feels when facing death' rather than fully healing him (180, emphasis mine). This aligns with the emphasis in certain popular trauma narratives on what we can call conscious escapism and Vonnegut's concept of 'comforting lies'. Sceptical scriptotherapy and naturalism in certain popular trauma texts then can be described as reworking the counterfactual form to represent trauma stemming from deterministic forces; characters imagine an alternate history of events as a means of escapism.

The OA

The OA is a particularly relevant case study of sceptical scriptotherapy due to its representation of diverse groups and their experience of trauma. The series is also diverse in terms of its production, being created by a woman and a queer man of colour. Debuting on Netflix in 2016, *The OA* is an American mystery drama television series containing science fiction, supernatural and fantasy elements, leading critics to describe the series as 'unclassifiable' in terms of genre (Doyle). *The OA* consists of two seasons of eight episodes each, created and produced by Marling and Batmanglij, having worked together on two previous films, *Sound of My Voice* (2011) and *The East* (2013). As with *Sense8*, *The OA* was planned to consist of five seasons but was cancelled by Netflix in 2019, leaving the series with a cliff-hanger ending. The cancellation prompted fan campaigns on Twitter (titled #SaveTheOA and #TheOAisReal), a change.org petition and protests in the form of hunger strikes and videos of viewers performing the magical dance that features in the series. The plot has been described by critics as bizarre, innovative and compelling (Doyle; Schedeen; Syme; Fienberg; Foutch; Gilbert). *The OA* centres on a formerly blind woman, Prairie Johnson (Brit Marling), who returns home having been kidnapped for seven years with her sight restored. Now calling herself The OA (The Original Angel), Prairie assembles a group of five locals, four high school boys and their teacher, to whom she reveals her story to recruit their help in rescuing her fellow captives. Prairie was abducted by a scientist named Hap (Jason Issacs) who locked her in an underground glass cage with four other individuals, and experimented upon them to research near-death experiences (NDEs). The four other captives include Homer Roberts (Emory Cohen), Scott Wilson (Will Brill), Rachel DeGrasso (Sharon Van Etten) and Renata Duarte (Paz Vega), each of whom was selected by Hap because they had an NDE. Hap's experiments involved repeatedly killing and reviving the inmates via drowning, during which they travelled to alternate dimensions. In these dimensions, the inmates attained knowledge of a magical dance called the Movements. The Movements are an ancient ritual comprising five steps that, when threaded together, form what appears to be an interpretive dance. When executed by five people in unison, the Movements can heal illness, reanimate the dead and open portals to other dimensions. Having been abandoned by Hap at a country road when Prairie later refuses to work with him, Hap informs her that he will jump dimensions with the remaining four captives. Prairie thus aims to teach the Movements to the five locals (referred to in this chapter as 'the new five') to transport her to another dimension. This chapter will predominantly focus on the first season of *The OA*, particularly as it more effectively demonstrates my framework of sceptical scriptotherapy.

The OA presents the viewer with two versions of events: a realist, tragic version in which Prairie is delusional or lying, using a science fiction narrative as a coping mechanism for a more plausible kind of sexual abuse she may have suffered in captivity, or a more palatable, supernatural alternative whereby Prairie is an interdimensional traveller. *The OA* contains both scenes that suggest Prairie is lying and telling the truth; the series presents both scenarios as 'real' and 'false' at different points in the narrative and it is up to the viewer to decide. *The OA* lends credence to Prairie's narrative in a number of ways, including Prairie legitimately regaining her sight, with her parents confirming that Prairie was blind as a child. This suggests that Prairie did jump dimensions when she died during Hap's experiments and regained her sight via otherworldly means. Conversely, Prairie's story can be taken as a fabrication. As Batmanglij notes: 'I believe the trauma in [Prairie's] story is true. Maybe she couldn't tell her story as it actually happened' (Birnbaum, *The OA*). For instance, the flashback scenes contrast to the sequences set in the present day. Laurie 'Lol' Crawley, *The OA*'s director of photography, says that the present-day scenes were shot to look more real, recognisable and 'rough-around-the-edge', similar to a documentary or found footage film, and that natural light was employed as much as possible, in addition to a 'responsive' handheld camera style. Crawley notes that the flashback sequences, conversely, have a more cinematic style, employing classical 'slow, tracking and Steadicam' camera movements. Ben Travers also observes that Prairie's trauma in captivity is presented like a 'fairy tale … far away and magical … like a person who's gone through an unimaginably painful experience and found a way to cope with it', and contrasts Prairie's flashback scenes to the gritty 'very real' sequences set in the present day. As noted, the series has been described as unclassifiable in terms of genre, incorporating elements of science fiction, fantasy, mystery and drama, which likewise suggest the fabrication of Prairie's story.

Certain scenes also suggest that the inmates are being abused by Hap rather than undergoing experiments. The inmate Scott ponders if Prairie had been raped when she attempted to escape, while Hap is frequently shown to leer at Prairie and exhibit jealousy over Prairie and Homer's closeness. Sexual assault is also suggested in the scene where Hap drags Prairie out of his car, pins her to the ground, cuts parts of her clothes and holds a knife to her neck. This part of the story appears the most difficult for Prairie to relay, as she describes it in a fragmentary manner: 'I'm lying there on the grass and I can't move. And then I feel the cold metal of the blade pressed against my throat ... Skies so big. Trees. And a road. Going somewhere' ('Invisible Self'). As noted, experimental forms such as narrative fragmentation are conventionally used to narrate trauma in fiction. However, as with the employment of the supernatural, this approach often results in silencing diverse individuals, where there may be a more urgent imperative to narrate their traumas in order to educate readers and viewers.

The OA subverts this convention and can be read instead in terms of sceptical scriptotherapy, as a marginalised trauma survivor reworking their experience. Prairie appears to revise the incident with Hap as she narrates it. The flashback sequence that plays out for the viewer and that of Prairie's retelling of it almost merge into one another as the scene interchanges rapidly between them, and while there is reference to sexual assault, it is not explicitly shown. The scene cuts back to that of Prairie with the new five when Hap pins Prairie to the ground in the flashback. When describing this moment to the group, Prairie holds a pocket knife and analogously cuts her clothes. She repeats her and Hap's conversation, and the motion of grabbing onto Hap's legs as he gets in his car, while screaming the words 'come back' to her listeners in the same manner as she did that day. Applying my concept of sceptical scriptotherapy and reading Prairie as revising a traumatic event into a more palatable, supernatural narrative, this scene is significant to feminist trauma theory on 'active' trauma recovery. The dual narratives and the ambiguity of the supernatural align with Walker's trauma theory in relation to film. Walker argues that the realistic mode of representation leaves cinematic texts 'within the binaristic paradigm', that is, that memory is either true or false (*Trauma* 59). For Walker, formally experimental texts demonstrate that traumatic memory 'eludes binaristic "it happened or it didn't" approaches' and instead straddles the categories of 'fantasy' and 'memory' ('False' 212). Walker says that trauma representation should acknowledge the 'vicissitudes of memory', particularly in regards to experiences such as sexual abuse, and 'confront the possibility that some memory claims or aspects of memory claims may indeed be mistaken' ('False' 212). Walker stresses that fantasy does 'not belie the truth' of the traumatic event but is 'connected to and produced' by it ('False' 212).

This approach appears to be taken throughout the series. For instance, the real-life case of Elizabeth Smart's kidnapping plays on Hap's radio, a survivor who famously likened rape to dying (*NBC News*). Prairie informs the new five that she and the inmates 'all died more times than I can count' ('Homecoming'). A further inspiration for the series' science fiction premise is Raymond Moody's concept of NDEs (Grow). Marling says that Moody noticed a convergence in near-death experiences: 'everybody talks about leaving the body and having this bird's eye point of view … and then maybe facing the choice of whether or not to return to the body' (Lopez). Moody's description of NDEs as an out-of-body experience draws strong parallels with dissociative symptoms of sexual abuse and aligns with Walker's theory on active traumatic memory, incorporating further feminist trauma theory on dissociation by Herman. Herman describes rape survivors as feeling 'as though the event is not happening to her, as though she is observing it from outside her body' (*Trauma* 43). Similarly, the inmate Rachel says her NDE in a car accident was like 'floating above the car' ('Champion').

In contrast to the conventional employment of the supernatural in trauma representations, the otherworldly metaphor of interdimensional travel is used to explore the psychological effects of abuse, specifically the need for victims to attain a feeling of agency. Hap's inmates imagine an alternative version of events as a means of coping with their abuse and captivity, regaining control over the narrative. Prairie convinces herself that she is not powerless, that the group 'aren't captives … we aren't lab rats … or unlucky. We're angels' ('Away'). The unique concept of angels in the series points to related themes of victimhood including guilt, forgiveness, redemption and transcendence. A common symptom of abuse-related trauma is that the victim feels responsible for their abuse. Indeed, the wing-like scars on the inmates' backs (Prairie and the group carve symbols representative of the Movements into their skin in case they forget them when they jump dimensions) are indicative of self-harm. Furthermore, rather than having Prairie transcribe her experience in a realistic or supernatural manner that transforms Hap into a monstrous figure, Prairie reworks the narrative and transforms the victims into empowered, supernatural beings with the capacity to retaliate (this also rejects the earlier, male perception of feminism as women being antagonistic towards men). The inmates' imaginations are presented as the only means at their disposal that is not subject to Hap's control. For instance, on Prairie's first night in captivity, Homer reassures her: 'You'll find your freedom in sleep, in your dreams. It's how we stay sane' ('New Colossus'). This concept is also evoked via the premise of other dimensions; Prairie conjures 'new worlds' where alternate versions of events take place. Prairie says that 'there are all these dimensions, worlds, alternate realities, and they're right on top of each other. Every time you make a choice, a decision, it forks off into a new possibility. ... The NDEs were like a way to travel through them, but temporarily' ('Forking Paths'). Prairie's use of the word 'temporarily' suggests interdimensional travel while flatlining to be fantasies of the inmates that provide brief escapism during Hap's abuse. Prairie travels to a dimension located on the rings of Saturn, where a woman, Khatun (Hiam Abbass), asks if Prairie will remain in this realm or return to the original world with the knowledge of one of the Movements. That each inmate travels to a different universe further evokes this idea; Homer's alternate world appears like an institution and Scott's is described as a filmset. However, regardless of whether interdimensional travel is real or fabricated, Prairie asserts these probable fantasies to be a means of liberation for the captives: 'The Movements would allow us to travel to a dimension permanently. ... We *wanted choices*, chances. ... A new life in a new world. *To us* that was freedom' ('Forking Paths', emphasis mine). Escapist fantasies are therefore therapeutic for Prairie and the other inmates. Further pointing to themes of victimhood and guilt, this emphasis on imagination can also be read along the lines of a Cartesian split between mind and body, one which emphasises the former over the latter. According to Suzannah Weiss, sexual abuse victims sometimes feel unclean and shameful despite having been subject to a force beyond their control and want to escape their bodies, that 'many survivors feel as if their bodies have betrayed them for responding to unwelcome stimulation'.

The group's quest to uncover all of the Movements to 'allow [them] to travel to a dimension permanently' ('Forking Paths') serves a similar therapeutic function, whereby the inmates retreat into fantasy as a means of regaining agency. Prairie compares what she considers to be Hap's less favourable position as captor to that of the captives, as he attempts to learn the Movements they practice each day in their cages through his security cameras: 'Every Movement we received [Hap] received as well. Right above us, Hap was learning each Movement on his own. ... At least we had each other. Hap was all by himself' ('Forking Paths'). Prairie also imagines Hap enviously observing how his captors' shared mission brings them closer together as a group: 'I found myself feeling resentful. ... My subjects seem so united. They have this tribalism. ... Rituals. ... I couldn't help feeling outside of it all, somehow' ('Forking Paths'). This type of recovery is especially significant in relation to women's trauma. While Prairie eventually enlists male students to help her rescue Hap's remaining inmates, and a number of these inmates are also male, it is Prairie who orchestrates and leads the group's mission to acquire the Movements. As noted, Marling aimed to depict a female character taking agency over her recovery. This approach is referred to when a journalist advises Prairie to document her experiences, describing it as healing and empowering: 'The process can sometimes help people to heal. Storytelling is cleansing. But I also want to make sure you control the narrative. That you profit from it' ('Champion'). *The OA* also critiques traditional, graphic depictions of women's trauma and sexual violence. Having returned home, a woman approaches Prairie and muses: 'you're so inspirational, being beaten and raped like that', after which Prairie's mother demands to know if Prairie was 'abused, beaten, hurt', despite believing she already knows this to be true ('Empire of Light'). Such responses act as a commentary on the type of stories the public demands from female trauma survivors, specifically how audiences crave conventionally violent trauma narratives with almost pornographic details of the survivor's suffering.

The New Five

Prairie's listeners, 'the new five' likewise consciously choose to believe her narrative as a means to heal the trauma to which they were subjected. The new five are diverse in terms of race, gender, sexuality, socio-economic status and age. According to Marling, each member is experiencing some kind of disintegration of the nuclear family, its trauma and its abuses (Jung). Steve Winchell (Patrick Gibson) is a school bully and drug dealer whose parents plan to send to military school; Buck Vu (Ian Alexander) is a trans-man of Asian-American descent whose father refuses to acknowledge his gender; Alfonso 'French' Sosa (Brandon Perea) is a gay Filipino-American who cares for his siblings in place of his alcoholic mother; Jesse Mills (Brendan Meyer) is impoverished and essentially orphaned; and the teacher at the boys' school, Betty Broderick-Allen (Phyllis Smith), is an older woman whose brother, Theo, has died. Indeed, when the school principal observes the group, he comments: 'that's quite an interesting group you're sitting with … I sort of pride myself on my high-school anthropology, but for the life of me I can't imagine what the five of you have in common' ('Paradise'). Similarly, Buck says to French when convincing him to join the new five, that society 'think[s] people like us will just slide into being criminals' and ponders, 'Don't you think that [Prairie] picked us for some reason? Like, Steve's probably a murderer, and Jesse's totally checked out of life, Ms Broderick-Allen is weird and sad and I'm, well, you know' ('New Colossus').

The group is continually torn between doubt and a desire to believe Prairie's implausible yet uplifting narrative in a manner that is prime for a sceptical scriptotherapical reading. The viewer is presented with two different versions of narrative events as the new five encounter what they consider conflicting evidence that Prairie is lying and telling the truth. They appear to share the perspectives of Hap's captives and supernaturally experience their traumas. The lives of the new five increasingly mirror those who they hear about in Prairie's story, appearing to take on the physical and emotional pain of Prairie's fellow captives by living through some of their past hardships. For instance, Buck witnesses a car accident that parallels the one described by Prairie's fellow inmate Rachel when she informs Prairie of her NDE. Rachel momentarily died in a car crash with her younger brother who had a red backpack with him at the time: 'the van flipped on the highway, collapsed, all around us. But I was floating above the car, and I could see my little brother's red backpack in the middle of the road' ('Champion'). In the car accident scene Buck witnesses, the rubble is filled with flares and shards of metal and tyres, and a red backpack lies in the middle. Such moments suggest that the new five are projecting their own interpretations onto Prairie's narrative as it plays out for the viewer, the flashback scenes being a combination of Prairie's memories and what the new five are imagining as they listen. The new five appear to similarly rework Prairie's narrative in their imaginations. When beginning the narrative, Prairie says 'imagine everything I tell you as if you're there yourself. … As if you are me' ('Homecoming'). Peter Debruge remarks, 'the narrative is constantly evolving before our eyes, it's almost impossible to get a grasp on what it is we're watching. … Are the flashbacks we see real, or do they represent [Prairie's] listeners' vivid imaginations?' Certainly, unusual details in Prairie's story imply a degree of interpretation, such as Prairie's eye colour being brown rather than blue in certain flashback scenes and Hap's archaic-looking technology. The latter is possibly Betty visualising a type of 'mad scientist's' equipment akin to 1970s science fiction that she grew up watching. The flashback that shows Hap playing heavy metal music similarly appears to be Betty's interpretation of events, as shortly before this scene is shown, Betty is reminded of her brother's love for the genre when Steve and Jesse uncover Theo's CDs. Also, Hap is previously claimed by Prairie in her narration to enjoy classical music. There are a number of further doublings, or moments in which the two groups' consciousnesses appear to seep into one another. The incident where Steve stabs Prairie with a pencil when she embraces him parallels Hap stabbing Prairie with an EpiPen when she first attempts to escape his house; Steve chasing the ambulance taking Prairie to the hospital when she is shot at the end of the first season, screaming to 'hold up, take me with you' ('Invisible Self'), mirrors Prairie's attempt to catch up to Hap's car when he abandons her; and the cut French gets on his forehead having engaged in a physical confrontation with Steve is similar to the cut on Hap's forehead that Prairie enquires about.

At the same time, the flashbacks can be interpreted as Prairie reworking into her story the incidents that occur to the new five. Prairie may have fabricated Hap's other captives, basing them on the new five.[2] French cannot find evidence of Homer's existence online, while his subsequent 'transformation' into Homer when he looks in the mirror can be read as French suspecting that Prairie based Homer on him. Just before his reflection morphs into that of Homer, French examines the cut on his forehead. This lucidity aligns with the sceptical scriptotherapical dual narrative form, as the narrative shifts not only between verifying and discrediting Prairie's narrative but also between the different characters' perspectives as they, too, rework a trauma narrative in their imagination. For instance, the members of the new five not only parallel members of the original group. Each member of the new five shares characteristics with more than one of the original inmates, as well as with Hap. French shares the cut on his forehead with both Homer and Hap, the latter of whom cuts his head when he murders his colleague. In addition to seeing Homer's reflection in the mirror, a number of French's scenes parallel shot-for-shot those of Hap, such as the scene where French watches Buck sing at the conference dinner, which plays out exactly as that in which Hap watches Renata play guitar at the Cuban hotel. These scenes also link Buck with Renata in regards to his musical talents, as Buck is a singer in the school choir and Renata returned from her NDE with an angelic singing voice. Further, Betty mirrors Rachel in losing her brother Theo, while Steve mirrors both Prairie and Hap in stabbing Prairie and chasing after the ambulance. In addition, parallels can also be drawn between the inmates and related individuals of the new five, and between the new five and individuals from Prairie's narrative outside of Hap and the original group. Buck echoes Prairie's father when eating ice cream in cold weather, remarking that he enjoys 'cold stuff in the cold' ('New Colossus'). This echoes Prairie's

[2] Prairie's recruitment of five individuals who resemble people from her story likewise suggests re-enactment and reworking of traumatic events.

father's line when he tries to rid Prairie of her nightmares by submerging herself in an ice hole they find in a nearby forest, telling Prairie she must become 'colder than cold' ('Homecoming'). Betty's brother Theo Allen, also referred to as Theo A, shares a name with Prairie's new identity as The OA, as well as echoes in his last voicemail to Betty Prairie's description of attempting to find her father and happiness in New York but encountering Hap and dangerous situations instead. Theo says: 'Hey … Just throwing out a line to see what comes back' ('Champion'), while Prairie says: 'The biggest mistake I made was believing that if I cast a beautiful net, I would only catch beautiful things' ('New Colossus'). Prairie's narrative, then, appears polyphonic and symbiotic, mirroring Marling's description of Prairie's relationship with the new five and wider trauma conceptions of testimony and recovery. Marling says that Prairie's connection with the new five is 'a very symbiotic relationship', asserting that the group not only has the capacity to help Prairie by 'receiving' and 'understand[ing] the story', but also that 'they desperately need it' (Birnbaum, *The OA*). This suggests that Prairie's narrative works as a means of communal healing amongst the group (the concept of sharing a trauma narrative with others), which has strong links with testimony as narrating traumatic experiences implies a listener or reader. Indeed, when asked by Steve: '[h]ow did you survive so long' in captivity, Prairie refers to the support she received from the original group: 'I survived because I wasn't alone' ('Empire of Light').

Moreover, French discovers books beneath Prairie's bed that prompts the group and viewer to question the veracity of her story, because Prairie's story appears to be based on the content of the books. The books are entitled: *The Oligarchs: Wealth and Power in the New Russia*; *Encyclopedia of Near-Death Experiences*; *The Book of Angels*; and Homer's *The Iliad*. Here, Prairie's FBI psychiatrist Elias Rahim (Riz Ahmed) informs French that Prairie's story is untrue. Elias informs French that the new five are experiencing secondary trauma having listened to Prairie's story: 'second-hand trauma is when you take somebody else's pain, so they can survive' ('Invisible Self'). This would explain why the new five literally experience the traumas of Prairie and her fellow captives, such as Buck witnessing the car accident. The apparent blending and conflation of the different characters' consciousness also evokes transmission (to appropriate a victim's experience, confuse self and other, and collapse all distinctions between them), as Prairie requested the group's empathy when beginning her story, instructing them to imagine they are her as she relays it. Yet, there are simultaneous suggestions that Elias planted these books, possibly under the instruction of Hap to discredit Prairie and keep Hap from prison. However, reading these scenes in terms of sceptical scriptotherapy, the legitimacy of the narrative is ultimately irrelevant as it grants the group escapism from trauma. As with Hap's captives, Prairie's story gives the traumatised new five a sense of agency as choosing to believe and rework it to incorporate their own interpretations is amongst the only aspect of their lives over which they have control and transforms them into empowered beings, whether literally or psychologically. Indeed, Marling asserts of the series' themes of faith, 'if you're going to have faith in something, you have to have it in the face of incredible doubt', but 'nobody can take your [faith] away' (Birnbaum, *The OA*).

In the season finale, the group performs the Movements at their school when a shooter breaks into the cafeteria. Beforehand, the group appears in a more stable, mentally healthy condition. Steve has managed to evade military school and is now happily eating lunch with his new girlfriend; Buck is studying with a new potential romantic interest; Jesse and French are laughing with their respective groups of friends; and Betty, despite having been fired, is evidently more self-assured. Prairie, too, transitions from an anxious, somewhat antisocial individual who refuses to be touched, to a more outgoing person unafraid of human contact. The series shows Prairie growing gradually closer to her narratees, embracing characters such as Steve when he is distressed, and describing the group as a 'family … built out of strange pieces' ('Champion'). When Prairie is injured in the school shooting in the finale of Season One, she says to Steve as she is wheeled out of the building on a stretcher: 'You did it. Don't you see? I have the will. Can't you feel it?' ('Invisible Self'). These words can be taken as confirmation of Prairie's recovery, having spent the days leading up to this incident constructing and sharing her story with the new five. The first episode in Season One of *The OA* opens with Prairie jumping from a highway bridge having been abandoned by Hap (the incident is presented through a recording on a civilian's phone). While Prairie describes this as an attempt to transport back to Hap's captives that he claimed will, by then, reside in another dimension with him, we can likewise read this in realist terms as a suicide attempt, having spent years in captivity. Prairie's claims of having the 'will' then can be taken as 'the will to live', that she is now ready to move on from her past experience having reworked her trauma into an empowering narrative. Marling says that 'the literal truth' and details of Prairie's story 'matter less' than the fact that telling it helped Prairie and the group to deal with their respective traumas (Birnbaum, *The OA*). For instance, when presented with apparent evidence that Prairie is lying via the books, Buck grasps the study on angels and says 'I'm keeping this one' ('Invisible Self'). The group's passionate performance of the Movements is also an apt metaphor for this approach to trauma recovery, visually establishing the concept of sceptical scriptotherapy—of rewriting traumatic events beyond individuals' control, in this instance gun violence—into empowering supernatural stories.

In addition, Marling says of the Movements that she aimed to 'create a language of movement' for inarticulable traumas, those that are difficult to talk about, 'a profound ritual and a language for communicating' (Leon). This is significant in terms of representing trauma and diversity in particular. The diverse new five gain the ability to more easily communicate their traumas to each other, which includes ostensibly taboo experiences of marginalised individuals that are frequently excluded from mainstream trauma discourse. This includes Prairie's possible sexual abuse by Hap, as noted; Buck's transition; Betty's feelings of invisibility, loneliness and irrelevance as an older woman; and French's questioning of his sexuality in the second season. Taylor Driggers notes:

> [As Prairie] finds a way to cope with her traumatic experience through the telling of her outlandish tale, her listeners also begin to find unexpected healing in their own lives. … Hearing her story of traumatic self-discovery … leads them to truths they desperately need.

For example, Buck, the youngest of the group, is inspired by French and sees him as the kind of man he aims to be; Steve reminds Betty of her brother, and she saves him from military school by giving the men trying to take him there her brother's 50,000 dollar inheritance cheque, seeing this as an opportunity to atone for her apparent 'failing' of Theo; and Steve and Jesse likewise help Betty collect her brother's belongings, where Betty and Jesse also bond over their lost relations. Marling describes the Movements as a 'technology' that Prairie 'introduces to the boys', an 'immediate … form of communication … for a deeper truth that is hard to get at with facts' (Bentley). This approach further reworks conventional trauma representation, *The OA* employing both the supernatural and experimental language (interpretive dance) to further explore the traumatic experiences of diverse characters rather than repressing them. The idea of the Movements as a means for communicating difficult topics is especially evident in the scene where Hap takes Homer to a hotel in Cuba in order to help him kidnap Renata. Homer, who has formed a relationship with Prairie in captivity, is unfaithful, having been instructed by Hap to have sex with Renata so Hap can drug her. When Homer returns to Hap's prison, Scott is dead and the captives perform the Movements in order to resurrect him. Here, Homer appears to communicate his apology to Prairie via the dance steps, while Prairie shifts from anger to sadness to forgiveness during the ritual. According to Marling, Prairie and Homer 'are having this pretty basic lover's quarrel', in which Homer 'touches some place of profound pain to show her how ashamed he is, and she forgives him, and they do all of this without any dialogue at all. They do all of it just moving through these movements, and somehow you understand it all and you understand it even more immediately than if they had used language' (Bentley).

As to whether the Movements magically defeated the assailant or distracted him long enough for a school staff member to tackle him is dependent upon whether the viewer interprets Prairie's narrative as true or false. This lucidity likewise has unique implications for the viewer's engagement with the trauma narrative. Similar to *The OA*'s characters, the viewer is presented with an overtly escapist narrative whereby they, too, can gain temporary comfort by consciously suspending disbelief and deciding the more positive, supernatural interpretation of events to be canon. Indeed, Marling confirms that storytelling rather than testimony as a means of healing is a central theme of the series and a comforting notion to instil in the viewer: 'We need storytellers now more than ever … to find a light … when things get … overwhelming' (Bonner). For instance, Prairie is shot and taken to hospital, but it is unclear if the new five have transported her to another dimension.[3] While 'teleporting' in the ambulance, Prairie muses 'they said it would be invisible, like jumping into an invisible current that just carries you away' ('Invisible Self'), and the final scene shows Prairie waking in a white room calling for Homer, which can be taken as either a hospital or Homer's NDE location.[4] Furthermore, the cafeteria dance scene is obviously outlandish, but *The OA* appears to encourage viewers to buy into it for the purposes of escapism. While the scene runs

[3] Prairie literally taking the bullet for the new five appears to visually reference second-hand trauma and *The OA*'s definition of the concept as 'taking on somebody else's pain'.

[4] The second season appears to take place within this location, which is presented as another dimension. However, this can also be taken logically as Prairie dreaming while in a coma.

the risk of being humorous, its serious tone, poignant music and the actors' earnest portrayals of the new five's belief in Prairie's narrative all appear part of an attempt to garner an emotional reaction and investment from viewers. Thus, my specific sceptical scriptotherapical approach demonstrates a new way to read such narratives, which is vital because stories, such as *The OA*, are not just about representing trauma in nuanced ways but also allowing the audience to visualise and engage with their own traumatic experience.

Mr Robot

As with *The OA*, Sam Esmail's *Mr Robot* is a relevant case study of sceptical scriptotherapy due to its diverse characters and their experience of trauma. The series is also diverse in terms of production. *Mr Robot*'s creator, Sam Esmail, was born to Egyptian immigrant parents in New Jersey and raised Muslim. Esmail cited the 2011 Arab Spring as an inspiration for developing the series' main character, Elliot Alderson (Rami Malek, also Egyptian-American). Esmail saw his own relatives' involvement in the Arab Spring and witnessed young people who were dissatisfied with their society using technology to make a positive change instead of using it as a tool of destruction, with Esmail noting that Elliot is a thinly veiled version of himself (Gross). Quickly becoming a cult hit and lauded for accurately portraying hacker culture, *Mr Robot* has received critical acclaim and received multiple accolades, including two Golden Globe Awards, three Primetime Emmy Awards and a Peabody Award. While widely praised for its technical accuracy, *Mr Robot* is also noted for attempting to accurately represent its protagonist's mental health issues. Malek worked closely with a psychologist during the series' production to learn about the different disorders Elliot experiences, which include dissociative identity disorder, clinical depression, delusions, paranoia, anger issues, social anxiety and drug abuse (Elliot is shown to take morphine, suboxone and ecstasy throughout the series). Esmail has acknowledged several major influences for *Mr Robot*, crediting David Fincher's *Fight Club* (1999) as an inspiration for Elliot's character in particular, as well as for the anti-consumerist, anti-establishment and anti-capitalist attitude of the series' characters. Nevertheless, Lauren Larson for *GQ* notes, '*Mr Robot* elevates the *Fight Club* formula: the show's mindfuckery lubes us up to think about society (Elliot's and ours) in a discerning way, but it is not the main event', with Elliot's mental illness instead being the central theme of the series.

Mr Robot follows Elliot's life as a cybersecurity engineer and secret vigilante hacker, with Elliot spending nights bringing society's hidden criminals to justice. In the pilot, Elliot is recruited by an insurrectionary anarchist known as Mr Robot (Christian Slater, who also plays Elliot's father Edward Alderson in flashbacks,), and joins his team of hacktivists known as fsociety. The group's main goal is to cancel all consumer debt by encrypting all of the data of one of the largest incorporations in the world, E Corp (which Elliot refers to as 'Evil Corp'). However, it is revealed that Elliot has created a number of alternate narratives as a coping mechanism for his various past and present-day traumas, presenting the viewer with a dual narrative structure. *Mr Robot* is therefore an appropriate text to read in terms of sceptical scriptotherapy. Elliot is a man of colour and survivor of childhood sexual abuse. While *Mr Robot* makes only brief references to Elliot's status as an Egyptian-American and Muslim-American culture, the series represents a marginalised trauma survivor reworking his trauma into an alternative, empowering narrative. Similar to *The OA*, the viewer is presented with two narratives: a realist, tragic narrative of childhood sexual abuse and its related traumas, and a more palatable, supernatural narrative wherein Elliot is a superhero-like character and concepts such as dimension-hopping are a reality. The alternate, superhero narrative in *Mr Robot* is used to explore the psychological effects of abuse, specifically the need for victims to attain a feeling of agency and control. Like Prairie reworking her story as she relays it to the new five, Elliot's internal life is revealed via voiceovers that provide insight into his mental state and his opinions on his surroundings, positioning the viewers as listeners to which he communicates his narrative. Elliot breaks the fourth wall and refers to the viewer as his 'imaginary friend', at times looking straight into the camera and asking viewers for reassurance of his perceptions. This technique pulls the viewer further into Elliot's point of view and the fiction of the series, and is similar to how both the viewers and characters within *The OA* are encouraged to willingly suspend disbelief and gain temporary comfort from the series' obviously escapist narrative.

Mr Robot's Persona as the Protector Personality

Because of Elliot's dissociative identity disorder, Mr Robot is a new manifestation of Elliot's deceased father, Edward Alderson, in the form of a hacker and idealised version of Edward. Mr Robot is also revealed to be Elliot's first alternate personality (the protector personality). Dissociative identity disorder (DID, previously known as multiple personality disorder) is when an individual has multiple, distinct personalities and the different identities control a person's behaviour at different times. DID is usually caused by past trauma during childhood (generally extreme and repetitive physical, sexual or emotional abuse) and the condition can cause memory loss, delusions or depression. The dissociative aspect is considered a coping mechanism whereby the person literally shuts off or dissociates themselves from an experience that is too traumatic to assimilate with their conscious self. Similar to dissociation, which, as discussed in Chap. 3, sufferers may 'look' at a traumatic event 'from a distance or disappear altogether', leaving other parts of their personality to experience and 'store' the event (van der Kolk, 'Intrusive' 168). To recall, Herman likewise notes that victims of sexual abuse not only 'feel as though the event is not happening to her, as though she is observing it from outside her body' (*Trauma* 43) but may 'begin to form separated personality fragments' (*Trauma* 103). The protector personality/Mr Robot was created to replace Elliot's father who molested him during childhood and 'to protect Elliot from intolerable situations' ('Whoami') such as his childhood sexual abuse, and subsequent violent and traumatic events. Similar to Prairie's narrative of angels, alternate dimensions and magical dance sequences, Elliot creating Mr Robot as a child (using his imagination) was the only way he could attain a sense of agency over his situation, granting him a way of retaliating against his oppressor. Mr Robot informs Elliot: 'The only reason I'm here is to make sure no one ever hurts you. That was supposed to be your father's job, but he failed. He was too weak. But you. You were strong. *You fought back. The only way you could.* You only brought me here to protect you from him' ('Whoami', emphasis mine). However, unlike more conventional trauma narratives, the series emphasises that this retreat into fantasy is beneficial to Elliot, as he informs Mr Robot 'you're nothing like him. That's why I created you. You're the father I needed. Not the father I had' ('Request Timeout'). By contrast, when Elliot's repressed memories of his father are uncovered, he informs his therapist that he wants to 'go back to forgetting' ('Request Timeout'). When Elliot's childhood friend and love interest Angela Moss (Portia Doubleday) discovers that he can conjure his late father in his mind, she likewise contemplates the apparent comfort of escapism: 'I envy you, I wish I could talk to my [deceased] mom again, even if she isn't real' ('eps1.8_m1rr0r1ng.qt').

Mr Robot also hides the memories of Edward's abuse by only showing Elliot the happy memories of his father, 'the memories when the two of [them] were friends before' ('Request Timeout'). Mr Robot stores 'the truth' so Elliot would 'never have to see it or feel it' ('Request Timeout'). For example, Elliot only remembers experiences including cinema trips with his father, their *Back to the Future* (Robert Zemeckis, 1985) Halloween costumes, and the incident where Edward did not scold Elliot for stealing money from one of the customers at Edward's computer store (the store was called 'Mr Robot', while stealing is a common symptom of childhood abuse). Mr Robot was initially created when Elliot, as a child, jumped out of his bedroom window to escape Edward's abuse, a memory Elliot/Mr Robot rewrites as Edward pushing Elliot out of a window because Elliot told his mother about Edward's leukaemia. According to Elliot, Edward revealed his sickness only to his son, swearing him to silence, and Edward's sickness was the reason he was fired from E Corp, where he and a number of other employees contracted leukaemia (including Angela's mother). Avenging his father's death is purportedly the reason Elliot wants to take down E Corp. However, it is also suggested that Elliot's father did not have leukaemia and that this condition is another screen memory Elliot employs to repress his father's abuse. For example, the flashback of the last interaction between Elliot and Edward shows Edward asking Elliot for forgiveness as Elliot accuses him of being 'just sick' and 'not want[ing] to admit it' ('eps3.7dont-delete-me.ko'). The topic of conversation in this scene can be interpreted as either Edward's leukaemia or abuse of his son. Analogous scenes include that in which the young Elliot is questioned by a doctor having fallen from the window, which abruptly cuts off as Elliot is about to explain the event, and the scene where Edward swears Elliot to secrecy about his illness in Edward's car, which can again be interpreted as Elliot replacing his father's paedophilia in his mind with leukaemia as Edward says to his son in this scene 'let's just keep that between us, okay? Don't even tell your mom. Just our little secret' ('eps2.4m4ster-s1ave.aes'). When adult Elliot is about to uncover his repressed memories of his childhood abuse, Mr Robot pleads with Elliot's psychiatrist Krista Gordon (Gloria Reuben) to change the subject and tries to distract Elliot from the conversation 'Elliot, look at me. ... Krista, if you do this, it will destroy him. ... I can't protect you anymore' ('Proxy Authentication Required').

Sitcom Episode

A pertinent example of the Mr Robot persona protecting Elliot from traumatic experiences is when Elliot is assaulted in prison (Elliot was arrested for hacking his therapist's cheating ex-boyfriend). Mr Robot transports Elliot to a late eighties/early nineties sitcom-like world, informing Elliot that they are in 'a place that makes everything better, a place that changes you' ('eps2.4_m4ster-s1ave.aes'). Here, Mr Robot encourages Elliot to retreat into fantasy so he does not have to feel the pain of the beating:

> It'll feel good if you let it. Believing it's real makes it so ... Sometimes lies can be useful, Elliot. Sometimes they protect you. ... When the truth is painful. ... A lie is the only remedy. 'Cause too much truth, too much honesty, that'll kill ya. ... Everything you see, it's all here for you. To help you. You should just try going along with it. ('eps2.4_m4ster-s1ave.aes')

The line 'it'll feel good if you let it' is evocative of what a predator may say to a child while inflicting sexual abuse, suggesting that Elliot is reworking his father's words into a more palatable alternative. As evident above, however, the topic quickly changes to the benefits of imagining alternative scenarios as a means of escapism from harsh realities. For the first fifteen minutes of this episode, *Mr Robot* is presented in a similar style to series such as Jeff Franklin's *Full House* (1987-1995) and William Bickley and Michael Warren's *Family Matters* (1989-1997). Saxophone-laden interstitial music plays, a low-quality green screen is employed, and the episode is presented in the 4:3 format. The upbeat song played over the opening credits reflects Elliot's paranoia and mistrust of authorial figures (both symptomatic of intra-familial childhood abuse), as well as Elliot's attempts to rewrite his traumatic memories: 'Used to be you could trust in the story, vilify the villains and celebrate the heroes. ... Those were better days. ... Everything's gonna be alright. ... Imagine yourself in a world numb with pain. ... Stand up tall and surely you'll survive. ... Let your mind just drift away.' These lyrics also align with what Katherine Cox calls a 'rhythmical mantra' recited by traumatised individuals in attempts to feel secure and downplay the severity of traumatic events (14). The opening credits feature 'caught in the act' introductions to the imaginary sitcom's cast, with each character forcibly smiling as the camera lingers in close-up, further suggesting concepts of denial and rewriting of reality.

The sitcom-esque episode begins with Elliot, Mr Robot/Edward, Elliot's mother Magda (Sandrine Holt) and Elliot's sister Darlene (Carly Chaikin) driving in a convertible. The image of Elliot being beaten in the real world is visible in the car's rear-view mirror and Darlene's game console. Mr Robot constantly tries to distract Elliot from these images and insists that 'it's best to stay focused on the road ahead', to which a live audience applauds. Darlene similarly refuses to show Elliot what is occurring in the real world. When Elliot asks to look at her Gameboy, she insists 'no way, you're not allowed. Your father told you to look ahead.' The characters' lines of dialogue and actions reflect Elliot's past and present-day traumas, and a canned laugh track plays in response to disturbing content. For example, Elliot's DID and the window incident are played as jokes. Darlene asks her mother, 'Mom, Elliot's hearing voices' to which Magda replies 'What else is new?', and the audience erupts with laughter. Magda then says 'If you're not careful, Dad's gonna push you out a window again!' which generates the same response from the audience. The violence Elliot's mother inflicted upon him and Darlene as children is also framed as comedic, as the audience laughs whenever Elliot's mother punches Darlene and exaggerated, cartoon punch sounds are employed. Magda questions Darlene 'Are your fingers broken, young lady?' to which Darlene quips 'Not yet, but in this family, it's only a matter of time! [audience laughs]'. Further traumatic incidents that have occurred in the series are repeated but in a more light-hearted manner, again suggesting that they are being reworked by Elliot into a more acceptable narrative. Elliot's boss Gideon Goddard (Michel Gill) was shot by a man who accused him of being involved in fsociety's takedown of E Corp and resulting financial meltdown. In Elliot's sitcom world, by contrast, Gideon is run over by a car driven by ALF, the Alien puppet from the American television sitcom *ALF* (Paul Fusco and Tom Patchett, 1986–1990), and Mr Robot advises Elliot that 'it's time to move past it'. Tyrell Welleck (Martin Wallström), the former Senior Vice President of Technology for E Corp who secretly works with fsociety, is also tied up in the trunk of the convertible. In the real world, Elliot fears he has murdered Tyrell when his mind was overtaken by Mr Robot, as Tyrell has gone missing and Elliot's last memory before he transformed into Mr Robot was reaching for a gun in front of Tyrell. In the sitcom world, Tyrell can be heard screaming from the trunk and comedically shouting 'I'm a businessman! A very important businessman!' Whenever Elliot questions Mr Robot about this, Mr Robot again insists that he ignores it. The therapeutic function of this evasive, fantasy world continues to be emphasised, however, when Elliot awakes in reality. Elliot collapses into Mr Robot's arms and whispers 'thank you'.

Mr Robot as the Superhero Personality, Escapism

As noted, Mr Robot is not only a surrogate father for Elliot but also one of Elliot's alter personalities. As noted, Mr Robot is played by the same actor who plays Elliot's father in flashbacks, Christian Slater, and the series shows either: shots of Mr Robot intercut with Elliot; Mr Robot talking to others while Elliot stands silently beside him; Elliot talking to himself; or Mr Robot in place of Elliot when he takes over Elliot's mind completely and controls it. For instance, when Angela dies, Mr Robot narrates to the viewer instead of Elliot, who is shown in the background as Mr Robot addresses the camera. Elliot has shut down and Mr Robot does not want Elliot to have to think about Angela's death. As Maria Guallar Comas points out, in scenes before Elliot and Mr Robot are revealed to be the same person, both characters are in the same quadrant of the frame in public spaces but are physically separated from the other people in the frame and are surrounded by negative space, in addition to being crammed into one side of the frame (23). Further, Elliot does not remember the moments when Mr Robot takes over, so Elliot has no recollection of starting fsociety and believes himself to have been recruited by Mr Robot. As noted, Elliot constructs Mr Robot as an off-the-grid leader of the underground hacker-collective called fsociety, which plans to bring down the world's largest conglomerate, E Corp, an act Elliot refers to as literally 'sav[ing] the world' ('eps1.8_m1rr0r1ng.qt'). This operation is referred to as the Five/Nine Hack and aims to erase consumer debt. In transforming himself into such an individual, then, Elliot refigures himself as an empowered being in the form of a superhero-like character who has the ability to achieve feats including 'the greatest redistribution of wealth in history' ('410 Gone') and 'the inevitable downfall of human civilisation' ('eps3.1undo.gz'). Superhero iconography is incorporated throughout the series. For instance, when planning fsociety with Darlene in a flashback, Elliot puts on his father's Mr Robot employee jacket and superhero music swells. Elliot also pairs the jacket with a Halloween Monopoly Man mask inspired by an obscure horror film from the 1980s that Elliot and his sister grew up watching (the mask is subsequently used in fsociety's video manifestos and video warnings about the group's upcoming actions). Like Prairie envisioning herself as The Original Angel in place of Hap's victim, Elliot's transformation grants him agency as he turns himself into a powerful figure. Elliot's empowering transformation into his father is also in contrast to texts explored in Chap. 3 such as *Twin Peaks*, in which the possessed Leland has no control over transforming into his childhood abuser BOB and the experience is shown to be traumatic.

Regarding escapism, Herman notes that an avoidance of traumatic memories in the patient 'leads to a stagnation in the recovery process, while approaching them too precipitately leads to a fruitless and damaging reliving of the trauma' (*Trauma* 176). Gibbs observes that both of these dynamics may be readily found in the fictional literature of trauma, as sufferer-narrators either 'deny, mislead, or elide details of traumatic events' or 'gradually edge towards confronting their pasts' (25). In such texts, the structure of the narrative can be interpreted as narrative procrastination, circling around a traumatic event as a form of evasive narration (Gibbs 52) (as discussed in relation to narrative crash and *The Shining*'s proliferation of narratives examined in Chap. 2). Elliot's Five/Nine Hack can be interpreted in a similar manner. As with the inmates' quest to uncover all of the Movements in *The OA*, the Hack serves a therapeutic function for Elliot whereby he gives himself an achievable goal. This goal is in contrast to overriding forces he cannot overcome such as his childhood abuse and thus a way of acquiring feelings of control. While the sceptical scriptotherapical approach I argue is exemplified in *Mr Robot* differs to conventional readings of escapism such as that of Herman's in that Elliot is shown to regret approaching his traumatic memories, Elliot's goal of taking down E Corp serves as a means of distraction from traumatic memories for him. A number of fsociety's activities are criminal and potentially dangerous to civilians, such as the secret operation the group refers to as Stage 2 which involves blowing up the building that houses the paper banking records of E Corp (a plan Elliot is unaware of, as Mr Robot organised it when he took over Elliot's mind). Nevertheless, that fsociety's and Elliot's attacks escalate aligns with how conventional trauma narrators deny, mislead or elide traumatic events, but by contrast appear healing (albeit severely misguided) for Elliot. For instance, when asked why he continues fsociety by Darlene, who insists that Elliot's goal is not to hurt others ('this is not who you are. You don't blow up buildings. You don't hurt people … what is this, then?'), Elliot responds 'I know … [but] there's something inside me that can't let go of what we started' ('eps3.3metadata.par2'). Mr Robot also says of these hacking activities that there will 'always be something else. Another symbol to destroy, more people to save. This is an *endless* war' ('eXit', emphasis mine).

Indeed, while Elliot convinces himself that the purpose of fsociety is to liberate the world from consumer debt and ensnaring the multinational in a fatal financial crisis, more than an appeal to justice or avenging his father, it is the promise of autonomy that most motivates Elliot (Volmar 3). When Elliot first 'meets' Mr Robot in the pilot, Mr Robot informs Elliot that fsociety will 'unravel' E Corp's 'delusion of control' and that he is here 'because you sense something wrong with the world, something you can't explain but you know it controls you and everyone you care about' ('eps1.0_hellofriend.mov'). Elliot's technical virtuosity also renders him almost omnipotent among others, whose personal accounts he hacks in what he justifies as 'protect[ing] them' ('Ones-and-zer0es.mpeg'). Elliot tells Krista 'I don't just hack you … I hack everyone—my friends, co-workers. But I've helped a lot of people' ('eps1.6v1ew-s0urce.flv'). For instance, in the pilot, Elliot hacks the owner of a Manhattan coffee shop who circulates child pornography. However, Elliot intercepts all of the traffic on the owner's network with his laptop and berates the owner that 'whoever is in control of the exit nodes is also in control of the traffic. Which makes me the one in control', after which Elliot pulls over his black hoodie in the manner of what Daniel Volmar describes as 'a night-time vigilante' (2). Elliot also hacks Angela's boyfriend, whom he discovers is cheating on her, but decides not to say anything as he is easier to 'manage' than her previous partners ('eps1.0_hellofriend.mov'). Krista theorises that one of Elliot's biggest issues is 'feeling like [he is] not in control' ('Ones-and-zer0es.mpeg'). In this scene, Elliot expresses he is able to exercise only limited agency, envisioning the world as a place in which free will exists but in the context of very limited choices, which may not even qualify as choices at all: 'How do we know if we're in control? That we're not just making the best of what comes at us and that's it. Trying to constantly pick between two shitty options … what the fuck is the difference … our choices are prepaid for us a long time ago' ('Ones-and-zer0es.mpeg'). Krista also diagnoses Elliot with 'delusions of grandeur' ('eps3.8_stage3.torrent'). This is evident in Elliot convincing himself that he can control the world via his god-like hacking abilities, and that he has the ability to 'set into motion' a new future ('eps3.0power-saver-mode.h'). Elliot's Mr Robot persona also convinces Tyrell to work with fsociety by telling him that they will become 'gods' ('eps2.4m4ster-s1ave.aes'). Later, when Elliot decides to undo the Five/Nine Hack, an operation that 'was meant to empower' fsociety ('eps3.1undo.gz'), he begins working for E Corp and 'purging' ('eps3.1undo.gz') the company of their immoral workers. Here, Elliot declares that he will 'fix the world I broke, and put it back together better than it was before' ('eps3.1undo.gz').

Alternate Reality, Oppressive Forces

The series uses both Elliot's superhero persona and the concept of alternate realities to further explore the theme of escapism as a means of regaining agency for marginalised trauma survivors. The penultimate and final episodes of the series ('Whoami' and 'Hello, Elliot') reveal that the Elliot the series centred on was not the real Elliot Alderson, but another of his constructed alter personalities called 'The Mastermind'.[5] To keep Elliot safe while he 'saved the world', this identity had locked Elliot away in an alternate reality. The Mastermind persona had become so in control of Elliot's mind that this alter forgot he was a persona of Elliot's DID. The Mastermind was a personality Elliot created to carry his rage about being abused and sought vengeance against anyone else that attempts to control Elliot, those who 'play God without permission' ('shutdown -r'). As a child, Elliot was subjected to overriding forces in the form of his father, so The Mastermind alter now tries to rid the world of other harmful, controlling forces such as paedophiles, pollution, mortgage scammers, pension embezzlers and sexual harassers. Forming fsociety was a further way for The Mastermind to rid Elliot's world of powerful forces such as consumer capitalism (specifically E Corp), organised religion (which The Mastermind refers to as 'the charlatans that want to run us' ('eps2.2init1.asec')) and other conglomerates that 'take advantage' of individuals including 'the FBI, NSA, CIA … all the world's leaders' ('eps3.0power-saver-mode.h').

[5] In 'Hello Elliot', it is also revealed that Elliot has created a number of other alternate personalities, which together resemble his family. These alters include 'The Mother Personality', an alter which resembles Elliot's mother and acts as a persecutor who 'blames Elliot for the abuse'. Indeed, Elliot has what resembles flashbacks or 'visions' of his mother physically harming his childhood self and chastising him ('I hate you. You're nothing. You're worthless. … He was weak, and you're just as weak as him'). Elliot also created a version of his younger self 'who emerged to handle the abuse he couldn't tolerate', analogous to splitting. The last personality revealed is the viewer, who Elliot refers to as 'the voyeurs'.

As Elliot/The Mastermind says of fsociety's goals, 'Sometimes I dream of saving the world, saving everyone from the invisible hand … at work controlling us even if it pushes us past our threshold of pain' ('eps1.0_hellofriend.mov'). Mr Robot also refers to these powerful groups as gods, 'a force that's bigger than you … our closest deities are the society of the richest, most influential men in existence … men who fuck over the rest of us for profit' ('eps3.8_stage3.torrent'). In the alternate reality, Elliot imagines Krista informing The Mastermind that Mr Robot wanted to 'shelter' Elliot by changing his past while The Mastermind wanted to save his future:

> it was his future you really wanted to protect. … That's why you went to such great lengths to take down all the evil that surrounded him in the real world. So you formed fsociety … you wanted to save the entire world so you could make it better for him, no matter the cost. That's why you hid him here, turning his harsh world into a fantasy. Trapping him in an endless loop. ('Hello, Elliot')

The fantasy referred to here is where the real Elliot's consciousness lives. As with the sitcom world, this place is 'a world where everything's better' ('Hello, Elliot'). The fantasy is an alternate reality in which Elliot's father is alive and never abused him, Magda did not physically assault or emotionally abuse Elliot growing up and Angela is still alive and engaged to Elliot. Elliot did not have an accident via the window and his mother informs him that she and Edward would 'never, ever hurt [him]' because they 'love [him] more than anything' ('Whoami'). Darlene does not exist in this world; The Mastermind removed her because she is Elliot's only family member in reality and may make him want to return to the real world. The Elliot in the fantasy world is confident and does not have any mental disorders or traumas resulting from his father's abuse such as social anxiety, as The Mastermind observes that Elliot has an active social life and many friends: 'this is what normal people do when they're happy, right? Get married, start a family, surround themselves with people they love, with people that love them' ('Whoami'). Here, Elliot also makes a good living and works for E Corp, which is a morally good company called F Corp (similar to 'fsociety') and is 'the best thing in everyone's lives' ('Whoami'). The fantasy world is a 'recursive loop' constructed to keep the real Elliot 'occupied' as The Mastermind took over Elliot's consciousness ('Hello, Elliot'). However, the benefits of this escapism are again stressed. The Elliot in this world says that he is 'stuck in a repetitive, boring routine that feels endless', consisting of morning routines and work, and that he would like 'to be someone with a more exciting life' ('Whoami'). Yet, he acknowledges that this situation is a better alternative: 'in the end, I know I'm lucky to be where I am' ('Whoami'). When Elliot's Mastermind persona travels to the alternate world, he meets the alternate Elliot who creates fan fiction and artwork about The Mastermind. This Elliot says that when he gets bored, he writes a story, which is the superhero-like narrative viewers were shown throughout the series about Elliot's vigilante-hacker adventures. Elliot says The Mastermind is 'someone with a more exciting life. Like a superhero, except his power would be computers. He's a cybersecurity engineer by day, vigilante hacker by night' ('Whoami'). However, Elliot asserts that while he sometimes 'fantasise[s] about being' this character, he does not actually want to be him because he is angry, alone, abnormal and 'has no life' ('Whoami').[6]

Further Characters: Agency and Escapism

Lack of agency is an experience expressed by further characters in *Mr Robot*, a number of whom like Elliot consciously rework traumatic events into more palatable, fantastical alternatives. As with *The OA*, these characters are likewise diverse in terms of race, gender and sexuality. For example, Tyrell joins fsociety because he wants god-like powers over the world, while Darlene joins because she wants to lead a revolution. Both characters are bisexual, underscoring their status as marginalised characters, and both are subjected to oppressive forces, Darlene's in the form of Magda's abuse and Tyrell's being his superiors at E Corp and later the Dark Army, a Chinese hacker group that participates in fsociety's attack on E Corp. Likewise, the main antagonist of *Mr Robot*, Whiterose (BD Wong), aims to construct a machine which she believes will enable people to enter a parallel universe. Whiterose is the leader of the all-powerful Dark Army. She also runs the Deus Group, which consists of the most powerful people in the world. Similar to *The OA*, Whiterose situates her machine under a power plant. She plans for this machine to blow up, resulting in the death

[6]This scene suggests that the real Elliot still has some degree of agency over The Mastermind persona when The Mastermind persona is in control.

of multitudes, but believes the explosion will result in everyone being reincarnated in the alternate reality: 'we will be found again as soon as this world around us transforms into a parallel world … we will be reborn as new, finally liberated from the horrific and brutal past that we've been shackled to for so long' ('eXit'). The project is referred to by Angela's father Phillip Price (Michael Cristofer) as 'an obsessive, psychotic denial of reality … [a] fantasy' ('409 Conflict'). Whiterose is a trans woman of colour who was not allowed to transition or marry the man she loved in her youth, who, in turn, killed himself when forced to marry another woman. In attempting to build a machine that will transport the world to an alternate reality where her lover is alive and she can live as a woman, Whiterose, like Elliot, resorts into fantasy as a means of regaining agency over these traumas. Whiterose says 'do you ever think that if you imagined or believed in something, it could come true. Simply by will?' and informs Elliot that she is 'tired' of the current world and 'the pain it causes', and wants to 'deliver us a better world' ('eXit'). When Elliot travels to Whiterose's plant in an attempt to stop her from causing the explosion, Whiterose gives Elliot the choice to activate the alternate world/instigate the explosion before shooting herself. Elliot must play a choose-your-own-adventure style point-and-click computer game which offers the choice to 'leave your friend or stay' (the choice-based game further evoking the series' central theme of agency). Elliot picks 'stay' and an earthquake begins. As with *The OA*, this scene lends credence to the series' depiction of the fantastic and presents the viewer with another dual narrative. Here, Elliot either gets knocked out and his subconscious within the alternate reality awakens or he actually travels to this place, simultaneously suggesting that the alternate reality is a real environment and a construct of Elliot's mind. While the supernatural alternative is less probable, the viewer and characters within the series can consciously choose to believe this more positive interpretation of events.

Angela also engages in conscious escapism as a means of evading trauma and acquiring control. Like Elliot, Angela says she wants 'to change the world' ('br4ve-trave1er.asf') and Doubleday says of her character that her ultimate goal is to garner 'power' (Birnbaum, *Mr Robot*). Angela reopens a lawsuit against E Corp for the death of her mother and later works for the conglomerate so as to change it from within, as a means of regaining agency over the trauma of her mother's death. Later, Whiterose brainwashes a number of people to recruit them into helping her with her powerplant project, and instructs Angela to blow up a number of E Corp buildings. Afterwards, Angela convinces herself that Whiterose's machine will reverse these deaths and bring back her mother from the dead when she travels to the alternate reality. Angela tells Elliot that Whiterose can 'make it like none of this ever happened … including what happened to our parents' ('eps3.0power-saver-mode.h'). Angela's escapism is underscored in the scene where she continuously rewinds the news segment of the buildings blowing up. She tells Darlene: 'See? They all came back. They're all fine. … Everyone's gonna be okay. Everyone's gonna be okay' ('eps3.6fredrick+tanya.chk'). The refrain of 'everyone's gonna be okay' here again reflects Cox's concept of the rhythmical mantra recited by traumatised individuals as a means of denial and comfort (14). The image of rewinding in trauma fiction has been noted by Gibbs. Gibbs points out how Billy in *Slaughterhouse-Five* experiences a war film backwards, a technique Gibbs also observes in later trauma texts such as Jonathan Safran Foer's *Extremely Loud and Incredibly Close*, Martin Amis' *Time's Arrow* and Sandra Gilbert's essay 'Writing Wrong' (60). Gibbs argues that the futility of this coping mechanism is underlined in *Slaughterhouse-Five* 'by the imagined reversal going to conspicuously absurd lengths' (61). For Gibbs, 'a careful reading demonstrates that Billy's attempt to use this reversal to escape from traumatic events is tacitly acknowledged to fail … preceding this he is described as seeing it backwards, then forwards again. Even from the outset, the fantasy of escape is denied' (61). In *Mr Robot*, by contrast, fantasy is the only means of survival for traumatised characters, as denying escapism is frequently shown to be a worse alternative. As noted, Whiterose commits suicide. Angela, when informed by her father that the casualties in the bombings will not be brought back to life in the alternate reality, cries that she had 'to believe there was a purpose' to their deaths ('409 Conflict') and goads Whiterose's workers into murdering her when advised by Philip 'to find a way to live with what you did' ('401 Unauthorized'). While the 'real' Elliot wakes up in the final scene of the series, his recovery is left ambiguous and the apparent comfort of escapism is still suggested as the voiceover of The Mastermind persona says that he and Mr Robot will '*always* be a part of Elliot Alderson … the best part because we're the part that always showed up … stayed … [and] changed him' ('Hello, Elliot'). As with *The OA*, then, sceptical scriptotherapy is a necessary framework through which to read more recent, popular texts by diverse writers, such as *Mr Robot*, that counter conventional readings of escapism.

Conclusion

This chapter read *The OA* and *Mr Robot* through sceptical scriptotherapy. Sceptical scriptotherapy is a type of writing that features characters consciously reworking traumatic events into fantastical alternatives rather than relaying them exactly as they happened as a means of healing. A number of further texts can be analysed in terms of sceptical scriptotherapy. An example of such is Marling and Batmanglij's film *Sound of My Voice*, the protagonist of which can be interpreted as either a time traveller or a traumatised con artist attempting to gain custody of her daughter. Similar to *Mr Robot*, Peele's *Us* features Black protagonists taking on new identities and displacing their traumatic experiences to more palatable, supernatural alternatives. The female protagonist of Prano Bailey-Bond's *Censor* (2021) reworks her kidnapping of an actress, murder of multiple film crew members and potential childhood killing of her sister into an alternate version of events whereby she returns her sister safely home to their parents, because, 'people construct stories to cope … you'd be surprised what the human brain can edit out when it can't handle the truth'. *Candyman*, examined in the previous chapter on polynarration, can likewise be read in terms of sceptical scriptotherapy, as the Candyman myth is employed by the Black community to process racial trauma. To recall, Burke informs Anthony that 'Candyman is how we deal with the fact that these things happened', and the Candyman Hive transforms murdered Black men into an empowered figure who retaliates against racial oppressors. Damon Lindelof and Tom Perrotta's television series *The Leftovers* (2014–2017) can likewise be read in terms of sceptical scriptotherapy. The series centres on a major traumatic event: the sudden evaporation of 2 per cent of the world's population. Major discourses decline, such as mainstream religion, in favour of newly formed cults and systems of belief, with the protagonists choosing to believe in obviously fictitious narratives as a means of soothing their personal and collective traumas. Perrotta refers to this strategy as 'embracing the healing fiction', which he says is employed in the postmodern world of extreme 'realists', those that 'view the world sceptically' (Robinson). The final episode shows the series' protagonists Kevin (Justin Theroux) and Nora (Carrie Coon) presenting one another with improbable but comforting narratives of travelling to another world, while at the same time making explicit that 'I'm not trying to sell you anything. It's just a nicer story' than the series' actual tragic events (Robinson). Perrotta likens this line of thinking to the postmodern view of grand narratives, specifically religion, a discourse increasingly considered fictional in the postmodern age, but one that individuals nevertheless buy into for the purposes of comfort:

> When Nora tells this story, she puts both Kevin and the viewer in the traditional position of the person who has been presented with a religious narrative. We have no proof. We have a choice to believe or not to believe … from a psychological perspective … life is so hard that sometimes you need a fiction in order to heal it. (Robinson)

Here, *The Leftovers* reworks the naturalist counterfactual form to represent trauma stemming from deterministic forces (Nick and Nora are traumatised by environmental forces in the form of a mass disaster-like event). These characters imagine an alternate history as a means of coping with this trauma, and the viewer is likewise presented with two different narratives: a more probable, tragic narrative and a 'nicer', fantastical alternative.

Ultimately, due to the increase in diversity and unique trauma representation in popular culture, new and more feminist trauma paradigms such as sceptical scriptotherapy and polynarration are vital in our reconsideration of the paradigms through which trauma narratives have traditionally been understood and read. My concept of sceptical scriptotherapy provides an original, critical challenge to dominant conceptions of trauma recovery; contributes to wider feminist trauma theory on active memory and recovery; and presents a new feminist framework for analysing more innovative and diverse trauma representations found in contemporary popular culture. As with the previous chapter on polynarration, examining texts such as *The OA* and *Mr Robot* establishes the importance of popular culture to the trauma discourse, in relation to both diversity and how it enables scholarship to uncover new trauma themes and techniques, therefore expanding the extent of trauma representation.

CHAPTER 6

Perpetrator Trauma in Video Games: Dan Salvato's *Doki Doki Literature Club* and Toby Fox's *Undertale*

Since the late 1990s, an extensive range of video games increasingly incorporate trauma as a theme, centring on traumatic events and granting players the ability to control traumatised protagonists. This includes both victim- and perpetrator-protagonists. This chapter explores perpetrator trauma in two metafictional video games: Dan Salvato's *Doki Doki Literature Club* (referred to here as *Doki Doki*) and Toby Fox's *Undertale*. Before analysing these texts, there are two issues that need addressing: the concept of transmissibility and how perpetrator trauma is defined in cultural trauma criticism.

Transmission and Perpetrator Trauma

To begin with the transmission argument, one of the goals of mainstream trauma narratives is to convey or transmit affect onto the reader the experiences of their protagonists, to employ experimental forms so as to make the reader feel, as close as possible, the symptoms of traumatised characters. As noted, this idea of 'transmissibility' is in accordance with the Caruthian model and remains influential upon trauma representations and cultural trauma criticism. It is important to distinguish transmission from vicarious trauma (also called second-hand or secondary trauma). Vicarious trauma may occur 'between victims and their listeners or viewers who are [disturbed] … to the extent of claiming' to be traumatised from engaging

S. Travers, *Trauma in American Popular Culture and Cult Texts, 1980–2020*, https://doi.org/10.1007/978-3-031-13287-2_6

with 'difficult material' (Luckhurst, *Trauma* 2). LaCapra distinguishes between the two. LaCapra claims that transmission is 'a kind of virtual experience through which one puts oneself in the other's position *while recognising the difference of that position*' (78, emphasis mine). By contrast, LaCapra describes vicarious trauma as the listener, reader or viewer appropriating the victim's experience, 'to confuse self and other, and collapse all distinctions' (21) between the victim and the listener, reader or viewer.

Regarding perpetrator trauma, this is a model of trauma that focuses on the traumatic experience of the perpetrator. While the experience of the perpetrator is important to the 1980 concept of PTSD (to recall, the concept was based in part on the experience of the Vietnam veterans), it is another type of trauma that has been largely excluded by cultural trauma theory (Gibbs 19). When discussing dominant cultural criticism's 'privileging of the representation of some traumas over others', Nick Hodgin and Amit Thakkar highlight the focus on the trauma of the victim 'over that of the perpetrator' (2). Raya Morag says that it is 'taken for granted that canonical psychological and psychiatric trauma research … has been carried out from the perspective of identification with the victim, preventing trauma research from offering the tools necessary to cope with the post-traumatic perpetrator' (8). Craps and Bond also point out that 'the dearth of research on representations of perpetrators has only just begun to be addressed', that cultural criticism tends to prioritise 'the experience of the victim' (9). According to Gibbs, cultural criticism's exclusion of perpetrator trauma is 'functionally political (in effect, if not intention)' in that it represents 'a denial of the US's wider status as a perpetrator' in relation to American armed forces such as Vietnam and Gulf War veterans (199). The denial of the US's status as perpetrator is 'a much wider phenomenon in contemporary American society' (199) and the exclusion of perpetrator trauma in cultural criticism 'has enabled the transformation of perpetrators into victims' (21). As Gibbs notes, 'if trauma is deliberately and exclusively associated with victimhood, then this dangerously excludes the possibility that if one suffers from trauma one can be a perpetrator' (16). For Gibbs, this practice is evident in American trauma fiction, whereby representations of perpetrator trauma tend to be characterised by both an 'inversion of perpetrator/victim status' (19) and 'linked to the notion of agency, in particular the denial of agency, as a means to slough off responsibility' (247). This kind of representation can be found in American war literature. Such texts tend to situate their narrator-protagonists, often members of US forces and perpetrators of violence, as individuals in a position of 'limited agency' (Gibbs 82) who are 'subject to the aggressive demands of military hierarchy' (Gibbs 22). Gibbs says, 'whatever deplorable actions in which they are directly or indirectly involved, they are nevertheless also simultaneously victims of traumatised circumstances over which they have no control' (167). Similarly, Tal, who is one of the few theorists to examine perpetrator trauma in depth (Gibbs 162), notes that 'the soldier in combat is both victim and victimiser' (Tal 10). This kind of representation, 'the conflation of perpetrator and victim', ameliorates the violence of US forces (Gibbs 178). Further, protagonists are often depicted as experiencing symptoms associated with victim trauma, such as flashbacks and nightmares, which are again presented in experimental forms to encourage the reader to empathise with these perpetrator-protagonists.

Morag's study claims that cinema also tends to represent perpetrator trauma in a similar way to victim trauma despite there being 'differences in real-world examples' (Morag 16–19 in Pheasant-Kelly, 'Signifying' 11). Morag compares perpetrator trauma to victim trauma and identifies a number of differences between them. For the perpetrator, these differences include: a 'preoccupation with the space' where the traumatic event took place instead of 'the time'; 'empathy and possible mourning for the victim of trauma'; 'a confession rather than a forgetting' of the traumatic event; and 'the experience of a profound moral contradiction rather than intrusive memories' (Morag 15–19 in Pheasant-Kelly, 'Signifying' 11). For Morag, 'the core of perpetrator trauma lies in the profound moral contradictions challenging the perpetrators rather than in their psychological disintegration or intrusive memories', as events perpetrators tend to face are not sudden overwhelming events, but events in which they participated and 'made a conscious decision to act', and sometimes were aware of in advance (16). While perpetrators may suffer from 'recurring belated symptoms' similar to those of trauma victims, they relate to 'the perplexity of denial of wrongdoing or the inability to prevent returning to the guilt-ridden experience rather than to the incomprehensibility of the traumatic event' (Morag 17). Therefore, perpetrator trauma, as Morag says, 'induces perpetrators to reflect on fissures in their own integrity' (17).

Indeed, Morag also identifies guilt as an integral symptom of perpetrator trauma. However, she points out that the type of guilt experienced by perpetrators is an 'active epistemic sense of guilt' that is motivated 'by empathy for the victims and characterised by assuming responsibility and looking "forward"' in the form of making reparations for atrocities, rather than 'guilt feelings' (16). Guilt feelings are characterised by 'identification, melancholic narcissism, self-pity, and looking "backward"' (16). Morag argues that guilt feelings 'indicate a pre-conceptualisation of the veterans as victims' (16), and, quoting from Robert Jay Lifton's writings on Vietnam War veterans in 'Survivor Experience and Traumatic Syndrome', these 'usually take the form of either an individual proclaiming their own evil in a self-enclosed fashion that permits little change or a numbed guilt that avoids confronting one's own culpability' (Lifton in Morag 15). Guilt is linked to victims as well in terms of survivor guilt, which refers to an individual feeling guilty because they survived a traumatic event when others did not (Morag 2). Further, it is important to emphasise that guilt and trauma are related but are not identical and therefore should not be conflated. As noted, perpetrator trauma is the name of the model of trauma that focuses on the traumatic experience of the perpetrator, and guilt is a symptom of this kind of trauma, as are a preoccupation with space, empathy and mourning for the trauma victim, feelings of responsibility, confession and moral contradiction.

Gibbs also identifies guilt as a symptom associated with perpetrator trauma. According to Gibbs, trauma amongst American veterans is often represented as 'linked to the guilt at their culpable role in the horrors they witnessed' (18). Furthermore, Gibbs argues that in certain texts, 'perpetrator trauma may be particularly marked by a gradual rather than instant or sudden process' (169). He claims that 'an insidious accretion of guilt coupled with the disillusionment about the case being fought for evidently prompts perpetrator trauma' in certain protagonists and that 'perpetrator trauma in this sense is often the result of guilt or shame over a series of acts of increasing intensity or depravity' (169). Therefore, while perpetrator trauma can certainly stem from a singular extraordinary event, the representation of perpetrator trauma in certain combat narratives is in contrast to the Freudian-Caruthian belatedness model and more in line with the alternative feminist and post-colonial trauma theories that argue for trauma as an ongoing experience. Indeed, Gibbs notes that a number of combat narratives 'represent the kind of insidious trauma discussed … in … Brown's theories that depart from the dominant model's insistence on sudden, event-based trauma' (48) and that 'the insidious nature of perpetrator trauma … is a defining difference from the dominant model' (175). Gibbs cites Anthony Swofford's *Jarhead*, Joel Turnipseed's *Baghdad Express*, Evan Wright's *Generation Kill*, Nathaniel Fick's *One Bullet Away* and Kayla William's *Love My Rifle More than You* as examples of this kind of perpetrator trauma representation. Gibbs observes that the protagonists in these texts 'regularly [perpetrate] acts of violence' (176) and are shown to experience a 'gradually worsening situation' (182) over a significant period of time, adding that the 'components of boredom and frustration in these soldiers' experiences' emphasise the 'insidious character of [their] perpetrator trauma' (174–175). For example, in *Baghdad Express*, Turnipseed's perpetrator trauma is described as 'gradual' (Gibbs 174), consisting of 'soul-rendering boredom, fear, the ache of lost love, murder, death' (Turnipseed 41). Similarly, Williams in *Love My Rifle More than You* says that 'deployment in Iraq was like [a] yearlong invitation to think ... you started to go crazy with the thinking and the waiting and the sitting around' (25).

Perpetrator Trauma in Video Games

While the dominant trauma model places a high importance on transmission when representing trauma victims, how trauma fiction and film might attempt to convey perpetrator trauma in this way has been somewhat overlooked in trauma criticism. By this I mean to simulate in the audience symptoms specifically associated with perpetrator trauma and characters who have committed violence and wrongdoings, such as feelings of responsibility, guilt and moral contradiction. However, the attempted transmission of perpetrator trauma can be found in popular culture, specifically video games. Because of the increased level of interactivity unique to the game form, the medium can more effectively encourage its audiences to identify and empathise with protagonists, and more directly experience traumatised perspectives (Smethurst, 'Playing Dead' 835). According to Smethurst, this increased level of interactivity and the way in which players have varying degrees of what is called narrative agency over the events and characters in these texts have been used as a means of transmitting to players symptoms associated with perpetrator trauma outlined above ('Playing Dead' 821). Smethurst and Craps identify interactivity as 'the most commonly referenced characteristic that marks games out as different from other media' and makes them particularly suited to do this ('Playing with Trauma' 271). Smethurst states:

> By innovating with the interactivity and player agency that define them as a medium, games have the power not only to match these trauma fictions in representing the trauma of the victim rhetorically but also to involve the

> player in the complicity, guilt, and potential trauma of the perpetrator through methods uniquely available to games. ('Playing Dead' 821)

Indeed, games are generally understood to 'require active engagement from an external agent (player) in order to function, since they gate their content behind manual skill- and/or puzzle-based challenges that ask the player to perform significant actions in order to progress through them' (Smethurst and Craps, 'Playing with Trauma' 271). Games offer players the opportunity to interact both with the secondary worlds and with characters that are already fully represented on the screen. The protagonist immediately responds to player commands, which can include moving to specific locations within the game's world and performing specific acts within it. Such abilities, the player's capacity to interact with the environment crafted by the game, are called the player's ludic agency.

Games can also enable players to impact the narrative of the text, which is called narrative agency. This includes abilities such as selecting parts of the dialogue of the controllable protagonist, in addition to making choices that alter the direction of the narrative, determine the content or scenes the game presents us with and influence the ending presented at the conclusion of the game.[1] In particular, games that interconnect ludic play and narrative engagement, or moral choice games that employ decision-making as one of their main mechanics, allow players to virtually perpetrate the violent and immoral acts which occur in the narrative or play out on our screens. This can be regarded as an attempt by the game to transmit to the player symptoms associated with perpetrator trauma such as feelings of responsibility, moral contradiction and guilt (commonly referred to as 'gamer guilt'). Dawn Stobbart adds that 'narrative agency arguably increases players' narrative and emotional investment' (116), bringing 'about immersion in games', which makes the player feel as though they are part of the game narrative and 'experience the actions taking place on the screen almost as if they are happening to the player' (8). The game feels real to the player because the world exists in that moment of playing, and moral choices carry a weight

[1] Regarding the dialogue of the controllable protagonist, certain games employ a gameplay mechanic called a dialogue tree or a conversation tree. When the controllable protagonist is speaking with another, non-playable character (NPC), the player can choose what the controllable protagonist says. A number of lines of pre-written dialogue are presented to the player during a conversation scene and the player selects one of these lines.

similar to real-world choices for the player despite affecting a secondary world. Immersion, then, can also be identified as a feature of games that makes them suitable for transmitting perpetrator trauma, as Stobbart notes that the narrative agency granted to players increases their 'narrative and emotional investment' (116), which 'can cause the player to mirror the feelings of the characters being controlled, such as fear, terror and horror, as well as giving a sense of accomplishment when achieving game milestones such as defeating an enemy, solving a puzzle or killing a "horrific monster"' (5–6).

The distinction between the 'game world' and the 'real world' is important to interrogate in terms of the psychological effect of in-game moral decisions. Terms such as 'secondary world' and 'virtual violence' are significant, underlining the idea that gaming is sufficiently bracketed off from 'reality' and that this is not real perpetrator trauma that the player experiences, but a simulated form of it. Smethurst summarises this idea when discussing Arnt Jensen's *Limbo* (2010):

> *Limbo* is not capable of traumatising the player directly. Rather *Limbo*'s visuals, sounds, and mechanics work in harmony to mount what Ian Bogost has called a 'procedural' argument about how it might feel to be traumatised—a virtual representation of the symptoms of trauma experienced by the player through play. Just as one experiences a book by reading it, or a testimony by listening to it. ('Playing Dead' 819)

My approach is similar to Smethurst and Craps' criticism. I argue that players at best experience a simulated form of perpetrator trauma symptoms, and that this is similar to the attempted transmission of trauma symptoms via experimental forms in trauma literature and film for which dominant, Caruthian cultural criticism argues. Indeed, Smethurst and Craps emphasise the importance of addressing both the differences and similarities between video games and more traditional media in terms of trauma representation as a means of further establishing games as a suitable medium for representing perpetrator trauma. For example, how games use the particular characteristics of the medium in order to uniquely 'represent the symptomatology ... of psychological trauma' (Smethurst and Craps, 'Playing with Trauma' 818), as well as how they 'borrow' from or extend the existing tropes of trauma representation in literature and cinema (Smethurst, 'Playing Dead' 819).

It is also important to interrogate the feasibility of the transmission argument in regards to both traditional media and games, and take into consideration the particular cultural factors that contribute to criticism on transmissibility. The notion of transmissibility in trauma fiction has been subject to criticism on multiple grounds, as Gibbs notes, 'not least that transmissibility is no more possible than representation' (28) (again, representation here refers to fictional forms such as literature and film). For Gibbs, to suggest that a text could somehow mimic 'the original experience of trauma for a reader, is deeply problematic' (28). Gibbs says, 'the transmission argument effaces the representational dimension of trauma narratives' (28) and elides the 'categorical difference between the experience of a trauma sufferer, a witness, and the second-hand reader' (29). Likewise, Wulf Kansteiner dismisses transmissibility, pointing out that there is a 'vast, uncharted psychological territory that lies between the experience of extreme trauma on the one hand and the much more frequent encounter with representations of violence on the other' (195). Anne Rothe criticises the 'empirically unsustainable idea' that successful trauma texts could communicate trauma 'so that the reader of this oxymoronically unmediated trauma narrative can experience it in its literal totality' (162). However, despite criticism from theorists such as Gibbs, Kansteiner and Rothe, the transmission argument is 'a major motivating force behind cultural trauma theory' (Gibbs 29). Indeed, Gibbs suggests that Caruth's theories regarding transmission are perhaps 'initially attractive precisely because as readers of trauma texts we desire affect and emotional response' (28).

We can consider the transmission of perpetrator trauma in games in a similar way. The questioning of players' moral framework does not actually translate to anything significant outside the environment of the video game. Players appear to experience a simulated form of perpetrator trauma. An example of this is a player feeling perpetrator-associated symptoms such as guilt, having negatively affected a virtual world or 'harmed' fictional characters. Certainly, players have attested to this phenomenon in game criticism and reviews. However, these reactions might again be the result of players' desire for affect and emotional response. That is, the interdependency between culture and audience whereby the desire for affect and response is either confused with or taken as evidence by critics/players as games successfully transmitting affect onto the player. In other words, critics claim that games simulate symptoms of perpetrator trauma, such as guilt, simply because the players want this to be the case, and because the players desire to be emotionally affected by texts; this desire is mistaken for games actually simulating these symptoms in the player, and, in turn, further establishes the argument that games have the capacity to do this.

Regarding the influence of the transmission argument, as Smethurst and Craps observe, we should take into account the assertion 'by proponents of literature that a good proportion of its value lies in its capacity to foster empathy and a greater understanding of other ... human beings' ('Playing with Trauma' 274). 'Unsurprisingly', Smethurst and Craps note, 'empathy is a hot topic in game studies discourse as well' ('Playing with Trauma' 274). It is perhaps possible that the extent to which game discourse confers value upon affect and emotional response has established the idea that this particular way of conceiving trauma in gaming is the only way, and critics, in turn, feel required to analyse games in these terms (i.e., the idea that a marker of a 'good' game is one that transmits affect onto the player). Furthermore, in addition to academic publications, much criticism on gaming is found online and outside of the academic sphere (in sources such as non-academic blogs, reviews and forums). Thus, the more emotionally charged and hyperbolic nature of online rhetoric should be taken into account here as well. For instance, commentators on forums may overstate their experience of playing horror games, claiming to be 'traumatised' as opposed to mildly disturbed; reviewers may similarly exaggerate their emotional reaction to a game narrative for promotional purposes. Regardless of whether games successfully transmit affect onto players and simulate in individuals perpetrator-associated symptoms, however, there is certainly an attempt made by these texts to do so, which marks these texts out as innovative in their approach to perpetrator trauma. I say innovative approach rather than representation here because while traumatised characters within a game text can be defined in terms of trauma representation, the concept of representation is not relevant to perpetrator trauma in the player who exists outside of the text.

Moral Choice Games

There are a variety of ways games attempt to induce perpetrator symptoms in players, the most common of which include feelings of responsibility, guilt and moral contradiction. A pertinent example of such are 'moral choice' games, which 'contain an interactive narrative wherein elements of the narrative respond to and are altered by the player's input and choices'

(Joyce). There are a number of different types of morality systems or ways in which games can present narrative choices to players. Games may contain a binary system of morality. This is where narrative choices are offered to players in pairs and the choices are obviously aligned with one of the two moral poles, enabling players to choose a 'good' or 'evil' path in the game story. Elements of the game narrative will differ depending upon our choices, such as its ending, the status of the protagonist as hero or villain and the relationship between the protagonist and the game's NPCs (non-playable characters, the game narrative's supporting cast). This kind of morality system forms the centre-piece of Ken Levine's and Alyssa Finley's *Bioshock* (2007), a dystopian-themed game that revolves around one moral conundrum: to have the protagonist rescue or kill the game world's remaining citizens, a group of ten-year-old girls called the 'Little Sisters'. Kill them and their life-force strengthens the protagonist's weapons (thereby making the game easier for the player to progress through), or spare them, which is an option that gives the protagonist less power but grants the player what Stobbart describes as a 'sense of accomplishment' and 'direct satisfaction' (Stobbart 192). *Bioshock* branches into two distinct possible endings depending on our choice: the 'good'/happy ending, which shows the protagonist living a happy life having raised the Sisters as his children, or the 'bad'/tragic ending, which shows the protagonist unleashing armoured super-soldiers onto the world.

Other types of moral choice games are more complex than those with a binary framework, in that they present the player with either a pair or selection of choices that are morally ambiguous. These games thrust most of the responsibility of deciphering right from wrong or good from evil choices onto the player by having one decide between, for example, equally unpleasant acts in ethical dilemmas or seemingly reasonable choices that have unexpected consequences later in the narrative. The titles from Telltale Games are prime examples of such. Telltale Games are episodic graphic adventure games and purely narrative titles, devoid of many of the ludic and RPG (role-playing game) elements of games such as *Bioshock*.[2] Instead, the focus of the game is to progress through the story via the use of 'decision points' where the narrative 'can split into multiple new

[2] An RPG or role-playing game is a game genre in which the player controls the actions of a character immersed in a well-defined world. A key feature of the genre is that characters grow in power and abilities, which increase each time the player accumulates a certain amount of experience, such as when they defeat a certain number of enemies.

branches, all of which are exclusive' (Heron and Belford). The choices may 'then feed into future choices' and alter elements 'of the story presented' (Heron and Belford). Player decisions in Telltale Games influence certain events in the narrative, but to a greater extent affect elements such as characterisation, theme and how the supporting characters in the game view the protagonist. Michael James Heron and Pauline Helen Belford point out, 'we may nuance the story told ... exploring variations on a theme', while at the same time not 'wander[ing] far from the main trunk of the story'. In other words, the general trajectory the player takes through the game is always the same, but the player can influence certain details of narrative events and how the protagonist reacts to them. Despite following a fairly linear narrative and apparent limitations in player agency, Telltale Games attempt to make the player feel that their decisions have consequences. For instance, because choices are not clearly grouped as good or evil, players are not only subjected to making difficult decisions, but left considering whether they made the right choice. However, this occurs only on the first playthrough, as the player is prevented from seeing the consequences of alternative choices (Smethurst and Craps, 'Playing with Trauma' 282).

Both the binary moral choice system and the branching narrative framework have been reported to simulate perpetrator trauma symptoms in players and include feelings of responsibility, guilt and moral contradiction. Regarding binary choice games such as *Bioshock*, Amanda Lange claims that only 10 per cent of players transgress conventional 'moral boundaries'. Regarding branching narrative games such as Telltale's *The Walking Dead: Season One* (2012), Stobbart notes that the decisions the player makes are often difficult and that the 'choice required for a positive outcome is not always the clearest or the easiest one', such as 'choosing who will eat, for example, when the survivors find food' (106). However, games that incorporate either the binary morality system or the branching narrative framework have been subject to criticism in terms of their linearity. Lange argues that because the player is offered 'obvious choices that map along an easily decipherable binary' of good and evil, their narrative agency is limited. Lindsey Joyce says that the player is led to believe that their choices 'will alter the course and outcome of the story', but 'beyond scoring a different morality, the outcomes of the player's choice' are 'too similar to generate a truly unique experience'. Telltale Games have received similar observations. The games enable player agency over characterisation and theme, but are limited in regards to player agency over plot, which is especially evident upon multiple playthroughs.

As with trauma fiction, critics such as Lange and Joyce suggest that games need to become more creative in their approach to morality and apparent transmission of perpetrator trauma. Indeed, there are a number of games that attempt to break out of the traditional conventions of video game moral decision-making. In particular, games extend morality mechanics and choice-based systems through a gameplay mechanic called the Butterfly Effect, which enables player actions and decisions to generate a chain of narrative events, leading individual players down drastically different paths in the game story and generating multiple different endings. For instance, an in-game action as minor as picking up an object can lead to a sequence of events that eventually result in the death of a major character. This technique is evident in games directed by David Cage such as *Detroit: Become Human* (2018). In the opening chapter, selecting the wrong dialogue choices results in the death of Connor, one of the game's protagonists, and absence of this character in the rest of the game. According to Joyce, it is this 'multiplicity' that is important for increasing feelings of agency for players, and, we can add, feelings of responsibility, guilt and moral contradiction. Joyce asserts: 'the story must … seem mutable. Developers must write multiple narrative beats and outcomes for the player to experience and have a sense of control … those component narrative pieces must also come together to form a whole given the player's input.'

However, while the multiplicity of games may increase players' narrative agency, the questioning of players' moral framework again does not seem to translate to anything significant outside of the environment of the video game. Thus, it still remains questionable if these games are successful in simulating perpetrator-related symptoms in players. One way of overcoming both issues in gaming (multiplicity and transmission) is the employment of metafiction and games interrogating these aspects of their medium. The employment of metafictional techniques and thematics in games is a trend that is becoming popular, particularly in moral choice indie games that seek new ways to increase player immersion and narrative agency.[3] Metafiction in more traditional narrative forms such as literature and film tends to work to distance audiences from the world of the text in

[3] Indie games are independently produced video games created by an individual or small team of game developers. Indie games' lack of controlling interests of mainstream developers frequently results in creative experimentation and innovation.

foregrounding its artifice, often for the purposes of parody or critiquing the particular discourse it works within. By contrast, games employ metafiction to both critique the medium and create greater audience immersion. Metafiction in gaming forces the player to reflect on their role as both the audience for and participant in the narrative. For instance, when a game makes a metafictional reference to the text as a game and chastises the player's violent in-game actions, as opposed to those of the controllable protagonist, the player is urged to consider the ways in which they engage with virtual violence (and by extension violent content more generally) for the purposes of entertainment. What is potentially explored successfully in games that employ metafiction, what we could call the 'moral point' of these texts, is players' capacity for immorality in relation to the game medium specifically; how, even though 'it's only a game', players engage with virtual violence for the purposes of entertainment.

Metafictional games reprimand players for in-game violence linked to expected play patterns of gamers, specifically, the player's contribution to the endorsement of violent media entertainment by engaging with such texts and expected play patterns of replayability. Replayability is the way in which users may play a game multiple times so as to see the results of choices that differ to those made in their first playthrough, to access narrative content they had missed (the differing narratives in games' alternative routes are referred to as potential and actualised textualities or narratives). While players usually play 'heroically' in moral choice games, a common tendency among gamers is that they play 'villainously' when replaying the game. Lange reports that players 'are willing to experiment with alternatives only on their second playthroughs', with over half of the participants she interviewed claiming to 'always play through first following the good storyline' and that 'evil is held for a second, lower priority playthrough after they've played the game "correctly"'. There are two reasons for this. Firstly, during an initial playthrough the player is 'apt to be more invested and feel more connected to the choices they make', whereas with repeat playthroughs, the player is 'selecting choices from a place of increased knowledge', and that knowledge the player 'possesses and brings to the narrative in repeat playthroughs lacks the necessity of critical reflection the first play experience attempts to provide' (Joyce). The second reason is curiosity and entertainment. In players' more detached replays of games, in-game decisions are not the result of their moral convictions but experimenting with narrative alternatives. For

Joyce, these tendencies for player replayability are undesirable for developers who wish to have the player think over their choices in a 'meaningful' way.

Perpetrator Trauma in Metafictional Video Games

It is well established, then, that players enjoy the ability afforded by games to explore their immorality and thus the glorification of violence. Yet, games' potential to translate their interrogation of players' moral framework to a real-world context has only begun to be explored. Overcoming this issue via metafiction has been considered by Smethurst and Stobbart, both of whom examine how Cory David's and Francois Coulon's *Spec Ops: The Line* (2012) questions players' culpability in the game's violence by 'punishing' them for playing the game. However, a thorough analysis of games' capacity to translate the interrogation of players' moral framework to a real-world context via metafiction remains wanting. This chapter will examine how *Doki Doki* and *Undertale* do this in a number of further, innovative ways; how these games employ metafictional techniques to interrogate players for their engagement with the wider game medium. Specifically, I examine how *Doki Doki* and *Undertale* use metafiction to explore player immorality in relation to expected play patterns of replayability and the medium's sensationalism of violence. Topics explored include *Doki Doki*'s and *Undertale*'s unique interactivity vis-à-vis player game saves and the game engine's recognition of player behaviours in real-time game play. I will discuss the games' collapse of the distinction between player and avatar, their references to the genre of moral choice games and their chastisement of the player for both engaging with these games and attempting to replay the game so as to undo certain actions and try out different in-game choices. The player in *Doki Doki* and *Undertale* then is made to feel perpetrator trauma symptoms including feelings of responsibility, guilt and moral contradiction, specifically for how they interact with games. In addition, I will demonstrate how Gibbs' characterisation of perpetrator trauma as insidious and 'gradual' (169) can be conveyed via 'the violent ludic structures of mainstream [games]' (Stobbart 64), whereby games like *Doki Doki* and *Undertale* require players to commit increasingly violent virtual killings in order to successfully progress through the game, and via the employment of increasingly disturbing content the further the player engages with the game.

Undertale

Undertale is a metafictional game that relies on player input to determine the outcomes of the narrative and characters, some of which are self-aware of their status as fictional NPCs and acknowledge the player as a separate entity from the protagonist. Released in 2015 by indie developer Toby Fox, *Undertale* is a 2D, RPG-inspired game in which the player controls a human child who has fallen into the Underground, an underground world populated by monsters. The player has the option to either murder the monsters they encounter, which is called the Genocide Route, or spare them via non-violent contextual means, such as befriending and helping them with their problems, which is called the Pacifist Route. The narrative differs markedly depending upon the player's actions. The Pacifist Route is a light-hearted adventure story with a happy ending whereby the protagonist can either break out of the Underground, or remain there and become adopted by Toriel, a goat-woman who acts as a guide throughout the game. The Pacifist Route concludes with either the protagonist enjoying a sunset outside or being tucked into bed by Toriel. If the Genocide Route is chosen, *Undertale* becomes a horror game and the player is the villain. The protagonist gains enormous power and the Underground's various towns are empty, as the NPCs fear the protagonist. The visual tone of the game changes from brightly coloured to grey scale, the humorous dialogue becomes pessimistic and the upbeat soundtrack becomes distorted. When the player empties the Underground of all its monster-inhabitants, *Undertale* ends with the protagonist destroying the game itself. There is also a range of Neutral Routes based upon specific choices, such as which and how many characters the player kills or spares, and how the player interacts with them during their playthrough.

I argue that *Undertale* attempts to transmit perpetrator trauma symptoms to the player in relation to their replayability and sensationalism of violence. As *Undertale* is an RPG, the game critiques in particular the violent ludic structures of mainstream games, whereby the player is not only required to commit virtual violence in order to progress (defeating enemies encountered) but rewarded for doing so in the form of granting the controllable protagonist increasing power and abilities (usually called experience points). *Undertale* simulates in the player feelings of responsibility, guilt and moral contradiction for this approach to gaming in a number of ways. In the Genocide Route, the player is punished rather than rewarded for their cumulative violence in the form of increasingly disturbing content, dialogue and imagery, undermining the usual power fantasies in RPGs and again evoking texts that represent perpetrator trauma as an 'insidious accretion of guilt … over a series of acts of increasing intensity or depravity' (Gibbs 169). How *Undertale* punishes the player in this way is a concept inherited from *Spec Ops: The Line*. According to Stobbart, games typically 'require the player to learn skills and offer a reward system for the successful implementation of those skills' (65). In *Spec Ops: The Line*, as 'the player controls the protagonist's journey deeper into' the game's environment, they begin to realise 'that the reward for the successful implementation of ludic skills' is instead 'a punishment' (65). The game's tone becomes darker and the player is subjected to 'scenes of escalating brutality' (65). Stobbart adds that 'while the game does not allow a diegetic choice, at each point in the game where actions are immoral … the player is offered a choice: to stop playing', that players' continuation of the game is 'a conscious choice' (69). That *Undertale* contains a number of Neutral Routes and endings further implicates the player in the horrific events taking place in the narrative, simulating in the player feelings of responsibility for the violence that unfolds onscreen as the player has the option at any time to cease killing the monsters they encounter and begin sparing them (sparing any character during the Genocide Route changes it to a Neutral Route and the player is presented with one of the Neutral Endings).

Killing monsters in *Undertale* is also in contrast to conventional in-game killings whereby the player progresses through repeated fight sequences with numerous faceless enemies, or as Tanya Krzywinska says, to kill 'without guilt or a second thought' (153). To return to Stobbart's suggestion that games such as *Spec Ops* challenge 'the usual video game rhetoric of shooting as playing for one of shooting as killing' (70), in turn foregrounding players' endorsement of violent media content, characters during *Undertale*'s Genocide Route plead with the player to spare them, while characters such as Papyrus, a skeleton monster the player befriends during the Pacifist/Neutral Routes, asserts that the player can do better as they murder him. Papyrus says: 'Well, that's not what I expected. But, st-still, I believe in you. You can do a little better.' Further, in enabling players to kill characters in the Genocide Route that they befriended and emotionally invested in during previous Pacifist or Neutral playthroughs, *Undertale* simulates guilt in the player specifically by acknowledging replayability tendencies, how players tend to play the 'good' path in their initial playthrough and the 'evil' path on their second in order to access additional narrative content. Indeed, *Undertale* makes use of the game medium's capacity to tell more slow-burning stories, enabling the player/protagonist to grow close to Papyrus over the course of the Pacifist or Neutral Routes. During these routes the character is gradually revealed to be inadequate in his profession as a member of the King's guard and without any friends, as well as have a mental disability that reduces his mind to a child-like state. Players can also phone Papyrus during their travels through the Underground, getting additional lines of the character's humorous dialogue and words of encouragement.

Certain self-aware characters make direct reference to players' replayability tendencies and endorsement of violent media content. These characters acknowledge the player as a separate entity from the protagonist that has the power to save and reload at will, and remark that the player is playing the Genocide Route because they are accustomed to the violent ludic structures of mainstream games and to satisfy their narrative curiosity. In the Genocide Route, Papyrus' brother Sans says to player: 'you're not doing this because you're evil. You're doing this because you can, and because you can you feel you have to', evoking the arbitrary nature of decision-making found in the ludic structures of games. Moreover, the game keeps track of players' saved files, with characters remembering and making reference to player actions performed before they loaded their saved game. Players who restart a game without saving to undo an in-game murder will find that characters are 'aware' of this and will berate the player for abusing their power of the save state and performing virtual violence as a means of experimentation. An instance of such occurs at the beginning of the game, where a common mistake for players is to accidentally kill Toriel during the tutorials wherein she teaches us about the game's rules and combat mechanics. When the player starts the game over to undo this act, the game's dialogue changes to reflect that they have already killed Toriel in their previous playthrough. Toriel comments on the protagonist's familiarity, that she feels as though she 'knows' them from somewhere, and recalls certain dialogue choices made by the player in their previous playthrough (such as the player's preferred choice of pie when Toriel offers the protagonist dessert). Flowey, a talking flower that can fully retain his memories between saves and one of the game's antagonists, also appears and whispers, 'You murdered her. And then you went back, because you regretted it', acknowledging the prior in-game killing as the player's rather than the controllable protagonist's.

Undertale also acknowledges when players start the entire game over to try a different route, with each playthrough affected by how they played previously. The order of playthroughs has varying consequences. When playing the Genocide Route after the Pacifist/Neutral Routes, Flowey condemns the player for undoing the happy ending the player previously achieved for the Underground's inhabitants. Here, Flowey reveals himself to have once been a player-like entity that has played through the game multiple times. Flowey became self-aware of his environment as a video game, gaining the ability to save and load the game, and likens himself to the player. He explains that he too turned evil out of ennui, bemoaning his boredom and claiming to have exhausted every possible in-game action and decision branch. He chastises the player for doing the same and denounces the wider game medium, making reference to in-game violence in direct relation to players' tendency for replayability. Flowey points out that the player's emotional impact is lessened upon repeat playthroughs and that replayability is driven by a sadistic narrative curiosity, that the need to complete a game 100 per cent tempts players to go back and play a game's evil route:

> I soon realised I didn't feel anything about anyone. My compassion had disappeared! … Interested, I decided to experiment. … At first, I used my powers for good. I became 'friends' with everyone. I solved all their problems … [that] was amusing. For a while. As time repeated, people proved themselves predictable. What would this person say if I gave them this? What would they do if I said this to them? … what would happen if I killed them. … It all started because I was curious. … You understand, [player's name]. I've done everything this world has to offer. … I've won every game. I've lost every game. I've appeased everyone. I've killed everyone. Sets of numbers. Lines of dialogue. I've seen them all.[4]

Flowey ponders if curiosity is an excuse for the power fantasy that games grant players, allowing one to exert total control over a virtual world and

[4] A similar ideology is at play in Jonathan Nolan and Lisa Joy's 2016 sci-fi series *Westworld*, in which protagonist William (Jimmi Simpson) is revealed to be the young Man in Black (Ed Harris), the antagonist of the series. *Westworld* is set in a technologically advanced Wild-West-themed amusement park, the equivalent of a live-action video game, and caters to paying guests who can indulge their fantasies within the park. The reveal of William's identity evokes player patterns of replayability: having visited Westworld for over thirty years and 'tried out' the role of the hero and all of the narrative routes that encompass, William is tempted to play the evil route to access different narrative content.

its inhabitants as a means of entertainment: 'what an excuse! You of all people must know how liberating it is to act this way.' Further, if the player goes through the Genocide Route again or multiple times, Flowey fittingly punishes the replay-minded player: he vows to remain silent from now onwards, refusing to give any more dialogue or new content and giving the player no incentive to play the Genocide Route again. Going beyond games such as *Spec Ops: The Line*, *Undertale* thwarts the player's narrative curiosity, acknowledging how players' tendencies for replayability are additionally motivated by this, and how players commit immoral in-game actions as a means of experimenting with narrative alternatives.

Playing the Genocide Route before the Pacifist also has unique effects on the narrative and again employs a number of innovative tactics to simulate in the player perpetrator symptoms for their replayability and engagement with violent video game content. Upon re-launching the game post-Genocide Route, the player is presented with a black screen with howling wind sound effects and the game's window is unnamed. Inputs have no effect and the player must wait ten minutes before engaging with the game. The use of a blank screen here (a reflective surface) can be interpreted as a mirror whereby the player must look at themselves and reflect upon their actions having played cruelly through the Genocide Route. This technique incorporates a further concept of perpetrator trauma, whereby the perpetrator reflects on the fissures of their own integrity rather than incomprehensibility of the traumatic event. When the ten-minute wait has passed, the player is given the option to reset the game world and play through it again. Here, the player is addressed by another self-aware character that looks almost identical to the game's protagonist. They question the player about the violence inherent to engaging with games, such as why one finds it entertaining to destroy a game world and recreate it, and if the player thinks they are above consequences when interacting with a virtual world. In further attempts by the game to make the player feel like a trauma perpetrator (albeit one that engages in virtual violence), this character is revealed to be the game's main antagonist and introduces themselves with the name the player purportedly gave to the controllable protagonist at the beginning of the game (while the controllable protagonist is revealed to be named 'Frisk'). Players conventionally use their own name when naming a controllable protagonist and if the player does so in *Undertale*, the name of the game's villain is literally that of the player. This character thanks the player for killing the inhabitants of the game and describes themselves as an inner demon of the controllable protagonist. This character informs the player that they were 'brought to life' by the controllable protagonist's killing, increasing power (the experience/execution points gained whenever a monster is killed) and, therefore, the player's sadistic curiosity.[5] This character says to the player: 'You. With your guidance … we eradicated. … Every time a number increases, that feeling. That's me. [player's name].' Indeed, Stobbart likewise notes that when games reveal the controllable protagonist as the narrative's antagonist, this makes the player feel further complicit in the game's violence (162).

Furthermore, if the player chooses to reset the game and try out the Pacifist/Neutral Routes, these routes are altered to incorporate references to the player's immoral acts in their previous Genocide playthrough. The player cannot undo their actions in the Genocide Route. Playing the Pacifist Route after the Genocide (entitled the Soulless Pacifist Route by the game) presents players with an altered version of the Pacifist/Neutral endings. As noted, the protagonist can either remain in the Underground with Toriel as her child, or go to the surface with the rest of the monsters, ending the game with the protagonist watching a sunset with the monsters or being tucked into bed by Toriel. The Soulless Pacifist route concludes with either the protagonist in bed facing the camera with glowing red eyes, accompanied by a low-pitched laugh and frightening music, or a photograph of the monsters with their faces crossed out, reminding the player that they murdered them in their previous playthrough. Ultimately then, these endings simulate in the player perpetrator trauma symptoms including feelings of responsibility, guilt and moral contradiction for their perpetration of virtual violence for entertainment and narrative curiosity.

Undertale's unique employment of interactivity and involvement of the player in a position of endorsement with violence has significant implications. What marks *Undertale* out as innovative in terms of these types of games is the player's greater degree of choice. The player can avoid violent content altogether in *Undertale* via the Pacifist and Neutral Routes, whereas, conventionally, players must follow the path laid out by the game's designers 'in order to experience the entire game and thereby actuate its potential as fully as possible' (Smethurst, *Spec* 206). In *Spec Ops: The Line*, players can justify their actions because 'they have no choice but to

[5] In game, the LV (or LOVE) usually stands for Level but in Undertale stands for Level of Violence. EXP, which usually stands for experience points, stands for Execution Points. During the Pacifist Route, players do not gain EXP or LV.

use violence in order to progress through the game' (*Spec* 211). While players have the option to stop playing *Spec Ops: The Line*, their continued interaction with the game is not voluntary. Smethurst argues that continued gameplay in *Spec Ops: The Line* is 'attributable not to the players' bloodthirst, but to the considerable psychological pressures involved when one is playing a game'; that 'one must also factor in the player's drive to go along with' the rules of the game in place: 'the authority is the player's contract with the game (i.e., their lusory attitude)' (*Spec* 215). Smethurst considers this a flaw in the game 'with regards to player choice' (*Spec* 215). This flaw is evident in other metafictional titles. Choices in Will Byles' *Until Dawn* (2015) frequently consist of forcing rather than inviting players to decide between enacting different violent actions in order to advance the narrative. Kotaro Uchikoshi's *Zero Escape: Zero Time Dilemma* (2016) contains interconnected 'good', 'evil' and 'neutral' pathways, so the player is required to play through all of these paths to access the narrative in totality and make sense of the game's story. Conversely, *Undertale*'s Pacifist and Neutral Routes provide the player with a fully realised narrative, a definitive ending and an average gameplay length (for an independent game, at least) of approximately ten hours. The Genocide Route is a wholly optional, separate story that takes place in an alternate timeline from the Pacifist/Neutral Routes. The Genocide Route can almost be considered a different game from the Pacifist/Neutral playthroughs, being a horror game (rather than adventure). Additionally, while the Genocide Route provides further narrative content, its narrative is largely about undoing the events of the Pacifist/Neutral Routes rather than adding to these narratives. Therefore, *Undertale* more clearly situates players as trauma perpetrators because players follow the genocide mode to completion without the kinds of external motivations found in other games. This exemplifies that games, because of their requirement of players' active input, can implicate audiences in on-screen violence in ways that more traditional media cannot. Films can only do this through metafictional reference to this idea of the viewer's role in the endorsement of violent media entertainment rather than more directly implicate audiences. For instance, Haneke's *Funny Games* similarly aims to interrogate the viewer's complicity in violent media, centring on two home invaders who take a family hostage for no apparent reason other than entertainment (they offer a number of bogus tragic backstories to explain their motivations). Addressing the audience via asides, the invaders are depicted as delivering upon thriller fans' desire to see on-screen violence. Metatextual slasher films including Wes Craven's *Scream* (1996) and *Wes Craven's New Nightmare* (1994) feature self-aware characters that are, like the viewer, fans of slasher films and enthusiastic about the genre's violent conventions.

This increased freedom runs the risk of players skipping *Undertale*'s Genocide Mode and representation of perpetrator trauma. However, *Undertale* appears to overcome this issue in a number of ways. The game has received critical acclaim: *Undertale* is among the best-selling games on Steam, was later released on consoles (PlayStation 4 and Nintendo Switch), and was nominated for several awards including the Innovation Award, Best Debut and Best Narrative at the Game Developers Choice Awards.[6] At the same time, the game has garnered a strong cult following and as such is discussed widely amongst players online. As Pheasant-Kelly notes, 'the term cult is usually understood through audience involvement' and 'cult engagement involves more intense displays of interest' than seen in usual textual engagement (95). The many mysteries Fox incorporated into *Undertale*'s Pacifist/Neutral Routes (such as secret side quests and areas to explore) encourage this kind of cult spectatorship, specifically online speculation. Resultantly, players are usually aware of the Genocide Route before engaging with *Undertale*. In the instance of rarer, blind playthroughs (playing *Undertale* with no prior knowledge of the game), *Undertale*'s varying mysteries prompt players to uncover as much of its content as possible, which may, in turn, include playing the Genocide Route. The game also takes into account players who solely play the Pacifist/Neutral Routes and watch the Genocide Route online. These players specifically are positioned as trauma perpetrators. If an individual is live streaming their playthrough on *YouTube*, Flowey claims that online viewers watching another gamer perform in-game violence are equally culpable in the violence taking place onscreen but are too cowardly to participate in these events: 'At least we're better than those sickos that stand around and watch it happen. Those pathetic people that want to see it, but are too weak to do it themselves. I bet someone like that's watching right now, aren't they?' This comment regarding the implication of online viewers simulates in the player or online viewer a further aspect of perpetrator trauma, specifically LaCapra's notion of the bystander. This is the grey area role of an individual who witnesses or is aware of a trauma being perpetrated by another

[6] Steam is a type of digital distribution platform which offers video gaming and social networking services.

individual and is thus not directly responsible for the act, but is at the same time implicated because they do nothing to prevent it. LaCapra discusses this in terms of the Holocaust, stating that: 'it is also important not to restrict responsibility for the Nazi genocide to Hitler and a small group of henchmen and instead to raise the larger question of the role and responsibility of ... "ordinary" people who went along with genocidal initiatives' (128). Michael Rothberg has a similar idea of what he calls the 'implicated subject', whereby an individual may not be a direct agent of harm but 'may still contribute to, inhabit, or benefit from regimes of domination that [they] neither set up nor control' (*Implicated* n.p.).

Undertale is also significant regarding debates around realistic representation in games in relation to trauma, specifically the argument that more lifelike, human-looking characters generate a stronger emotional effect in players. This has been increasingly contested by critics as unnecessary, while photorealistic graphics have been found to hinder players' emotional resonance. For instance, *Until Dawn* employs motion capture and has been described by players in terms of the uncanny valley, whereby the characters almost resemble real people but not entirely, inducing feelings of 'revulsion' rather than 'increased affinity' (Sparks). Instead, it has been observed that players tend to remember what happens in games rather than their appearance. Alex Fox notes, 'we describe the story moments in the game, not the ... realistic graphics'. Kyle Orland similarly asserts that emotional resonance is driven by 'strong world-building, compelling, believable writing and engaging scenarios that make the player's actions feel integral to the experience'. *Undertale*'s exploitation of the medium's capacity to tell more slow-burning stories and the creation of well-developed characters have been found to make it particularly difficult for players to harm them. William Hughes comments that *Undertale* 'does everything in [its] power to make the various monsters feel like vibrant, real people, and the player feel like the worst sort of sociopath for taking their lives'. This is important in terms of advancing realism in games specifically. Alexander Galloway argues that because games are an active medium that require constant physical input by the player, a realistic game 'must be realist in doing, in action ... rather than in looking, as it is with cinema'. Galloway says games are realist in terms of 'a congruence between the social reality depicted in the game and the social reality known and lived by the gamer'. While *Undertale* features heavily stylised monster characters, among the reasons the game has been found by players to be emotionally resonant is because it incorporates universally relatable themes, including loneliness, anxiety, friendship and community. That *Undertale* reprimands players for their engagement with the game medium itself means it more closely resembles 'the real social context' (Galloway) in which players live, making the game, by Galloway's characterisation, more realistic.

Doki Doki Literature Club

Doki Doki Literature Club is an American freeware visual novel developed by Team Salvato, a team led by Dan Salvato, for PC in 2017. The plot that follows the story of an unseen male high school student who joins his school's literature club and interacts with its four female members, the apparent goal of the game being for him to gain the affections of one of the girls. The characters include Sayori, Yuri, Natsuki and Monika, the club's leader whom the player does not have the option to romance. The structure of *Doki Doki*'s narrative is largely linear with branching paths depending upon the girl one's character pursues, which affects the narrative's cutscenes and ending.[7] While *Doki Doki* purports to be a conventional dating simulator, it gradually reveals itself as a psychological meta-horror.[8] The initial stages of the game involve attending the literature club and sharing poetry with its members, and each of the girls is gradually revealed to be going through some type of crisis: Sayori suffers from depression, Yuri is a masochist, Natsuki is abused by her father and Monika has entered an existential crisis having realised she is trapped in a video game. Whereas troubled love interests are a trope of the visual romance genre, with players often having to solve their emotional problems, *Doki Doki* undermines this convention as the issues of its characters cannot be solved by having the player romance them. Incorporating trauma as a theme, whichever girl the player pursues has a tragic outcome whereby the girl commits suicide.

For example, if the player has their character pursue Sayori, she constantly bemoans her feelings of inadequacy and sadness, and eventually confesses her love to the protagonist. The player has the option of reciprocating or rejecting her feelings, but regardless of the player's response,

[7] A cutscene is a non-interactive cinematic scene in a game that develops the game's narrative.

[8] Dating simulators are games whereby the player controls an avatar surrounded by several NPCs, the common objective being to achieve a romantic relationship with one of them.

Sayori hangs herself in her bedroom the following day. Upon encountering Sayori's suicide, the game begins to glitch, the music becomes heavily distorted and the protagonist prompts the player to restart the game, suggesting that choosing the other option when hearing Sayori's confession would have prevented her suicide. As noted, this is a common tendency in players when engaging with moral choice games: players, who usually save their game before making significant decisions that cause the plot to diverge, quit the game and go back to take a different route. By contrast, *Doki Doki* thwarts the player from doing so and forcefully brings them back to the main menu, where the 'New Game' option is replaced with a line of jumbled text and previously saved files become inaccessible. Here, the game reprimands the player for their replayability and desensitised approach to violent media content, therefore inducing in the player perpetrator trauma symptoms such as feelings of responsibility and guilt, but in relation to video gaming specifically. As Stobbart notes:

> the ability to save a videogame at any point also changed the way players view death ... render[ing] death a minor inconvenience, rather than a significant setback in the narrative and ludic progress of the game ... with no consequences other than frustration. (178)

Conversely, clicking the pixelated link in *Doki Doki* seemingly starts the narrative again, but with the Sayori character permanently erased from the game's world.

Similar to *Undertale* and its apparent attempt to simulate in the player symptoms of perpetrator trauma, *Doki Doki*'s tone becomes increasingly darker the further the player engages with it. *Doki Doki* appears to punish the player for their continuation of the game and complicity in the endorsement of violent media entertainment, the player's very engagement with the game becoming a moral dilemma. Again, we can align this concept with *Spec Ops: The Line*, whereby the player's continuation of the game is a conscious choice and each time they chose to continue playing, 'the game "rewards" them with horror in the form of more death, more destruction, more discomfort and more uneasy complicity in [the controllable protagonist's] unethical actions' (Stobbart 69). Similarly, in *Doki Doki*, the player is subjected to a series of increasingly disturbing imagery and narrative events. The game's other romantic options begin to behave uncharacteristically as Yuri and Natsuki gradually become aggravated towards each other. These characters' animation also becomes pixelated and warped, and unusual imagery is incorporated into their design at random moments, creating frightening jumpscares.[9] Yuri frequently zooms into the screen, such as when she eerily 'stares' out of the screen at the player and asks if we like her poem, while Natsuki's eyes and mouth are at times overlaid with black pixels, or all of her facial features disappear. As noted, romancing Yuri and Natsuki likewise results in these characters' suicide. Natsuki reacts by complaining that the protagonist is spending too much time with the other girls and begs us to 'play with her'. The character then glitches (her eyes and mouth distort), snaps her neck and runs towards the screen, which turns black with the word 'END' spelled backwards across it. Yuri stabs herself with a kitchen knife regardless of whether we accept her confession of love for the protagonist, and we are then forced to look at an image of Yuri's bloody corpse for an extended period of time. Stobbart's observation on death in gaming is also relevant here, as she notes that death in games is 'not only used as a tool for play', but as a 'method of teaching a player how to complete a game successfully' (186). However, Stobbart argues that death can also be 'a visceral, grotesque aspect of gaming, where the visual representation is shocking, challenging the player's own role as complicit in these moments' (186).

These scenes in *Doki Doki* contrast with more conventional games in that, as with *Undertale*, cutscenes usually provide the player with a reward for their progression in the game in the form of satisfying their desire to know what happens next in the game's narrative. Going beyond games such as *Spec Ops* then, *Doki Doki* also thwarts the player's narrative curiosity, acknowledging how players' tendencies for replayability are additionally motivated by this, and how players commit immoral in-game actions as a means of experimenting with narrative alternatives. *Doki Doki* employs a number of formal techniques so as to simulate the break-down or crashing of the game, and thwart the player's engagement with the narrative. The game speeds through text and dialogue too fast for the player to read; some of the characters' text is blacked out and overwritten with black gibberish text; and certain scenes rewind and fast forward. *Doki Doki* eventually reveals Monika to have been tampering with the game's programming and script in an attempt to romance the protagonist herself, and eventually the player (recall, Monika is not available for the player as a romantic option). As noted, Monika has an existential crisis having realised she

[9] The sudden appearance of a frightening or shocking image, frequently accompanied by a burst of loud music.

exists within a dating simulator game, a fictional world, and this knowledge grants her the ability to alter the game's story and events, erase characters and save files and 'break the fourth wall', whereby she can address the player directly. The glitches and apparent crashing of the game are represented as due to Monika's constant manipulation of its data in pursuit of the player. It is also disclosed that Monika, with the intention of making these characters less desirable to the player and eliminating the competition, edited the files of the other club members so as to change their dialogue and appearance, amplify their negative traits and make them suicidal.

In *Doki Doki*'s final act, Monika destroys the entire game and the player is presented with a scene where Monika is sitting at a table facing the screen. The classroom where the game is set is empty, with a space-like background beyond the windows (representative of cyberspace). This scene makes various attempts to simulate in the player perpetrator trauma symptoms including feelings of responsibility, guilt and moral contradiction, but again in relation to their status as a player outside of the game. For instance, Monika outlines her awareness of her status as a character in a game and the protagonist as a separate entity from the player. Monika knows what application the player is using to play the game (such as Steam) and the real name of the player by finding the name of the administrator of the player's computer:

> I'm not even talking to that person anymore, am I? That 'you' in the game, whatever you want to call him. I'm talking to *you*, [player's username within the game]. Or. Do you actually go by [player's real name] or something?

Here, the player can choose to delete Monika's character by accessing the game's files, or continue speaking with her. The dialogue incorporates multiple light-hearted topics such as vegetarianism and the weather. However, the conversation becomes increasingly disturbing. Monika berates the player for both engaging with the game and ceasing to interact with it, as she likens the player's action of quitting the game to killing her character. The latter draws upon the idea established by game criticism that the player 'endows a game character with life' and when they cease to interact with the game, 'the character stands still and lifeless until the player returns to the game' (Stobbart 170). According to Stobbart, this idea is often exploited in horror games to remind the player of the 'spectre of death that exists on the fringes of gameplay' (170). Conversely, Monika then begs the player to play *Doki Doki* indefinitely, as quitting the game puts her in a void where she is 'endlessly hammered' by colours, lights and noise. If the player quits the game, Monika will acknowledge this and make remarks such as 'What just happened? … it almost feels like I've been killed or something. … It seems to happen whenever you quit the game … avoid doing that.' The more times the player closes *Doki Doki*, the more aggravated Monika becomes: 'I know I asked already, but can you seriously please try not to do that so much. … Why would you do that to me? … stay here with me from now on, okay?' If the player decides to delete Monika from the game via the game files, the character will glitch out, becoming a disembodied entity and angrily expressing her disgust at the player. At the conclusion of the game, however, Monika realises that she will never escape the game world and 'erases' the game files from the player's computer.

Doki Doki continues to 'punish' the player here for their continuation of the game, as the disturbing content escalates the further the player journeys into the final act. Indeed, Monika's pleading to keep her alive becomes more desperate and the ending of the game again subjects the player to watching a character's suicide in Monika's erasure of the game. Additionally, Monika's berating of the player for playing the game exacerbates and the game's horror elements are heightened. As with *Undertale*, if the player is live streaming their playthrough of the game, Monika becomes aware of this and contorts her face into a frightening facial expression, and has the game zoom into her face as she does this, again incorporating the trauma concept of the bystander. Also similar to *Undertale* is how Monika's lengthy and dramatic death is in contrast to more conventional, guilt-free in-game killings whereby the player is invited to kill multiple times. For Stobbart, this further pulls 'the player's actions out of the diegetic world and into the real world', highlighting the violence inherent to conventional ludic structures of gaming whereby the player is required to kill in order to progress (70). Indeed, as Monika deletes the game files and dies, she expresses remorse for her actions and performs a song she wrote for the player during the game's closing credits (Monika is for the first time enabled to communicate vocally with the player here; as per usual with dating simulators, *Doki Doki* is text-based and has thereby been devoid of voice acting up to this point). In *Doki Doki*'s prolonged ending then, the player is made to contemplate the notion of performing virtual violence for entertainment and narrative curiosity, and made to feel perpetrator trauma symptoms such as feelings of responsibility, guilt and moral contradiction for doing so, the game's interrogation of the player's moral framework translating to a real-world context. Moreover, that *Doki Doki* becomes increasingly disturbing as the player progresses through the game, as the final act establishes, can be further linked to this chapter's reading of the game as attempting to transmit perpetrator trauma. This aspect of the game corresponds with Gibbs' argument that perpetrator is represented in certain texts as an ongoing experience, as an 'insidious accretion of guilt ... over a series of acts of increasing intensity or depravity' (169), rather than stemming from a singular extraordinary event. Certainly, the final act contains the most frightening content in the game, featuring discussion of dark topics such as violence and death, horror imagery in Monika's contorted facial expression and a lengthy suicide scene. Also significant to this aspect of *Doki Doki*'s representation of perpetrator trauma is that of the game more frequently refers to the player rather than the controllable protagonist the further the player continues the game.

Doki Doki's unique interactivity and metafictional references to the player's endorsement of violent media entertainment again have significant implications. While *Doki Doki* is not as mutable as *Undertale* in terms of player choice, the game's violent content in the final act is likewise optional as the player can, at any point, cease interacting with Monika and delete her character ('harming' Monika via exiting and re-entering the game is also elective). As with *Undertale*, however, *Doki Doki* makes a number of attempts to overcome the issue of players skipping the game's violent content and prompts them to engage with it without the types of external motivation conventionally present in games. This, in turn, more clearly situates players as trauma perpetrators. For instance, *Doki Doki* contains two disclaimers at the beginning of the game which warn the player of disturbing content. While these disclaimers are necessary for younger players and those who require trigger warnings for topics such as anxiety, depression and suicide, they also appear deliberately designed to spark curiosity about this disturbing content amongst players, prompting the player to play the entirety of the game narrative in order to uncover it. *Doki Doki*'s violence also became the game's unique selling point within weeks of its release, with *Doki Doki*'s large online following being due mainly to its unusual mix of dating simulator tropes and aesthetics with horror. Popular video game streamers—including PewDiePie, Jacksepticeye, Markiplier, Game Grumps and Etika—helped the game to receive additional attention via their Let's Play playthroughs, and their videos promoted the horror aspects of *Doki Doki* in particular. For instance, Jacksepticeye entitled the opening video of his playthrough 'Don't Trust This Game, *Doki Doki Literature Club*, Part 1'. Further promoting *Doki Doki*'s more disturbing content, Monika, whose route is the most violent, is the character primarily used in promotional imagery for the game, and subsequently became the most popular character amongst players, becoming the subject of multiple fan works, such as the mod *Monika After Story*.

Doki Doki, like *Undertale*, is also significant regarding debates around realistic representation in games in relation to trauma, employing an unrealistic, animé-style character design. However, this aspect of *Doki Doki* raises a further, important issue regarding perpetrator trauma and how individuals interact with the game medium. Similar to how *Undertale* critiques the violent ludic structures of RPGs, *Doki Doki* chastises the disturbing tropes specific to dating simulators in such a way that the player feels guilty for engaging with the game. For instance, one of Monika's conversation topics in the final act is the sexism inherent to the genre of *Doki Doki*: 'What is it about these character archetypes that people find so appealing, anyway? Their personalities are just completely unrealistic. … I'm not judging or anything! … Maybe I just feel a little insecure because you're playing this game in the first place.' Lack of agency and stereotypes for female characters have been highlighted as among dating simulators' sexist archetypes, particularly prevalent in animé-style visual novels. The cast of *Doki Doki*'s characters initially appear to conform to animé waifu stereotypes (animé term for love interest): Sayori is the cheerful childhood friend; Natsuki is the tsundere (animé term for a character that is initially cold and prideful before becoming infatuated with the protagonist); Yuri is the shy, mysterious 'goth' girl with a dark side; and Monkia is the 'popular' girl depicted as out of the protagonist's league. Regarding agency, the genre usually casts female characters solely as love interests for a male protagonist and their main goal is to date said protagonist. As Jenna January notes of dating sims, 'girls are automatically yours for the choosing'. *Doki Doki* incorporates and subverts these archetypes here and indeed throughout the game. Characters vie for the protagonist's attention, but to the extent that they are willing to murder one another; the problems of the girls cannot be solved by the protagonist or by the protagonist's romantic interest; the protagonist/player never actually gets to date any of the girls; and Monika is literally lacking in agency in the revelation of her character as a self-aware NPC. For instance, Monika demonstrates her lack of free will when she attempts and fails to change the game's music in the final act, and begins speaking of topics she has no knowledge of such as other video games, suggesting she is ultimately subject to the game's creators: 'Was I programmed to talk about that? Because I have no idea what that is. Ahaha! Sometimes I feel like I'm not in control, and it's kind of scary. But if you have some way to contact the people who created me, maybe they'll know why I started saying that.' Monika's fixation on the player also serves as a criticism of the possessiveness that players of dating sims often romanticise, further guilting the player for their engagement with a genre whereby players can literally decide the direction of female characters' narratives and have their affection for particular characters automatically reciprocated. Gamer_152, moderator at the gaming blog *Giant Bomb*, observes that there is 'a lack of titles in the dating sim space which give their female characters desires and preferences independent of the wants of a presumed male, heterosexual player'. Monika's berating of the player and attempts to guilt players into continuing conversing with her/playing the game reflects how dating sim players subject virtual love interests to similarly controlling behaviour, in addition to the inversion of perpetrator/victim status linked to a denial of agency that Gibbs identifies as characteristic of perpetrator trauma representations. Analogous moments include when the player is asked to choose a girl to make their partner but is only given the option 'Just Monika', and when the player's cursor is forcibly moved towards Monika's name when given a selection of characters to choose from. Further reflecting the dating sim player, the possessive Monika sits at a desk in the final act and is positioned similarly to a player facing a computer; she is shot in close up and stares out of the screen. This framing of the character is suggestive of the player's self-reflection, paralleling *Undertale*'s mirror-like blank screen at the end of the Genocide Route and reflecting trauma perpetrators' reflection upon their integrity.

Conclusion

Due to *Doki Doki*'s and *Undertale*'s innovation, my analysis focused on the metacognitive operation of these two types of atypical game play and their relationship to perpetrator trauma representation, specifically in relation to individuals' interaction with the game medium and sensationalism of violence. However, this approach is found in other titles and is therefore significant to wider game studies. For instance, in the first two *Danganronpa* games (Takayuki Sugawara's *Danganronpa: Trigger Happy*

Havoc (2010) and *Danganronpa 2: Goodbye Despair* (2012)), the antagonist Junko Enoshima becomes a terrorist out of boredom, her goal being to simply spread despair throughout the world. Among her acts is to organise and broadcast a killing game whereby kidnapped students are forced to murder one another. The world of *Danganronpa V3: Killing Harmony* (Shun Sasaki 2017) is revealed to be a fictitious series whose audience is an in-fiction representation of the player, who is framed as a Junko-like villain in that by playing the game, the player too puts characters through suffering for entertainment. Similarly, while player choice is restricted in *Until Dawn* in comparison to *Undertale*, the former likewise works to position the player as a trauma perpetrator. The game enables players to commit virtual violence as a means of experimenting with narrative alternatives, such as presenting players with decisions that will obviously result in the demise of certain characters, and makes a number of metafictional references which align the player with the game's killer, such as having certain characters describe the killer's acts as a 'game' consisting of 'actively triggering events that lead to someone's death'.

Through the medium's capacity for interactivity, video games attempt to transmit to players perpetrator trauma symptoms including feelings of responsibility, guilt and moral contradiction, while also incorporating further concepts specific to perpetrator trauma including trauma as an ongoing experience and self-reflection. As with trauma literature, this notion of transmission in games is questionable, even in regards to more recent indie games such as *Doki Doki* and *Undertale*. However, the employment of metafictional techniques in these titles represents at least an attempt at overcoming the issue that games' questioning of players' moral framework does not translate to anything significant outside the environment of the game. Regardless of whether these titles successfully transmit affect onto players and simulate in them symptoms common to trauma perpetrators, that they even attempt to do this marks these games out as highly innovative trauma texts. Ultimately, this chapter aimed to extend existing explorations of perpetrator trauma and transmission in metafictional games, and uncover new ways the medium represents trauma.

CHAPTER 7

Conclusion

This book examined five original paradigms through which to understand trauma in popular texts, the ultimate aim being to add to existing scholarship on trauma in contemporary American popular culture, and to uncover new themes and formal techniques of trauma representation. To briefly reiterate the major findings of this book, Chap. 2 examined popular trauma texts' engagement with postmodern perspectives in *House of Leaves* and *The Shining*. Contemporary American popular culture and cult texts produce innovative trauma representations through the engagement with postmodern themes and perspectives rather than solely its experimental aesthetic. Chapter 3 explored a framework that I term competitive narration in two early 1990s works, *Batman Returns* and *Twin Peaks*. Through this framework, I analysed how certain popular and cult texts critique fiction's neglect and mythologisation of women's trauma. Chapter 4 investigated the representation of trauma and diverse characters in popular texts by gender and ethnically diverse writers, through a framework termed polynarration. *Sense8*, *Steven Universe* and *Candyman* feature diverse groups of characters acquiring interconnectivity abilities that enable them to supernaturally share traumatic experiences and help one another recover. These texts produce unique narratives where a singular traumatic event is told from a range of diverse perspectives as characters' consciousnesses and/or bodies amalgamate. *Sense8*, *Steven Universe* and *Candyman* are in line with contemporary conceptions of feminism by women as communal and intersectional rather than earlier, male conceptions of feminism

S. Travers, *Trauma in American Popular Culture and Cult Texts, 1980–2020*, https://doi.org/10.1007/978-3-031-13287-2_7

by men as individualistic, competitive and antagonistic towards men, as expressed in *Batman Returns* and *Twin Peaks.* Chapter 5 discussed a framework that I term sceptical scriptotherapy, again in texts by writers diverse in terms of gender, race and sexuality: *The OA* and *Mr Robot.* Sceptical scriptotherapy features characters narrating traumatic events by reworking them into alternate, therapeutic narratives. In contrast to conventional trauma fiction, escapist fantasies are depicted as the only way victim-protagonists can take agency over their recovery, because the trauma experienced by diverse groups are frequently structural traumas beyond individuals' control. Chapter 6 investigated the transmission of perpetrator trauma in two metafictional games: *Doki Doki Literature Club* and *Undertale.* This chapter examined how both games employ metafiction as a means of exploring player immorality in relation to the game medium specifically, interrogating players' culpability in the medium's sensationalism of violence and expected play patterns of replayability.

To briefly look towards further developments in American popular trauma narratives, trauma continues to be a focus point in contemporary American popular culture, and contemporary American popular culture continues to expand the modes of trauma representation. As we have seen, the conclusion of each chapter in this study pointed towards additional, recent textual examples of the five original paradigms explored. Further developments include horror films which explore the intersection of nihilism and the traumatic experience of grief, such as Robert Egger's *The Witch* (2015), Ari Aster's *Hereditary* (2018), David Bruckner's *The Night House* (2020) and Mike Flanagan's *Midnight Mass* (2021). Ron Breton, for example, calls the 2010s the 'Decade of Grief Horror'. David Church likewise points out grief as a central theme of twenty-first-century horror (n.p.).

Trauma fiction in contemporary American popular culture continues to see an increase in diverse representation and production. Themes and approaches not explored in this study include these texts' representation of trauma through comedy and surrealism, as evident in works of television including Tina Fey's and Robert Carlock's *Unbreakable Kimmy Schmidt* (2015–2019), Lisa Hawnawalt's *Tuca and Bertie* (2019) and Maya Erskine's and Anna Konkle's *PEN15* (2019-2021). These series examine ongoing traumas resulting from the structural violence of racism and sexism, and experiences such as sexual coercion, sexual assault and kidnapping. The employment of supernatural metaphors to further explore rather than repress ostensibly taboo traumas commonly experienced by women such as gaslighting and emotional abuse is also recurring, evident in Ari Aster's *Midsommar* (2019) and Leigh Whannell's *The Invisible Man* (2020). Trauma texts also increasingly draw upon ideas from literary naturalism. Gibbs notes that central components of naturalism such as determinism are integrated into the narrative structure and thematic concerns of a number of American television series, including Shawn Ryan's *The Shield* (2002–2008), James Manos, Jr.'s *Dexter* (2006–2013) and Vince Gilligan's *Breaking Bad* (2008–2013), the protagonists of which are absolved from moral responsibility because their actions are depicted as involuntarily determined by external forces (Gibbs 246). Regarding games and trauma, game designers are developing new ways to increase immersion in players, which, as noted, is considered among the essential components of representing trauma in games. An example of such is VR (virtual reality) games. The player wears a headset and the 'borders of the screen' are removed, which 'marks off a bounded reality' between the game and the real world (Stobbart 19). According to Stobbart, through VR, the player is more 'fully contained in the game world' and 'potentially able, through this immersion, to more readily identify as the character' in the game (19). An example of this type of game is Nik Bowen's *The Inpatient* (2018).

It is also important to consider trauma representation in the 2020s, considering the global societal crises and political, social and cultural dynamics of the past number of years. There have been a number of traumas that have gripped the world during the course of this book's production. These include traumas relating to climate change, the coronavirus/COVID-19 pandemic, Internet culture and engaged citizenship in a networked world, the Black Lives Matter Movement, the Stop Asian Hate movement that arose during the pandemic, and inequality and social inclusion. Multiple texts produced in American popular culture have responded to these issues over the past number of years and they are points for further possible directions for future trauma criticism. COVID-19 has resulted in massive economic and social disruption, in addition to lockdowns, shortages and political and cultural turmoil. Individuals may seek peaceful escapism via popular culture. Conversely, COVID-19 has driven some viewers towards fictional pandemics as an alternative means of escapism. Narratives of zombie apocalypses have plagued popular culture since the nineteenth century, but the trope is being re-examined in terms of both the pandemic and climate change, such as in Frank Darabont's *The Walking Dead* and Stephen King's *The Stand* and its televisual adaptation

The Stand (Josh Boone and Benjamin Cavell, 2020–2021). Overt references to the COVID-19 pandemic in popular culture began in 2020, such as Shonda Rhimes' *Grey's Anatomy* (2005–present), Dan Fogelman's *This Is Us* (2016–2022), David Shore's *The Good Doctor* (2017–present) and Adam Mason's *Songbird* (2022). Other popular works reference the pandemic either metaphorically or obliquely via themes of contagion, isolation, loss of control and mob mentality, such as David Gordon Green's *Halloween Kills* (2021) and Dan Erickson's *Severance* (2022–present). Climate change films have been ongoing throughout the twenty-first century, including Roland Emmerich's *The Day After Tomorrow* (2004) and Alex Garland's *Annihilation* (2018), culminating in 2020s films such as John Krasinski's *A Quiet Place Part II* (2020) and Adam McKay's *Don't Look Up* (2021). The Black Lives Matter Movement and police brutality are reflected in a range of films and series beyond *Candyman* discussed in this study, including *Atlanta*, *Us* and Jordan Peele's *The Twilight Zone* (2019–2020), Damon Lindelof's *Watchmen* (2019) and Mariama Diallo's *Master* (2021). As with *PEN15*, positive, comedic and fantastical portrayals of Asian-American characters have increased as a response to the rise of anti-Asian violence during the pandemic, including Dan Kwan's and Daniel Scheinert's *Everything Everywhere All at Once* (2022), Domee Shi's *Turning Red* (2022), Destin Daniel Cretton's *Shang-Chi and The Legend of The Ten Rings* (2021) and Awkwafina's and Teresa Hsiao's *Awkwafina is Nora from Queens* (2020–present). A number of these texts explore topics including diversity, Asian-American identity, racism, intersectional feminism and inter-generational trauma. A relative issue in terms of future scholarship is globalisation, how US popular texts compare to their international counterparts in terms of trauma representation. This topic is now an essential one to explore due to the current increasing globalisation. The past decade has seen increasing globalisation in terms of communication (the Internet and social media), trauma (traumatic events which effect the entire world such as the pandemic and climate change) and popular culture (the rise of streaming platforms offers easy access to world cinema alongside Hollywood blockbusters, ultimately upending the global media landscape). For instance, Netflix's South Korean viral sensation *Squid Game* (Hwang Dong-hyuk 2021) and hit US horror series *Midnight Mass* were released within ten days of each other and, in turn, were frequently examined together in online pop cultural criticism and reviews.

The above examples are merely a brief range of contemporary American popular culture's continual engagement with trauma and innovation when representing it, and further establish what I hope this book has demonstrated overall. That is, as critics of trauma in popular culture continue to argue, when we look to the popular, we uncover new themes and techniques of trauma representation that have yet to be uncovered in existing criticism. We also recognise the different media involved in representing trauma, thereby increasing the extent of trauma representation. As noted in this study's Introduction, my book ultimately aims to add to existing trauma studies on contemporary popular culture, and to encourage critics and theorists of trauma to do the same.

Works Cited

A Quiet Place Part II. John Krasinski. Paramount Pictures, 2020.

A Nightmare on Elm Street. Dir. Wes Craven. New Line Cinema, 1984.

Ager, Rob. '"Mazes, Mirrors, Deception and Denial": An In-Depth Analysis of Stanley Kubrick's *The Shining*'. *Collative Learning.* 2008. <https://www.collativelearning.com/the%20shining.html>.

Alemoru, Kemi. 'The New *Candyman*, like the Black horror genre in general, is having an identity crisis'. *gal-dem.* 2 Sept. 2021. <https://gal-dem.com/candyman-black-horror-review/>.

ALF. Paul Fusco and Tom Patchett. Warner Bros. Domestic Television Distribution, 1986-1990.

Allen, Graham. 'The Unempty Wasps' Nest: Kubrick's *The Shining*, Adaptation, Chance, Interpretation'. *Adaptation* 8.3 (2015): 361-371.

'Alone Together'. Dir. Ian Jones-Quartey. 15 Jan. 2015. *Steven Universe.* Rebecca Sugar. Warner Bros. Television Distribution, 2013-2019.

Alsup, Janet. 'A Pedagogy of Trauma (or a Crisis of Cynicism): Teaching, Writing and the Holocaust'. *Witnessing the Disaster: Essays on Representation and the Holocaust.* Eds. Michael Bernard-Donals and Richard Glejzer. University of Wisconsin Press, 2003. 75-89.

American Psychiatric Association. *Diagnostic and Statistical Manual of Mental Disorders: DSM-5.* American Psychiatric Association, 2013.

American Psycho. Dir. Mary Harron. Lions Gate Films, 2000.

Amis, Martin. *Time's Arrow, or the Nature of the Offence.* Penguin Books in association with Jonathan Cape, 1992.

Annihilation. Alex Garland. Paramount Pictures, 2018.

S. Travers, *Trauma in American Popular Culture and Cult Texts, 1980–2020*, https://doi.org/10.1007/978-3-031-13287-2

'Arbitrary Law'. Dir. Tim Hunter. 1 Dec. 1990. *Twin Peaks.* David Lynch and Mark Frost. CBS Television Distribution, 1990-1991.

Atlanta. Donald Glover. 20th Television and Disney-ABC Domestic Television, 2016-present.

Auster, Paul. *Man in the Dark.* Faber & Faber, 2008.

—. *Oracle Night.* Henry Holt and Company, 2009.

Awkwafina is Nora from Queens. Awkwafina and Teresa Hsiao. Viacom CBS Domestic Media Networks, 2020-present.

A.X.S. 'In *Sense8* an empathetic outlook is an advanced form of humanity'. *The Economist.* May 5. 2017. <https://www.economist.com/prospero/2017/05/05/in-sense8-an-empathetic-outlook-is-an-advanced-form-of-humanity>.

Aydin, Ciano. 'How to Forget the Unforgettable? On Collective Trauma, Cultural Identity, and Mnemotechnologies'. *An International Journal of Theory and Research* 17.3 (2017): 125-137.

'BAATN: The Black, African and Asian Therapy Network'. <https://www.baatn.org.uk/>.

'Back to the Barn'. Dir. Joe Johston et al. 8 Oct. 2015.

Back to the Future. Robert Zemeckis. Universal Pictures, 1985.

Bailey, Dale. *American Nightmares: The Haunted House Formula in American Popular Fiction.* The University of Wisconsin Press, 1999.

Bakhtin, Mikhail. *Problems of Dostoevsky's Poetics.* University of Minnesota Press, 1984.

Barker, Clive. 'The Forbidden'. *Books of Blood: Volume One.* Berkley, 1986.

Barth, John. 'Lost in the Funhouse'. *Lost in the Funhouse: Fiction for Print, Tape, Live Voice.* Anchor Press, 1968.

—. 'The Literature of Exhaustion'. *The Friday Book: Essays and Other Nonfiction.* Putnam, 1984. 62-76.

Barthes, Roland. 'The Death of the Author'. *Image, Music, Text.* Trans. Stephen Heath. Fontana Press, 1997.

Batman. Dir. Tim Burton. Warner Bros. Pictures, 1989.

Batman Begins. Dir. Christopher Nolan. Warner Bros. Pictures, 2005.

Batman Returns. Dir. Tim Burton. Warner Bros. Pictures, 1992.

Beebe, Maurice. 'The Fall of the House of Pynchon'. *Nineteenth-Century Fiction* 11.1 (1956): 1-17.

Beckett, Samuel. *Endgame.* Faber and Faber, 2009.

—. *Waiting for Godot.* Grove Press, 1954.

Belville, Maria. *Gothic-postmodernism: Voicing the Terrors of Postmodernity.* Rodopi, 2009.

Bemong, Nele. 'Exploration # 6: The Uncanny in Mark Z. Danielewski's '*House of Leaves*''. *Image and Narrative: Online Magazine of the Visual Narrative* 5 (2003). <http://www.imageandnarrative.be/inarchive/uncanny/nele-bemong.htm>.

Benshoff, Harry M. and Sean Griffin. *America on Film: Representing Race, Class, Gender, and Sexuality at the Movies.* Wiley-Blackwell, 2009.

Better Call Saul. Vince Gilligan. AMC, 2015-present.

Biggs, John. 'The new age of empathy'. *Techcrunch.* 2 Aug. 2016. <https://techcrunch.com/2016/08/02/the-new-age-of-empathy/?guccounter=1&guce_referrer=aHR0cHM6Ly93d3cuZ29vZ2xlLmNvbS8&guce_referrer_sig=AQAAAF_EXJONZL_-f2rTU8ExRn_7z2epwURgvWXUDMo3ztZOarXl-kELVLDn3yE2_oxwHADYsmmP_9A9mfZEIFyBg6Z1zcBam2nsDf32bZ0l-7N4JUjqATZRBpUBQRmT7oXUPaVoubQdKTHbwqnMKxyzvFx3eql2PGvjmYctLDwcOJUd>.

Bioshock. Writ. Ken Levine and Alyssa Finley. 2K Games, 2007.

Black, Sarah-Tai. 'Slavery-era horror film *Antebellum* is a smug and dishonest genre exercise'. *The Globe and Mail.* 17 Sept. 2020. <https://www.theglobeandmail.com/arts/film/reviews/article-slavery-era-horror-film-antebellum-is-a-smug-and-dishonest-genre/>.

Blake, Linnie. *The Wounds of Nations: Horror Cinema, Historical Trauma and National Identity.* Manchester University Press, 2008.

Blumenfeld, Zach. 'Comic-Con: Rebecca Sugar on *Steven Universe*'s Emmy Nomination and Rejecting Gendered TV for Kids'. *Paste.* 25 Jul. 2017. <https://www.pastemagazine.com/tv/steven-universe/comic-con-rebecca-sugar-on-steven-universes-emmy-n/>.

Boeing, Geoff. 'Visual Analysis of Nonlinear Dynamical Systems: Chaos, Fractals, Self-Similarity and the Limits of Prediction'. *Systems* 4.4 (2016): 37-54.

BoJack Horseman. Raphael Bob-Waksberg. Netflix, 2014-2020.

Bond, Lucy and Stef Craps. *Trauma.* Taylor and Francis Group, 2019.

Borges, Jorge Luis. 'The Circular Ruins'. *Collected Fictions.* Trans. Andrew Hurley. Penguin, 1998.

Botting, Fred. *Gothic.* Routledge, 1996.

Bradley, Laura. 'How *BoJack Horseman* Uses Animation to Express the Surreal Misery of Trauma'. *Vanity Fair.* 14. Sept. 2018. <https://www.vanityfair.com/hollywood/2018/09/bojack-horseman-season-5-lisa-hanawalt-interview>.

Breaking Bad. Vince Gilligan. AMC, 2008-2013.

Brennert, Alan. *The Brave and the Bold Vol 1 #197.* DC Comics, 1983.

Brent, Elizabeth et al. 'Postmodernism and Television: Speaking of *Twin Peaks*'. *Full of Secrets: Critical Approaches to Twin Peaks.* Ed. David Lavery. Wayne State University Press, 1995. 173-195.

Breton, Ron. 'The Decade of Grief Horror: Reflecting on Shared Themes in the Horror Movies of the 2010s'. *Bloody Disgusting.* 20 Jul. 2021. <https://bloody-disgusting.com/editorials/3675480/decade-grief-horror-reflecting-shared-themes-horror-movies-2010s/>.

Brick, Martin. 'Blueprint(s): Rubric for a Deconstructed Age in *House of Leaves*'. *Philament* 2 (2004). 20 Sept. 2015.

Bridges, Tristan. 'Why Nerds Are So Sexist'. Conducted by Diana Tourjee. *Vice.* 13 Apr. 2016. <https://www.vice.com/en/article/wnwvgx/why-nerds-are-so-sexist>.
Brown, Laura S. 'Outside the Range'. *Trauma: Explorations in Memory.* Ed. Cathy Caruth. Johns Hopkins University Press, 1995. 3-12.
'br4ve-trave1er.asf'. Dir. Deborah Chow. 29 Jul. 2015. *Mr Robot.* Sam Esmail. US Network, 2015-2019.
Brownmiller, Susan. *Against Our Will: Men, Women, and Rape.* Fawcett Books, 1993.
Burton, Tim and Mark Salisbury. *Burton on Burton.* Conducted by Mark Salisbury. Faber & Faber, 2008.
Butler, Judith. 'Performative Acts and Gender Constitution: An Essay in Phenomenology and Feminist Theory.' *Theatre Journal* 40.4 (1988): 519-531.
Campbell, Donna M. 'American Literary Naturalism: Critical Perspectives.' *Literature Compass* 8.8 (2011): 499-513.
Candyman. Dir. Clive Barker. TriStar Pictures, 1992.
Candyman. Dir. Nia DaCosta. Universal Pictures, 2021.
Candyman: Farewell to the Flesh. Dir. Bill Condon. Gramercy Pictures, 1995.
Candyman 3: Day of the Dead. Dir. Turi. HBO, 1999.
Cape Fear. Dir. Martin Scorsese. Universal Pictures, 1991.
Captain Marvel. Dir. Anna Boden and Ryan Fleck. Walt Disney Studios Motion Pictures, 2019.
Caruth, Cathy. 'Trauma and Experience: Introduction'. Caruth, *Trauma* 3-12.
—. *Unclaimed Experience: Trauma, Narrative, and History.* Johns Hopkins University Press, 1996.
Censor. Dir. Prano Bailey-Bond. Vertigo Releasing, 2021.
Chabon, Michael. *The Yiddish Policemen's Union.* Harper Collins, 2007.
Chandler, Marilyn. *Dwelling in the Text: Houses in American Fiction.* University of California Press, 1991.
Chaney, Cassandra and Ray V. Robertson. 'Chains of Psychological Enslavement: Olivia Pope and the Celebration of the Black Mistress in ABC *Scandal*'. *Africology: The Journal of Pan African Studies* 9.3 (2016): 126-153.
Chion, Michel. *David Lynch.* Trans. Robert Julian. BFI, 2006.
Chioneso, Nkechinyelum A. et al. 'Community Healing and Resistance Through Storytelling: A Framework to Address Racial Trauma in Africana Communities'. *Journal of Black Psychology.* 2020.
Christopher, Renny. *The Viet Nam War/The American War.* University of Massachusetts Press, 1995.
Church, David. *Post-Horror: Art, Genre and Cultural Elevation.* Edinburgh University Press, 2021.
Cocks, Geoffrey, et al. 'Introduction: Deep Focus'. *Depth of Field: Stanley Kubrick, Film, and the Uses of History.* University of Wisconsin Press, 2005.

Cocks, Geoffrey. *The Wolf at the Door: Stanley Kubrick, History and the Holocaust.* Peter Lang, 2004.

Comas, Maria Guallar. 'Storytelling in Different Media: The Narrative Strategies of *Fight Club* and *Mr Robot*'. University of Barcelona. Diss. 11 Jun. 2019. 1-27.

Community. Dan Harmon. Sony Pictures Television, 2009-2015.

Cooley, Kevin. 'Drawing Queerness Forward: Fusion, Futurity, and *Steven Universe*'. *Representation in Steven Universe.* Ed. John R. Ziegler and Leah Richards. Springer Nature, 2020. 45-68.

Cooper, Ian, Nia DaCosta and Yahya Adbul-Mateen II. 'Reviving *Candyman*: How Jordan Peele and Nia DaCosta made more than a sequel'. *Los Angeles Times.* Conducted by Sonaiya Kelley. 26 Aug. 2021.

Cox, Katherine. 'What Has Made Me? Locating the Mother in the Textual Labyrinth of Mark Z. Danielewski's *House of Leaves*'. *Critical Survey* 18.2 (2006): 4-15.

Craps, Stef and Gert Buelens. 'Introduction: Postcolonial Trauma Novels'. *Studies in the Novel* 40.1 & 2 (2008): 1-12.

Craps, Stef. *Postcolonial Witnessing: Trauma Out of Bounds.* Palgrave Macmillan, 2013.

Crawley, Laurie 'Lol'. 'Other Worlds'. *British Cinematographer*, 2016. <https://britishcinematographer.co.uk/lol-crawley-bsc-oa/>.

Crazy Ex-Girlfriend. Rachel Bloom and Aline Brosh McKenna. Warner Bros. Television Distribution, 2015-2019.

Creeber, Glen. *The Television Genre Book.* BFI, 2001.

Creed, Barbara. 'From Here to Modernity: Feminism and Postmodernism'. *Screen* 28.2 (1987): 47-68.

Crenshaw, Kimberlé. "Mapping the Margins: Intersectionality, Identity Politics, and Violence against Women of Colour." *Stanford Law Review*, vol. 43, no. 6, July 1991, pp. 1241-1299.

Danganronpa: Trigger Happy Havoc. Takayuki Sugawara. Spike Chunsoft, 2010.

Danganronpa V3: Killing Harmony. Dir. Shun Sasaki. Spike Chunsoft, 2017.

Danganronpa 2: Goodbye Despair. Takayuki Sugawara. Spike Chunsoft, 2012.

Danielewski, Mark Z. 'A Conversation with Mark Z. Danielewski'. Conducted by Sophie Cottrell. *Bold Type.* 2000a. <http://www.randomhouse.com/boldtype/0400/danielewski/interview.html>.

—. 'Haunted House: An Interview with Mark Z. Danielewski'. Conducted by Larry McCaffery and Sinda Gregory. *Critique: Studies in Contemporary Fiction* 44.2 (2003): 99-135.

—. *House of Leaves.* New York, 2000b.

Daredevil. Dew Goddard. Netflix, 2015-2018.

Daria. Glenn Eichler and Susie Lewis Lynn. MTV, 1997-2002.

Davenport, Randi. 'The Knowing Spectator of *Twin Peaks*: Culture, Feminism, and Family Violence.' *Literature Film Quarterly* 4 (1993): 255-259.

Dawson, Conor Michael. "The Horror! The Horror!': Traumatic Repetition in Joseph Conrad's *Heart of Darkness* and Mark Z. Danielewski's *House of Leaves*'. *Postgraduate English: A Journal and Forum for Postgraduates in English* 25 (2012): 1-31.

De Saussure, Ferdinand. *Ferdinand de Saussure: Course in General Linguistics*. Trans. Roy Harris. Duckworth, 1983.

Debruge, Peter. "Why *The OA* Is One of the Year's Most Important Films." *Variety*. 24 December 2016. <https://variety.com/2016/tv/columns/the-oa-netflix-brit-marling-film-critic-appreciation-1201948242/>.

'Demons'. Dir. Lesli Linka Glatter. 3 Nov. 1990.

'Demons'. *Sense8*. Dir. The Wachowskis. 5 Jun. 2015. *Sense8*. Dir. The Wachowskis. Netflix, 2015-2018.

Dennis, Jeffery P. '"The Same Thing We Do Every Night": Signifying Same-Sex Desire in Television Cartoons'. *Journal of Popular Film & Television* 31.3 (2003): 132–133.

Desmet, Christy. 'The Canonisation of Laura Palmer'. *Secrets*, Lavery 93-108.

Desmond, Jane. 'Embodying Difference: Issues in Dance and Cultural Studies'. *Cultural Critique* 26 (1994): 33–63.

Detroit: Become Human. Dir. David Cage. Quantic Dream, 2018.

Dexter. James Manos Jr. CBS Television Distribution, 2006-2013.

Diaz-Oritz, Claire. 'The Digital World is Warmer than You Think. Here's How Social Media Builds Empathy'. Conducted by Elizabeth Tenety. *The Washington Post*. 24 February 2015. <https://www.washingtonpost.com/news/inspired-life/wp/2015/02/24/the-digital-world-is-warmer-than-you-think-heres-how-social-media-builds-empathy/>.

'Dispute Between Brothers'. Dir. Tina Rathborne. 8 Dec. 1990.

Dmytryk, Edward. *On Film Editing*. Abingdon-on-Thames: Taylor and Francis, 2012.

Doane, Mary Ann. 'Subjectivity and Desire: An(other) Way of Looking'. *Contemporary Film Theory*. Ed. Antony Easthope. Longman, 1993. 162– 178.

Doctor Sleep. Dir. Mike Flanagan. Warner Bros. Pictures, 2019.

Doctorow, E. L. *The Book of Daniel*. Random House Trade, 2007.

Don't Look Up. Adam McKay. Netflix, 2021.

Deadpool. Dir. Tim Miller. 20th Century Fox, 2016.

Doki Doki Literature Club. Dan Salvato. Team Salvato, 2017.

Dolan, Marc. 'The Peaks and Valleys of Serial Creativity: What Happened to/on *Twin Peaks*'. *Secrets*, Lavery 30-50.

Doubleday, Portia. '*Mr Robot* Star Portia Doubleday on Angela's Motives, Her Love for Elliot, and What's Ahead for Season 3'. *Variety*. Debra Birnbaum. 23 Sept. 2016. <https://variety.com/2016/tv/news/mr-robot-season-finale-portia-doubleday-angela-1201869212/>.

Doyle, John, 'Netflix's mysterious *The OA* is mind-bending drama'. *The Globe and Mail.* 18 Dec. 2016. <https://www.theglobeandmail.com/arts/television/doyle-netflixs-mysterious-the-oa-is-mind-bending-astounding-drama/article33344922/>.

Driggers, Taylor. 'Failure Fiction: *The OA* and the Healing Breakdown of Narrative'. *Dancing in the Desert.* 7 Feb. 2017. <https://dancinginthedesertblog.wordpress.com/2017/02/07/failure-fiction-the-oa-and-the-healing-breakdown-of-narrative/>.

Dunn, Eli. '*Steven Universe*, Fusion Magic, and the Queer Cartoon Carnivalesque'. *Gender Forum* 56 (2016): 44–57.

Duquette, Kelly. 'Bruce Wayne's Traumatic Past and Batman's New History: Ego-Ideal and Ideal Ego in the Batman Origin Myth'. Thesis. University of Florida, 2010.

Duras, Marguerite. *The Lover.* Pantheon Books, 1997.

Dyer, Richard. *Only Entertainment.* Routledge, 2002.

Ebert, Roger. '*The Shining* (1980)'. *Chicago Sun-Times.* 18 Jun. 2006. <https://www.rogerebert.com/reviews/great-movie-the-shining-1980>.

Eco, Umberto. *The Name of the Rose.* Harcourt Brace, 1994.

Ellis, Emma Grey. 'What Brought *Sense8* Back – and What Killed It in the First Place'. *Wired.* 12 Sept. 2020. <https://www.wired.com/story/sense8-finale-death-of-weird-sci-fi/>.

Ellis, Bret Easton. *Lunar Park.* Knopf, 2005.

Elsaesser, Thomas. 'Postmodernism as Mourning Work'. *Screen* 42.2 (2002): 193-201.

Erikson, Kai. 'Notes on Trauma and Community'. Caruth, *Trauma* 183-199.

'eps1.0_hellofriend.mov'. Dir. Niels Arden Oplev. 24 Jun. 2015.

'eps1.6v1ew-s0urce.flv'. Dir. Sam Esmail. 5 Aug. 2015.

'eps1.8_m1rr0r1ng.qt'. Dir. Tricia Brock. 19 Aug. 2015.

'eps2.2init1.asec'. Dir. Sam Esmail. 27 Jul. 2016.

'eps2.4m4ster-s1ave.aes'. Dir. Sam Esmail. 10 Aug. 2016.

'eps3.0power-saver-mode.h'. Dir. Sam Esmail. 11 Oct. 2017.

'eps3.1undo.gz'. Dir. Sam Esmail. 18 Oct. 2017.

'eps3.3metadata.par2'. Dir. Sam Esmail. 1 Nov. 2017.

'eps3.6fredrick+tanya.chk'. Dir. Sam Esmail. 22 Nov. 2017.

'eps3.7dont-delete-me.ko'. Dir. Sam Esmail. 29 Nov. 2017.

'eps3.8_stage3.torrent'. Dir. Sam Esmail. 6 Dec. 2017.

Everything Everywhere All at Once. Dan Kwan and Daniel Scheinert. A24, 2022.

Evil Dead. Dir. Sam Raimi. New Line Cinema, 1981.

'eXit'. Dir. Sam Esmail. 15 Dec. 2019.

Fahy, Thomas. 'Introduction'. *The Philosophy of Horror.* Ed. Thomas Fahy. University Press of Kentucky, 2010. 1-14.

Falsetto, Mario. *Stanley Kubrick: A Narrative and Stylistic Analysis.* Greenwood Publishing Group, 2001.
Family Matters. William Bickley and Michael Warren. Warner Bros. Television Distribution, 1989-1997.
Felman, Shoshana. 'Education and Crisis, or the Vicissitudes of Teaching'. Caruth, *Trauma* 13-60.
Ferris Bueller's Day Off. Dir. John Hughes. Paramount Pictures, 1986.
Fick, Nathaniel. *One Bullet Away.* Houghton Mifflin Harcourt, 2006.
Fienberg, Daniel. '*The OA* Season 2: TV Review'. *The Hollywood Reporter.* 21 Mar. 2019.
Fight Club. Dir David Fincher. 20th Century Fox, 1999.
Foer, Jonathan Safran. *Extremely Loud and Incredibly Close.* Mariner Books, 2006.
Foucault, Michel. 'The Subject and Power'. *Critical Inquiry* 8.4 (1982): 777-795.
Foutch, Haleigh. '*The OA* Season 2 Review: An Ambitious, Wondrous Exercise in WTF Storytelling'. *Collider.* 22 Mar. 2019. <https://collider.com/the-oa-season-2-review/>.
Fox, Alex. 'Why Video Games Should Abandon Realistic Graphics'. *Forever Geek.* <https://www.forevergeek.com/why-video-games-should-abandon-realistic-graphics/>
Frankenstein. Dir. James Whale. Universal Pictures, 1931.
Freeland, Cynthia A. 'Feminist Frameworks for Horror Films'. *Post-Theory: Reconstructing Film Studies.* Eds. David Bordwell and Noel Carroll. University of Wisconsin Press, 1996. 195-218.
Freese, Peter. 'Vonnegut's Invented Religions as Sense-Making Systems'. *Kurt Vonnegut's Cat's Cradle.* Ed. Harold Bloom. Chelsea House, 2002. 91-112.
Freud, Sigmund. 'An Autobiographical Study'. *The Standard Edition of the Complete Psychological Works of Sigmund Freud.* Trans. James Strachey. Vol. 20. Hogarth Press, 1959.
—. *Moses and Monotheism.* Trans. Katherine Jones. Vintage, 1939.
—. 'Screen Memories'. *Sigmund Freud: The Uncanny.* Trans. David McLintock. Introd. Hugh Haughton. Penguin Books, 2003.
—. *The Origins of Psychoanalysis: Sigmund Freud's Letters to Wilhelm Fliess, Drafts and Notes, 1887-1902.* Eds. Marie Bonaparte et al. Imago, 1954.
—. 'The Uncanny'. *The Standard Edition of the Complete Psychological Works of Sigmund Freud.* Trans. James Strachey. Hogarth Press and the Institute of Psycho-Analysis, 1955. 219-252.
Full House. Jeff Franklin. Warner Bros. Television Distribution, 1987-1995.
Funny Games. Dir. Michael Haneke. Warner Independent Pictures, 2007.
'Fusion Cuisine'. Dir. Ian Jones-Quartey et al. 6 Nov. 2014.
Galloway, Alexander. 'Social Realism in Gaming'. *Game Studies* 4.1 (2004).

Gamarra, Edward A. Jr. '*The Shining* as Postmodern Horror'. *Discovering Stephen King's The Shining: Essays on the Bestselling Novel by America's Premier Horror Writer*. Ed. Tony Magistrale. Wildside Press LLC, 2006. 95-106.

Game of Thrones. Benioff, David and Daniel Brett Weiss. Warner Bros. Television Distribution, 2011-2019.

George, Diana Hume. 'Lynching Women: A Feminist Reading of *Twin Peaks*'. *Secrets*, Lavery 109-119.

Gergen, Kenneth. *The Saturated Self: Dilemmas of Identity in Contemporary Life*. BasicBooks, 1991.

Get Out. Dir. Jordan Peele. Universal Pictures, 2017.

Giampietro, Rob. 'Spaces and Storytelling in *The Shining*'. *Lined and Unlined*. 2000. <https://linedandunlined.com/archive/spaces-and-storytelling/>.

'Giant Woman'. Dir. Ian Jones-Quartey et al. 24. Feb. 2014.

Gilbert, Sandra M. 'Writing wrong'. *a/b: Auto/Biography Studies* 14.1 (1999): 108-117.

Gilbert, Sophie. 'The Radical Sincerity of *The OA*'. *The Atlantic*. 19 Mar. 2019. <https://www.theatlantic.com/entertainment/archive/2019/03/the-return-of-the-oa-tvs-strangest-most-sincere-show/585208/>.

Giorgis, Hannah. 'Who Wants to Watch Black Pain?' *The Atlantic*. 17 Apr. 2021. <https://www.theatlantic.com/culture/archive/2021/04/black-horror-racism-them/618632/>.

Gibbs, Alan. *Contemporary American Trauma Narratives*. Edinburgh University Press, 2014.

—. 'Violence, Determinism and the Beset White Male in Twenty-First Century US Television: *The Shield*, *Dexter*, and *Breaking Bad*'. *CASiLaC*. 8 Apr. 2018. <http://casilac.ie/portfolio-item/april-18-2018-violence-determinism-and-the-beset-while-male-in-twenty-first-century-us-television-the-shield-dexter-and-breaking-bad/>.

Grady, Constance. 'The waves of feminism, and why people keep fighting over them, explained'. *Vox*. 20 Jul. 2018. <https://www.vox.com/2018/3/20/16955588/feminism-waves-explained-first-second-third-fourth>.

Grey's Anatomy. Shonda Rhimes. ABC, 2005-present.

Gross, Terry. '*Mr Robot* Creator Says His Own Anxiety and Hacking Helped Inspire The Show'. *NPR*. 30 Oct. 2019. <https://www.npr.org/2019/10/30/774691659/mr-robot-creator-says-his-own-anxiety-and-hacking-helped-inspire-the-show#:~:text='Mr.-,Robot'%20Creator%20Sam%20Esmail%20Says%20Anxiety%20And%20Hacking%20Inspired%20The,to%20create%20his%20hit%20show>.

Grow, Kory. "*The OA*: Behind the Scenes of Netflix's Mysterious New Hit Series." *The Mary Sue*. 23 December 2016. <https://www.themarysue.com/the-oa-the-sound-of-my-voice-and-believing-women/>.

Haas, Bob, et al. 'Sit and Shine'. *Discovering*, Magistrale 107-122.
Hague, Angela. 'Infinite Games: The Derationalisation of Detection in *Twin Peaks*'. *Secrets*, Lavery 130-143.
Hala, James. 'Kubrick's *The Shining*: The Spectres and the Critics'. *The Shining Reader*. Ed Tony Magistrale. Starmont House, 1991. 203-216.
Halfyard, Janet K. *Danny Elfman's Batman: A Film Score Guide*. Scarecrow Press, 2004.
Halloween Kills. David Gordon Green. Universal Pictures, 2021.
Hannibal. Bryan Fuller. Sony Pictures Television, 2013-2015.
Happiness. Dir. Todd Solondz. Good Machine Releasing, 1998.
Hardy, Phil. *The BFI Companion to Crime*. University of California Press, 1997.
Hassler-Forest, Dan A. 'Redefining Superheroes in Post-9/11 Hollywood'. *Comics as a Nexus of Cultures: Essays on the Interplay of Media, Disciplines and International Perspectives*. Eds. Jochen Ecke and Gideon Haberkorn. McFarland, 2010. 33-44.
Hastings, Reed. '6 Things You Need to Know About How Netflix Built Its Powerful Culture'. Conducted by Andrea Huspeni. *Entrepreneur*. 29 Jun. 2017. <https://www.entrepreneur.com/article/296209>.
Hawthorne, Nathaniel. *The Scarlet Letter*. Holt, Rinehart and Winston, 1947.
Hayles, N. Katherine. 'Saving the Subject: Remediation in *House of Leaves*'. *American Literature* 74.4 (2002): 779-806.
Hayward, Susan. *Cinema Studies: The Key Concepts*. Psychology Press, 2000.
Heberle, Mark A. *A Trauma Artist: Tim O'Brien and the Fiction of Vietnam*. University of Iowa Press, 2001.
Heinemann, Larry. *Paco's Story*. Vintage Contemporaries, 2005.
Heldenfels, Richard D. 'More Than The Hood Was Red: The Joker as Marxist'. *The Joker: A Serious Study of the Clown Prince of Crime*. Eds. Robert Moses Peaslee and Robert G. Weiner. University Press of Mississippi, 2015. 94-108.
Heller, Joseph. *Catch-22*. The Modern Library, 1961.
'Hello, Elliot'. Dir. Sam Esmail. 22 Dec. 2019a.
Henke, Suzette. *Shattered Subjects: Trauma and Testimony in Women's Life-Writing*. St. Martin's, 2000.
Hereditary. Dir. Ari Aster. A24, 2018.
Herman, Judith Lewis. *Father-Daughter Incest*. Harvard University Press, 1981. Print.
—. *Trauma and Recovery*. BasicBooks, 1997. Print.
Heron, Michael James and Pauline Helen Belford. 'All of Your Co-Workers are Gone: Story, Substance, and the Empathic Puzzler'. *Journal of Games Criticism* 2.1 (2015): 1-29.
Householder, April Kalogeropoulos and Adrienne Trier-Bieniek. *Feminist Perspectives on Orange is the New Black: Thirteen Critical Essays*. McFarland, 2016.
House of Cards. Beau Willimon. Sony Pictures Television, 2013-2018.

Hibbs, Thomas S. *Shows about Nothing: Nihilism in Popular Culture*. Baylor University Press, 2012.

Hodgin, Nick and Amit Thakkar. *Scars and Wounds: Film and Legacies of Trauma*. Springer International Publishing, 2017.

Horror Noire: A History of Black Horror. Shudder, 2019.

Hughes, William. 'Undertale dares players to make a mistake they can never take back'. *AV Club*. 9 Dec. 2015. <https://www.avclub.com/undertale-dares-players-to-make-a-mistake-they-can-neve-1798287299>

Hunt, Nigel C. *Memory, War and Trauma*. Cambridge University Press, 2010.

Hutcheon, Linda. *The Politics of Postmodernism*. Routledge, 2002.

'I Am Also A We'. *Sense8*. Dir. The Wachowskis. 5 Jun. 2015.

'I Have No Room in My Heart for Hate'. *Sense8*. Dir. James McTeigue. 5 May. 2017.

I Love Lucy. Writ. Jess Oppenheimer et al. CBS Films, 1967-1968.

I'm Thinking of Ending Things. Dir. Charlie Kaufman. Netflix, 2020.

Inland Empire. Dir. David Lynch. 518 Media, 2006.

Inside. Dir. Arnt Jensen. Playdead, 2016.

Iron Man 3. Dir. Shane Black. Walt Disney Studios Motion Pictures, 2013.

Isn't It Romantic. Dir. Todd Strauss-Schulson. Warner Bros. Pictures, 2019.

Jacksepticeye. 'Don't Trust This Game, *Doki Doki Literature Club*, Part 1'. *YouTube*. 27 Nov. 2017. <https://www.youtube.com/watch?v=jKgNdM1jPe0>

Jameson, Fredric. 'Historicism in *The Shining* (1981)'. *Signatures of the Visible*. Routledge, 1992. 82-98.

—. *Postmodernism, or, The cultural logic of late capitalism*. Duke University Press, 1991.

Jancovich, Mark and Nathan Hunt. 'The Mainstream, Distinctions and Cult TV'. *Cult Television*. Eds. Sara Gwenllian-Jones and Roberta E. Pearson. University of Minnesota Press, 2004. 27-44.

Jeffries, Dru. 'Kubrick and Curation: Inside TIFF's *Stanley Kubrick: The Exhibition*'. *The Kubrick Legacy*. Ed. Mick Broderick. Routledge, 2019. 7-21.

Jessica Jones. Melissa Rosenberg. Netflix, 2015-2019.

Johnson, Diane and Jan Harlan. '*The Shining* Producer Explains Ending Changes'. Conducted by James Hibberd. *Entertainment Weekly*. 30 Mar. 2017. <https://ew.com/movies/2017/03/30/shining-ending-explained/>.

Johnson, Diane. 'Writing *The Shining*'. Cocks et al. 55-61.

Joyce, James. *Finnegans Wake*. Penguin, 1973.

Joyce, Lindsey. 'Assessing *Mass Effect 2 and Elder Scrolls V: Skyrim*: Using Collaborative Criteria for Player Agency in Interactive Narratives'. *Journal of Games Criticism* 3.1 (2016).

Jung, E. Alex. "The Gentle Queerness of Netflix's *The OA*." *Vulture*. 6 January 2017. <https://www.vulture.com/2017/01/oa-netflix-gentle-queerness.html>.

'Jungle Moon'. Dir. Ki-Yong Bae et al. 5 Jan. 2018.

Kael, Pauline. 'Excerpts from the New Yorker Review of *The Shining*'. *The New Yorker Magazine.* 9 June. 1980. <https://www.newyorker.com/culture/culture-desk/come-play-with-the-shining>.

Kaplan, E Ann. 'Melodrama, Cinema and Trauma'. *Screen* 42.2 (2001): 201-205.

Kaplan, E. Ann and Ben Wang. *Trauma and Cinema: Cross-Cultural Explorations.* Hong Kong University Press, 2004.

Kay, Wallace G. 'Blake, Baudelaire, Beckett: The Romantics of Nihilism'. *Southern Quarterly: A Journal of the Arts in the South* 9 (1971): 253-59.

Keegan, Cáel M. *Lana and Lilly Wachowski: Sensing Transgender.* University of Illinois Press, 2018.

—. 'Tongues without bodies: the Wachowskis' *Sense8*'. Transgender Studies Quarterly 3.3-4 (2016): 605-610.

Kelley, Sonaiya. 'Reviving *Candyman*: How Jordan Peele and Nia DaCosta made more than a sequel'. *Los Angeles Times.* 26 Aug. 2021. <https://www.latimes.com/entertainment-arts/movies/story/2021-08-26/candyman-sequel-explained-nia-dacosta-jordan-peele/>.

*Kevin can F**k Himself.* Valerie Armstrong. AMC, 2021.

King, Stephen. *Carrie.* Pocket Books, 1999.

—. *Gerald's Game.* Viking, 1992.

—. *IT.* Simon and Schuster, 1986.

—. 'The Library Policeman'. *Four Past Midnight.* Viking, 1990.

—. *The Shining.* Doubleday, 1977.

—. *The Stand.* Knopf Doubleday Publishing Group, 2008.

Kroker, Arthur. *The Will to Technology and the Culture of Nihilism: Heidegger, Nietzsche and Marx.* University of Toronto Press, 2004.

Kolker, Robert. *A Cinema of Loneliness.* Oxford University Press, 2011.

Krzywinska, Tanya. 'Zombies in Gamespace: Form Context, and Meaning in Zombie-Based Video Games'. *Zombie Culture: Autopsies of the Living Dead.* Eds. Shawn McIntosh and Mark Leverette. The Scarecrow Press Inc., 2008. 153-68.

Kubrick, Stanley. 'Kubrick: Exclusive Interview'. Conducted by John Hofsess. *Cinephilia & Beyond.* 1980a. <https://cinephiliabeyond.org/stanley-kubricks-treatment-of-the-shining/>.

—. 'Kubrick on *The Shining*: An Interview with Michel Ciment'. Conducted by Michel Ciment. *The Kubrick Site.* 1980b. <http://www.visual-memory.co.uk/amk/doc/interview.ts.html>.

—. 'Stanley Kubrick *The Shining* Interview'. Conducted by Michel Ciment. *Stanley Kubrick A Vox Nue.* 1980c. <https://cinephiliabeyond.org/stanley-kubricks-treatment-of-the-shining/>.

Kuzniar, Alice. 'Double Talk in *Twin Peaks*'. *Secrets,* Lavery 16-29.

Lacan, Jacques. *Ecrits: The First Complete Edition in English*. Trans. Bruce Fink. W.W. Norton & Company, 2006.

LaCapra, Dominick. *Writing History, Writing Trauma*. Johns Hopkins University Press, 2014.

Lachenal, Jessica. 'Lilly Wachowski Acknowledges Re-Examination of The Matrix With Lens Focused on Transness'. *The Mary Sue*. 5 Apr. 2016. <https://www.themarysue.com/the-matrix-trans-lens/>.

Lange, Amanda. "You're Just Gonna Be Nice': How Players Engage with Moral Choice Systems'. *Journal of Games Criticism* 1.1 (2014).

Larson, Lauren. 'How *Mr Robot*'s Rami Malek Hacked His Way into Hollywood'. *GQ*. 11 Jul. 2016. <https://www.gq.com/story/mr-robot-rami-malek-hacked-hollywood>.

Lee, Meera. 'Psychoanalysis and 'Imaginary Ethnography''. *Verge: Studies in Global Asias* 1.1 (2015): 69-73.

Leibowitz, Flo and Lynn Jeffress. 'Stanley Kubrick's *The Shining*: Review by Flo Leibowitz and Lynn Jeffress'. *Film Quarterly* 34.3 (1981): 45-51.

Leon, Melissa. 'Secrets of *The OA*': Co-Creator Brit Marling Explains What the Hell is Happening in the Netflix Sci-Fi Mystery'. *Daily Beast*. 12 Jul. 2017. <https://www.thedailybeast.com/secrets-of-the-oa-co-creator-brit-marling-explains-what-the-hell-is-happening-in-the-netflix-sci-fi-mystery>.

Levesley, David. 'Here's the Best Queer Scene in *Sense8*'. *Slate*. 22 Jun. 2015. <https://slate.com/human-interest/2015/06/in-sense8-netflix-has-created-a-queer-masterpiece.html>.

Lewis, Rachel Charlene, and Marina Watanabe. '*Steven Universe* Future Hasn't Backed down from Mental Health'. *Bitch Media*. 19 Mar. 2020. <https://www.bitchmedia.org/article/steven-universe-future-review-mental-health-ptsd#:~:text=%E2%80%9CSteven%20Universe%20Future%E2%80%9D%20Hasn't%20Backed%20down%20from%20Mental%20Health&text=In%20Steven%20Universe%20Future's%20first,sign%20of%20his%20internalized%20pain>.

Leys, Ruth. *Trauma: A Genealogy*. University of Chicago Press, 2000.

Lifton, Jay. 'Survivor Experience and Traumatic Syndrome'. *The Broken Connection: On Death and the Continuity of Life*. American Psychiatric Pub, 1966. 163-78.

Light, Clare. '*Sense8* and the Failure of Global Imagination'. *Nerds of Colour*. 10 Jun.2015.<https://thenerdsofcolor.org/2015/06/10/sense8-and-the-failure-of-global-imagination/>.

Limbo. Dir. Arnt Jensen. Playdead, 2010.

Lindelof, Damon and Tom Perrotta. 'Did *The Leftovers* Finale Answer What Happened to the Departed?' Conducted by Joanna Robinson. *Vanity Fair*. 5 Jun. 2017. <https://www.vanityfair.com/hollywood/2017/06/leftovers-finale-recap-what-happened-to-the-departed-truth-lindelof-interview>.

—. *The Leftovers*. HBO, 2014-2017.

Little, William G. 'Nothing to Write Home About: Impossible Reception in Mark Z. Danielewski's *House of Leaves*'. *Postmodern Studies* 40 (2007): 169-199.

Livingstone, Jo. '*Candyman* Grapples With the Horror of Selling Trauma'. *Critical Mass*. 27 Aug. 2021. <https://newrepublic.com/article/163449/candyman-grapples-horror-selling-trauma-movie-review>.

'Lonely Souls'. Dir. Lynch. 10 Nov. 1990.

Lowenstein, Adam. *Shocking Representation: Historical Trauma, National Cinema, and the Modern Horror Film*. Columbia University Press, 2005.

Luckhurst, Roger. 'In War Times: Fictionalising Iraq'. *Contemporary Literature* 53.4 (2012): 713-737.

—. *The Shining (BFI Film Classics)*. Bloomsbury Academic, 2013.

—. *The Trauma Question*. Routledge, 2008.

Lutz, John. 'From Domestic Nightmares to the Nightmare of History'. *Philosophy*, Fahy 161-178.

Lynch, Jennifer. *The Secret Diary of Laura Palmer*. Pocket Books, 1990a.

Lyotard, Jean-Francois. *The Postmodern Condition: A Report on Knowledge*. Trans. Arthur Goldhammer. University of Minnesota Press, 1984.

Macklin, Anthony F. 'Understanding Kubrick: *The Shining*'. *Journal of Popular Film and Television* 9.2 (1981): 93-95.

Madigan, Mark J. "Orders from the House': Kubrick's *The Shining* and Kafka's *The Metamorphosis*'. *Discovering*, Magistrale 74-81.

Magistrale, Tony. 'Introduction'. *Discovering*, Magistrale 5-18.

Mamatas, Nick. 'Holy Signifier, Batman!' *Batman Unauthorised: Vigilantes, Jokers, and Heroes in Gotham City*. Eds. Dennis O'Neil and Leah Wilson. BenBella Books, 2008. 47-54.

Manchel, Frank. 'What About Jack? Another Perspective on Family Relationships in Stanley Kubrick's *The Shining*'. *Discovering*, Magistrale 82-94.

Marling, Brit. "Brit Marling Mediates on Life and (Near) Death in *The OA*." Conducted by Kristina Lopez. *WUNC 91.5: North Carolina Public Radio*. 20 January 2017. <https://www.kcbx.org/post/brit-marling-meditates-life-and-near-death-oa#stream/0>.

—. "Brit Marling Spills on Her Mysterious New Netflix Show *The OA*." Conducted by Maria Bonner. *Marie Claire*. 16 December 2016. <https://www.marieclaire.com/culture/interviews/a24243/brit-marling-the-oa-interview/>.

Marling, Brit and Zal Batmanglij, creators. *The OA*, season 1, Netflix, 2016-2019.

—. 'Secrets of *The OA* Co-Creator Brit Marling Explains What the Hell is Happening in the Netflix Sci-Fi Mystery'. Conducted by Melissa Leon. *Daily Beast*. 21 December 2017. <https://www.thedailybeast.com/secrets-of-the-oa-co-creator-brit-marling-explains-what-the-hell-is-happening-in-the-netflix-sci-fi-mystery>.

—. '*The OA* Creators Explain Netflix's Mysterious New Drama'. Conducted by Debra Birnbaum. *Variety*. 16 December 2016. <https://variety.com/2016/tv/news/the-oa-producers-netflix-brit-marling-zal-batmanglij-1201942744/>.

Maslin, Janet. 'Nicholson and Shelley Duvall in Kubrick's *The Shining*'. *Film Review*. 23 May. 1980. <https://archive.nytimes.com/www.nytimes.com/library/film/052380kubrick-shining.html>.

Master. Mariama Diallo. Amazon Studios, 2021.

Mayer, So. 'Dancing in the Streets: The Politics of Sense8's Pleasure Activism'. *Sense8: Transcending Television*. Eds. Deborah Shaw and Rob Stone. Bloomsbury Academic, 2021. 177-196.

McDonnell, Chris, and Cartoon Network Enterprises. *Steven Universe: Art & Origins*. Abrams, 2017.

McGowan, Todd. *The Impossible David Lynch*. Columbia University Press, 2007.

McHale, Brian. *Postmodernist Fiction*. Methuen, 1987.

McNally, Richard J. 'Conceptual Problems with the DSM-IV Criteria for Posttraumatic Stress Disorder'. *Posttraumatic Stress Disorder: Issues and Controversies*. Ed. Gerald M. Rosen. John Wiley and Sons Ltd, 2004. 1-14.

Melley, Timothy. 'Postmodern Amnesia: Trauma and Forgetting in Tim O'Brien's *In the Lake of the Woods*'. *Contemporary Literature* 44:1 (2003): 106-131.

Midnight Mass. Dir. Mike Flanagan. Netflix, 2021.

Midsommar. Dir. Ari Aster. A24, 2019.

Miles, Robert. *Gothic Writing, 1750-1820: A Genealogy*. Manchester University Press Series, 2002.

Miller, Frank. *Batman: Year One*. DC Comics, 1987.

'Mindful Education'. Dir. Joe Johnston et al. 25 Aug. 2016a.

Monika After Story. Monika After Mod Team. 2017.

Moody, Raymond. *Life After Life*. Rider, 2001.

Moonlighting. Glenn Gordon Caron. ABC Distribution Company, 1985-1989.

Mooney, Darren. '*Candyman* Is About Art About Trauma'. *The Escapist*. 27 Aug. 2021. <https://www.escapistmagazine.com/candyman-is-about-art-about-trauma/>.

Moore, Lorrie. *A Gate at the Stairs*. Random House, 2009.

Morag, Raya. *Waltzing with Bashir: Perpetrator Trauma and Cinema*I. B. Tauris, 2013.

Morrison, Toni. *Beloved*. Knopf, 1987.

Mother! Dir. Darren Aronofsky. Paramount Pictures, 2017.

Mulkern, Patrick. '*Doctor Who*: The God Complex'. *Radio Times*. 18 Sept. 2011. <https://www.radiotimes.com/tv/sci-fi/doctor-who-guide/doctor-who-the-god-complex/>.

Mulvey, Laura. 'Visual Pleasure and Narrative Cinema.' *Visual and Other Pleasures*. Palgrave Macmillan, 1989. 14-26.

Nabokov, Vladimir. *Lolita*. Random House US, 2010.
Naremore, James. *On Kubrick*. British Film Institute, 2007.
Neale, Steven. 'Masculinity as Spectacle: Reflections on Men and Mainstream Cinema'. *Screening the Male: Exploring Masculinities in Hollywood Cinema*. Eds. Steve Cohan and Ina Rae Hark. Routledge, 1993. 9– 22.
Neela, Debnath. 'Review of *Doctor Who* "The God Complex"'. *The Independent*. 8 May. 2012. <https://web.archive.org/web/20120508010005/http://blogs.independent.co.uk/2011/09/18/review-of-doctor-who-%E2%80%98the-god-complex%E2%80%99/>.
Nelson, Thomas Allen. 'Remembrance of Things Forgotten: *The Shining*'. *Kubrick: Inside a Film Artist's Artist's Maze*. Indiana University Press, 1982. 195-227.
Newby, Richard. 'Unpacking *Candyman* and Its Darkest Revelation'. *The Hollywood Reporter*. 30 Aug. 2021. <https://www.hollywoodreporter.com/movies/movie-features/candyman-jordan-peele-nia-dacosta-1235005120/>.
Newell, Mindy. *Catwoman*. DC Comics, 1989.
Nicol, Bran. *The Cambridge Introduction to Postmodern Fiction*. Cambridge University Press, 2009.
Nietzsche, Friedrich. *The Will To Power*. Trans. Walter Kaufman and R.J. Hollingdale. Vintage Books, 1968.
Nochimson, Martha. 'Desire Under the Douglas Firs: Entering the Body of Reality in *Twin Peaks*'. *Secrets*, Lavery 144-159.
O'Brien, Tim. *In the Lake of the Woods*. Penguin Books, 1995.
Okoya, Wenimo. 'Community Healing is the Systemic Change People of Colour Need'. *Children's Health Fund*. 3 Aug. 2020. <https://www.childrenshealthfund.org/community-healing-is-the-systemic-change-people-of-color-need/>
'Ones-and-zer0es.mpeg'. Dir. Niels Arden Oplev. 1 Jul. 2015.
Orange is the New Black. Jenji Kohan. Netflix, 2013-2019.
Orland,Kyle.'Op-ed:whyphotorealismisn'tthekeytoemotionalgamingexperiences'. *ArsTechnica*. 2 Aug. 2012. <https://arstechnica.com/gaming/2012/08/op-ed-why-photorealism-isnt-the-key-to-emotional-gaming-experiences/>
Owens, Craig. 'The Discourse of Others: Feminists and Postmodernism'. *The Anti-Aesthetic: Essays on Postmodern Culture*. Ed. Hal Foster. New Press, 1985. 57-82.
Pan's Labyrinth. Dir. Guillermo del Toro. Warno Bros., 2006.
Pederson, Joshua. 'Speak, Trauma: Toward a Revised Understanding of Literary Trauma Theory'. *Narrative* 22.3 (2014): 333-353.
PEN15. Maya Erskine and Anna Konkle. Hulu, 2019-2021.
Perkins Gilman, Charlotte. 'The Yellow Wallpaper'. *The Charlotte Perkins Gilman Reader: The Yellow Wallpaper, and Other Fiction*. Pantheon Books, 1980.
Pezzotta, Elisa. *Stanley Kubrick: Adapting the Sublime*. Mississippi: University Press of Mississippi, 2013.

Pheasant-Kelly, Frances. 'Strange Spaces: Cult Topographies in *Twin Peaks*'. *Fan Phenomena: Twin Peaks*. Eds. Marisa C. Hayes, Franck Boulegue. Intellect Books, 2013. 94-107.

—. *Fantasy Film Post 9/11*. New York: Springer, 2016.

—. 'Reframing Gender and Visual Pleasure: New Signifying Practices in Contemporary Cinema'. *Sensational Pleasures in Cinema, Literature and Visual Culture*. Palgrave Macmillan, London, 2014. 195-212.

—. 'Signifying Trauma in the Post-9/11 Combat Film: *The Hurt Locker* and In the *Valley of Elah*'. *Journal of War & Culture Studies* (2019): 1-21.

'Pilot: Northwest Passage'. Dir. David Lynch. 8 April. 1990b.

Pinedo, Isabel Cristina. 'Postmodern Elements of the Contemporary Horror Film'. *The Horror Film*. Ed. Stephen Prince. Rutgers University Press, 2004. 85-117.

—. *Recreational Terror: Women and the Pleasures of Viewing*. State of New York Press, 1977.

Pitre, Jake. 'Queer Transformation, Contested Authorship, and Fluid Fandom'. *Representation*, Ziegler and Richards 19-44.

Poe, Edgar Allan. 'The Fall of the House of Usher'. *The Works of Edgar Allan Poe*. Harper and Bros, 1910.

Pratt, Alan. 'Nihilism'. *Internet Encyclopedia of Philosophy*. (2005). <https://iep.utm.edu/nihilism/>.

Pratt, Kellee. '"Battle of the Sexes" Is a Reminder That Feminism Doesn't Mean Beating Men'. *Verily*. 25 Sept. 2017. <https://verilymag.com/2017/09/battle-of-the-sexes-feminism-is-about-men-and-women-working-together-09262017>.

Praxmarer, Matthew. 'Kurt Vonnegut's Early Novels: Searching for Meaning in a Meaningless World'. Thesis. Governors State University, Illinois, 2011.

'Proxy Authentication Required'. Dir. Sam Esmail. 17 Nov. 2019b.

Psycho. Dir. Alfred Hitchcock. Paramount Pictures, 1960.

Pynchon, Thomas. *Gravity's Rainbow*. Viking Press, 1973.

—. *The Crying of Lot 49*. Lippincott, 1966.

Radstone, Susannah. 'Trauma and Screen Studies: Opening the Debate'. *Screen* 42.2 (2001): 188-193.

—. 'Trauma Theory: Contexts, Politics, Ethics'. *Paragraph* 30.1 (2007): 9-29.

Ramadanovic, Petar. "From Haunting to Trauma: Nietzsche's Active Forgetting and Blanchot's Writing of the Disaster." *Postmodern Culture* 11.2 (2001).

Rauscher, Andreas. 'The Marvel Universe on Screen: A New Wave of Superhero Movies?' *Comics as a Nexus of Cultures: Essays on the Interplay of Media, Disciplines and International Perspectives*. Eds. Mark Berninger, Jochen Ecke and Gideon Haberkorn. McFarland, 2010. 33-45.

Rayborn, Tim and Abigail Keyes. *Jessica Jones, Scarred Superhero: Essays on Gender, Trauma and Addiction in the Netflix Series*. McFarland, 2018. Print.

Reddy, Helen. 'I am Woman'. *I Don't Know How to Love Him.* Capitol Records, 1971.

'Request Timeout'. Dir. Sam Esmail. 23 Nov. 2019c.

Requiem for a Dream. Dir. Darren Aronofsky. Artisan Entertainment, 2000.

Richardson, John. '*Laura* and *Twin Peaks*: Postmodern Parody and the Musical Reconstruction of the Absent Femme Fatale'. *The Cinema of David Lynch: American Dreams, Nightmare Visions.* Eds. Erica Sheen and Annette Davison. Wallflower Press, 2004. 77-92.

Rick and Morty. Justin Roiland and Dan Harmon. Warner Bros. Television Distribution, 2013-present.

Rodley, Chris. *Lynch on Lynch.* Faber and Faber, 1997.

Room 237. Dir. Rodney Ascher. IFC Films, 2012.

Roth, Philip. *The Plot Against America.* Vintage International, 2005.

Rothberg, Michael. *Multidirectional Memory: Remembering the Holocaust in the Age of Decolonisation.* Stanford University Press, 2009.

—. *The Implicated Subject: Beyond Victims and Perpetrators.* Stanford University Press, 2019.

Rothe, Anne. *Popular Trauma Culture: Selling the Pain of Others in the Mass Media.* Rutgers University Press, 2011.

Royle, Nicholas. *The Uncanny.* Manchester University Press, 2002.

Ryan, Gail. 'Victim to Victimiser: Rethinking Victim Treatment'. Abstract. *Journal of Interpersonal Violence* 4.3 (1989): 325-341.

Sartre, Jean-Paul. *Existentialism is a Humanism.* Trans. Philip Mairet. Yale University Press, 1975.

Saw. Dir. James Wan. Lions Gate Films, 2004.

Schedeen, Jesse. 'Netflix's *The OA* Season 2 Review'. *IGN.* 29 Oct. 2019. <https://www.ign.com/articles/2019/03/23/netflixs-the-oa-season-2-review>.

Scream. Dir. Wes Craven. Woods Entertainment, 1996.

Scream 3. Dir. Wes Craven. Dimension Films, 2000.

Seinfeld. Larry David and Jerry Seinfeld. Columbia Pictures Television, 1989-1998.

Sense8. Lana and Lily Wachowski. Netflix, 2015-2018.

Severance. Dan Erickson. Apple Inc., 2022-present.

Shang-Chi and The Legend of The Ten Rings. Destin Daniel Cretton. Walt Disney Studios Motion Pictures, 2021.

Shastri, Sudha. 'Return to the beginning: *House of Leaves* by Mark Z. Danielewski'. *Atenea* 26.2 (2006): 81-94.

Shelley, Mary. *Frankenstein.* Oxford University Press, 1998.

Shoah. Dir. Claude Lanzmann. New Yorker Films, 1985.

'shutdown -r'. Dir. Sam Esmail. 6 Dec. 2017.

Sizemore-Barber, April, Elizabeth Velez and Hanna Chan. 'Feminists from 3 different generations talk #MeToo'. *Vox.* 31 Jan. 2018. <https://www.

vox.com/conversations/2018/1/31/16952380/me-too-second-third-wave-feminism-backlash>.

Sloboda, Nicholas. 'Heteroglossia and collage: Donald Barthelme's "Snow White"'. *Mosaic: A journal for the interdisciplinary study of literature* 30.4 (1997): 109+. <gale.com/apps/doc/A20403103/LitRC?u=anon~8a127950&sid=googleScholar&xid=2110afcf>.

Slocombe, Will. 'Postmodern Nihilism: Theory and Literature'. *Nihilism and the Sublime Postmodern: The (Hi) Story of a Difficult Relationship*. Abingdon-on-Thames: Routledge, 2006.

—. "This is Not for You': Nihilism and the House that Jacques Built'. *Modern Fiction Studies* 51.1 (2005): 88-109.

Smart, Elizabeth. "'I was broken beyond repair': Elizabeth Smart recalls kidnapping ordeal." *NBC News*. Tracy Jarrett. 5 October 2013. <https://www.nbcnews.com/news/us-news/i-was-broken-beyond-repair-elizabeth-smart-recalls-kidnapping-ordeal-flna8C11336267>.

Smethurst, Tobi and Stef Craps. 'Playing with Trauma: Interreactivity, empathy, and complicity in *The Walking Dead* video game'. *Games and Culture* 10.3 (2015): 269-290.

Smethurst, Tobi. 'Playing Dead in Videogames: Trauma in *Limbo*'. *The Journal of Popular Culture* 48.5 (2015): 817-835.

Smith, Anthony N. 'Pursuing 'Generation Snowflake': Mr Robot and the USA Network's Mission for Millennials'. *Television & New Media* 20.5 (2019): 443-459.

Songbird. Adam Mason. STXfilms, 2022.

Sound of My Voice. Writ. Brit Marling and Zal Batmanglij. Fox Screenlight Pictures, 2011.

Sparks, Matt. 'Metafocus: Avoiding the Uncanny Valley in VR & Serious Games'. *Learning Solutions*. 26 Dec. 2019. <https://learningsolutionsmag.com/articles/metafocus-avoiding-the-uncanny-valley-in-vr-serious-games>

Spec Ops: The Line. Dir. Cory David and Francois Coulon. 2K Games, 2012. Game.

Sperb, Jason. *The Kubrick Façade: Faces and Voices in the Films of Stanley Kubrick*. Scarecrow Press, 2006.

Spider-Man. Dir. Sam Raimi. Sony Pictures Releasing, 2002.

Spider-Man 2. Dir. Sam Raimi. Sony Pictures Releasing, 2004.

Spider-Man 3. Dir. Sam Raimi. Sony Pictures Releasing, 2007.

Squid Game. Hwang Dong-hyuk. Netflix, 2021.

Stacey, Jackie. *Star Gazing: Hollywood Cinema and Female Spectatorship*. Routledge, 1994.

Staiger, Janet. *Perverse Spectators: The Practices of Film Reception*. New York University Press, 2000.

Stepić, Nikola N. 'Spectacles of Shame: Ryan Murphy as Curator of Queer Cultural Memory'. *Proceedings of the Faculty of Philosophy* 47.3 (2017): 71-86.

Steven Universe Future. Rebecca Sugar. Warner Bros. Domestic Television Distribution, 2019-2020.

Steven Universe: The Movie. Rebecca Sugar. Warner Bros. Domestic Television Distribution, 2019.

Stevenson, Diane. 'Family Romance, Family Violence, and the Fantastic in *Twin Peaks*'. *Secrets*, Lavery 70-81.

Stobbart, Dawn. *Videogames and Horror: From Amnesia to Zombies, Run!* University of Wales Press, 2019.

Strengell, Heidi. *Dissecting Stephen King: From the Gothic to Literary Naturalism*. Popular Press, 2005.

Strenger, Carlos. *The Fear of Insignificance: Searching for Meaning in the Twenty-First Century*. Palgrave-Macmillan, 2010.

'Super Watermelon Island'. Dir. Joe Johnston et al. 12 May. 2016b.

Swafford, Anthony. *Jarhead*. New York: Scribner, 2003.

Syme, Rachel. 'The Best, Most Inaccessible Show on Television'. *The News Republic*. 28 Mar. 2019. <https://newrepublic.com/article/153410/best-inaccessible-show-television>.

Tal, Kalí. *Worlds of Hurt: Reading the Literatures of Trauma*. Cambridge University Press, 1996.

Tanis, Martin. "Online Social Support Groups." *Oxford Handbook of Internet Psychology*. Ed. by Adam Joinson et al. Oxford University Press, 2007. Pp. 139-154.

Tehrani, Noreen. 'Psychological well-being and workability in child abuse investigations'. *Occupational Medicine* 68.3 (2018): 165-170.

Telotte, Jay P. 'The Dis-order of Things in *Twin Peaks*'. *Secrets*, Lavery 160-172.

The Big Lebowski. Dirs. Joel and Ethan Coen. Gramercy Pictures, 1988.

The Blair Witch Project. Dirs. Daniel Myrick and Eduardo Sánchez. Artisan Entertainment, 1999.

The Bourne Identity. Dir. Doug Liman. Universal Pictures, 2002.

The Cabin in the Woods. Joss Whedon. Lionsgate, 2012.

The Chronicles of Narnia: The Lion, the Witch and the Wardrobe. Dir. Andrew Adamson. Buena Vista Pictures, 2005.

The Dark Knight. Dir. Christopher Nolan. Warner Bros. Pictures, 2008.

The Day After Tomorrow. Roland Emmerich. 20th Century Fox, 2004.

The Good Doctor. David Shore. ABC, 2017-present.

The Inpatient. Dir. Nik Bowen. Supermassive Games, 2018. Game.

The Invisible Man. Dir. Leigh Whannell. Universal Pictures, 2020.

'The Kindergarten Kid'. Dir. Kat Morris et al. 11 Aug. 2016.

The Leftovers. Damon Lindelof and Tom Perrotta. Warner Bros. Television Distribution, 2014-2017.

The Matrix. Dir. The Wachowskis. Warner Bros., 1999.

The Melancholy of Haruhi Suzumiya. Tatsuya Ishihara. Kyoto Animation, 2006-2009.

The Night House. Dir. David Bruckner. Searchlight Pictures, 2020.

The OA. Brit Marling and Zal Batmanglij. Netflix, 2016-2019.

'*The OA* Creators Defend the Series' Most Controversial Twist: The Movements'. Jean Bentley. *The Hollywood Reporter*. <27 Dec. 2016. https://www.hollywoodreporter.com/tv/tv-news/oa-creators-defend-movements-959026/>

The Outsider. Richard Price. HBO, 2020.

The Ring. Dir. Gore Verbinski. DreamWorks Pictures, 2002.

The Shield. Shawn Ryan. 20th Television, 2002-2008.

The Shining. Dir. Stanley Kubrick. Warner Bros., 1980.

The Sinner. Derek Simonds. NBC Universal Television Distribution, 2017-2020.

The Stand. Josh Boone and Benjamin Cavell. CBS All Access, 2020-2021.

The Texas Chain Saw Massacre. Dir. Tobe Hooper. Bryanston Distributing Company, 1974.

The Truman Show. Dir. Peter Weir. Paramount Pictures, 1998.

The Twilight Zone. Jordan Peele CBS All Access. 2019-2020.

The Walking Dead. Frank Darabont. Fox Networks Group, 2010-present.

The Walking Dead: Season One. Telltale, 2012.

The Witch. Dir. Robert Eggers. A24, 2015.

This is Us. Dan Fogelman. NBC, 2016-2022.

Thomas, Kevin. 'Kubrick's Shining: A Freudian Picnic'. Los Angeles Times. 23 May. 1980. <https://notices.californiatimes.com/gdpr/latimes.com/>.

Thornhill, Dreebs. '*House of Leaves* changed my life: the cult novel at 20'. Conducted by Andrew Lloyd. *The Guardian*. 2 Apr. 2020. <https://www.theguardian.com/books/2020/apr/02/house-of-leaves-changed-my-life-the-cult-novel-at-20>.

'Together Alone'. Dir. Kat Morris et al. 31 Dec. 2018.

Travers, Ben. '*The OA* Ending: What's Good, Bad, and Offensive About a Final That Demands To Be Seen'. *IndieWire*. 20 Dec. 2016. <https://www.indiewire.com/2016/12/the-oa-ending-spoilers-netflix-1201760740/>.

Tuca and Bertie. Lisa Hawnawalt. Tornante Productions, LLC, 2019.

Turim, Maureen. 'The Trauma of History: Flashbacks Upon Flashbacks'. *Screen* 42.2 (2001): 205-210.

Turning Red. Domee Shi. Walt Disney Studios Motion Pictures, 2022.

Turnipseed, Joel. *Baghdad Express*. Penguin Books, 2003.

Twin Peaks: *Fire Walk with Me*. David Lynch and Mark Frost. New Line Cinema, 1992.

Twin Peaks: *The Return*. David Lynch and Mark Frost. Showtime, 2017.

Unbreakable Kimmy Schmidt. Tina Fey and Robert Carlock. NBC Universal Television Distribution, 2015-2019.

Undertale. Toby Fox. GameMaker Studio, 2015.

Until Dawn. Will Byles. Supermassive Games, 2015.

Us. Dir. Jordan Peele. Universal Pictures, 2019.

'USS Callister'. *Black Mirror*. Writ. Charlie Brooker and William Bridges. Netflix, 2017.

Valenti, Jessica. 'Fourth-Wave Feminism: Questions for Jessica Valenti'. Conducted by Deborah Solomon. *The New York Times Magazine*. 13 Nov. 2009.

Van der Kolk, Bessel A and Onno van der Hart. 'The Intrusive Past: The Flexibility of Memory and the Engraving of Trauma'. Caruth, *Trauma* 158-182.

Van der Kolk, Bessel A. *Psychological Trauma*. American Psychiatric Pub, 2003.

Van Der Ster, Jelle. 'Lost in the Funhouse: Postmodern meta-reflections in videogames'. *Uni>ersia*. 24 Sept. 2009. <http://citeseerx.ist.psu.edu/viewdoc/summary?doi=10.1.1.94.4737>.

VanDerWerff, Emily. 'Netflix's *Sense8* is Complete Nonsense, but Deeply Lovable'. *Vox*. 7 May 2017. <https://www.vox.com/culture/2017/5/7/15563788/sense8-season-2-review-netflix>.

Vees-Gulani, Susanne. 'Diagnosing Billy Pilgrim: A psychiatric approach to Kurt Vonnegut's *Slaughterhouse-Five*.' *Critique: Studies in Contemporary Fiction* 44.2 (2003): 175-184.

Vickroy, Laurie. *Trauma and Survival in Contemporary Fiction*. University of Virginia Press, 2002.

Vidler, Anthony. *The Architectural Uncanny: Essays in the Modern Unhomely*. MIT Press, 1992.

Viruet, Pilot. 'In Season 2, *Dear White People* takes on trauma and the Internet'. *The Verge*. 4 May. 2018. <https://www.theverge.com/2018/5/4/17320358/netflix-dear-white-people-season-2-justin-simien-internet-trolls-racism-online-bullying>.

Volmar, Daniel. 'Far from the lonely crowd: the trenchant techno-cynicism of *Mr Robot*'. *Endeavour* 41.4 (2017): 208-210.

Vonnegut, Kurt. *Cat's Cradle*. Dial Press Trade Paperbacks, 2010.

—. *Conversations with Kurt Vonnegut*. Ed. William Richard Allen. University Press of Mississippi, 1988.

—. *Slaughterhouse-Five*. Dial Press, 2005.

Walker, Janet. *Trauma Cinema: Documenting Incest and the Holocaust*. University of California Press, 2005.

—. 'Trauma Cinema: False Memories and True Experience'. *Screen* 42.2 (2001): 211-216.

WandaVision. Jac Shaeffer. Disney Platform Distribution, 2021.

Watchmen. Damon Lindelof. HBO, 2019.

Weinstein, Arnold. *Nobody's Home: Speech, Self, and Place in American Fiction from Hawthorne to DeLillo*. Oxford University Press, 1993.

Weiss, Penny A. 'Introduction'. *Feminism and Community*. Eds. Penny A. Weiss and Marilyn Friedman. Temple University Press, 1995. 3-18.

Weiss, Suzannah. “I Didn’t Want To Be Aroused By My Sexual Assault, But I Was.” *The Establishment.* 29 Aug, 2018. <https://medium.com/the-establishment/i-didnt-want-to-be-aroused-by-my-sexual-assault-but-i-was-ec5b9e9c04c1>.

Wes Craven’s New Nightmare. Dir. Wes Craven. New Line Cinema, 1994.

Westworld. Jonathan Nolan and Lisa Joy. Warner Bros. Television Distribution, 2016-present.

We Were Soldiers. Dir. Randall Wallace. Paramount Pictures, 2002.

‘What is Hive Mentality’. *WebMD.* <https://www.webmd.com/mental-health/what-is-hive-mentality>.

Wheatley, Helen. *Gothic Television.* Manchester University Press, 2006.

Whitehead, Anne. *Trauma Fiction.* Edinburgh University Press, 2004.

‘Whoami’. Dir. Sam Esmail. 22 Dec. 2019.

Williams, Janet B. W. and American Psychiatric Association. *Diagnostic and Statistical Manual of Mental Disorders: DSM-III-R.* 3th ed. American Psychiatric Association, 1987.

Williams, Jordan. ‘All 6 Candymen Explained: Origins, Differences, Real Meanings’. *Screen Rant.* 31 Aug. 2021. <https://screenrant.com/candyman-2021-different-candymen-characters-origins-meaning/>.

Williams, Kayla. *Love My Rifle More Than You.* W. W. Norton, 2005.

Williams, Linda. ‘When the woman looks’. *Re-vision: Essays in Feminist Film Criticism.* Eds. Mary Anne Doane and Patricia Mellencamp. University Publications of America, 1984.

Williams, Monnica. ‘Racism’s Psychological Toll’. *New York Times.* Conducted by Jenna Wortham. 24 Jun. 2015. <https://www.nytimes.com/2015/06/24/magazine/racisms-psychological-toll.html>.

Wood, Robin. ‘*Psycho*’. Alfred Hitchcock’s Psycho: A Casebook’. Ed. Robert Kolker. Ebrary, 2006. 74-84.

Woodward, Ashley. ‘Nihilism and the Postmodern in Vattimo’s Nietzsche’. *Minerva – An Internet Journal of Philosophy* 6 (2002): 51-67.

—. *Nihilism in Postmodernity: Lyotard, Baudrillard, Vattimo.* Davies Group, Publishers, 2009.

—. ‘Postmodern’. *Internet Encyclopedia of Philosophy.* (2005). <https://iep.utm.edu/lyotard/>.

Wright, Evan. *Generation Kill.* Penguin Publishing Group, 2004.

Wright, Jarrell D. ‘Reconsidering Fidelity and Considering Genre in (and with) *The Shining*’. *Stabley Kubrick: Essays on his Films and Legacy.* Ed. Gary D. Rhodes. McFarland, 2015.

—. ‘Shades of Horror: Fidelity and Genre in Stanley Kubrick’s *The Shining*’. *True to the Spirit: Film Adaptation and the Question of Fidelity.* Eds. MacCabe et al. Oxford University Press, 2011.

Wulf, Kansteiner. 'Genealogy of a category mistake: a critical intellectual history of the cultural trauma metaphor'. *Rethinking History* 8.2 (2004): 193-221.

Wyman, Bill. 'Come Play with *The Shining*'. *The New Yorker*. 29 Mar. 2013. <https://www.newyorker.com/culture/culture-desk/come-play-with-the-shining>.

Young, Allan. *The Harmony of Illusions: Inventing Post-Traumatic Stress Disorder*. Princeton University Press. 1997.

Young Frankenstein. Dir. Mel Brooks. 20th Century Fox, 1974.

'Zen, or the Skill to Catch a Killer'. Dir. Lynch. 19 Apr. 1990.

Zero Escape*: Zero Time Dilemma*. Dir. Kotaro Uchikoshi. Chunsoft, 2016.

Ziegler, John R. and Leah Richards. 'Introduction'. *Representation*, Ziegler and Richards 1-18.

Zolciak, Olivia. '"I Am a Conversation": Gem Fusion, Privilege, and Intersectionality'. *Representation*, Ziegler and Richards 69-88.

'401 Unauthorized'. Dir. Sam Esmail. 6 Oct. 2019.

'409 Conflict'. Dir. Sam Esmail. 1 Dec. 2019.

'410 Gone'. Dir. Sam Esmail. 8 Dec. 2019.

INDEX[1]

[1] Note: Page numbers followed by 'n' refer to notes.

S. Travers, *Trauma in American Popular Culture and Cult Texts, 1980–2020*, https://doi.org/10.1007/978-3-031-13287-2

C

Milton Keynes UK
Ingram Content Group UK Ltd.
UKHW040639050923
428087UK00001B/102

9 783031 132889